Redescribing Relations

REDESCRIBING RELATIONS

Strathernian Conversations on Ethnography,
Knowledge and Politics

Edited by
Ashley Lebner

berghahn
NEW YORK · OXFORD
www.berghahnbooks.com

Published in 2017 by
Berghahn Books
www.berghahnbooks.com

Library of Congress Cataloging-in-Publication Data
Names: Lebner, Ashley, editor. Title: Redescribing relations : Strathernian
conversations on ethnography, knowledge and politics / edited by Ashley
Lebner. Description: New York : Berghahn Books, 2017. | Includes
bibliographical references and index.
Identifiers: LCCN 2016053214 (print) | LCCN 2016055842 (ebook) | ISBN
9781785333927 (hardback) | ISBN 9781785334573 (pbk.) | ISBN
9781785333934 (ebook)
Subjects: LCSH: Ethnology–Philosophy. | Anthropological ethics. |
Knowledge, Sociology of. | Strathern, Marilyn. Classification: LCC
GN345 .R435 2017 (print) | LCC GN345 (ebook) | DDC 305.8001–dc23
LC record available at https://lccn.loc.gov/2016053214

British Library Cataloguing in Publication Data
A catalogue record for this book is available from the British Library

ISBN 978-1-78533-392-7 (hardback)
ISBN 978-1-78533-457-3 (paperback)
ISBN 978-1-78533-393-4 (ebook)

Contents

Acknowledgements

This book is dedicated to Marilyn Strathern, whose intellectual and personal generosity has inspired so many, especially the contributors and supporters of this volume.

Redescribing Relations would not have come into existence without Marion Berghahn's unqualified enthusiasm for the book's proposal and for her ongoing support during a longer than expected gestation period. Duncan Ranselm, also at Berghahn, similarly provided vital encouragement, facilitating this volume's shaping and completion. Michael Lambek's advice when I was an SSHRC postdoctoral fellow at the University of Toronto was also very helpful. The volume's final form ultimately owes much to Erik Mueggler, who commented on a version of the introduction and listened patiently to reflections on the volume over time, making me consider practical matters that turned into good decisions. I also thank Annabel Pinker and Patrice Ladwig, who both offered key advice at crucial junctures.

Each in their own ways, the contributing authors have also helped bring this volume to fruition, not least by staying committed to the project over time. Yael Navaro is owed particular thanks for her dedication from early on, as is Alberto Corsín Jiménez for his reading of the introduction and his subsequent advocacy for the project, which helped bring Sarah Green on board and generate wider interest. Stuart Kirsch's ongoing support of the project, as well as his detailed comments on the introduction, have been invaluable and heartening, as have Casper Bruun Jensen's suggestions and Carol Greenhouse and Britt Ross Winthereik's consistent encouragement. I am especially grateful to Eduardo Viveiros de Castro, Marcio Goldman, and Carlos Fausto for their generous willingness to share their engagements with Marilyn's work.

The introduction has also benefitted from comments from Elizabeth Roberts and participants in the University of Michigan's Socio-Cultural Anthropology Workshop, as well as five (initially) anonymous reviewers for Berghahn and the journal *L'Homme*, where a shorter version was published in French in 2016. I thank them all and especially those subsequently revealed to me – Andrew Barry, Barbara Bodenhorn and Emilia Sanabria – for asking good questions, which pushed me to find more answers.

I am most grateful to Marilyn herself, not only for her heartening words on different versions of the introduction but also for supporting the project from its first iteration, when it was conceived as a special issue for *Cambridge Anthropology* (now called *The Cambridge Journal of Anthropology*) to mark her retirement. Of course without her support, it would never have gotten off of the ground. Deep thanks also go to Sabine Deiringer, who was my coeditor throughout that initial period and in the early stages of the present volume. I remain grateful to her for that stimulating period of collaboration. I am also especially indebted to Lee Wilson, who was on the editorial board of Cambridge Anthropology with me at the time and who provided vital support to make that special issue happen.

While the current volume draws stimulus from its predecessor, the aim here has been to extend and connect the earlier focus on bureaucracy and knowledge to more general issues in Strathern's thinking on ethnography and politics, which have been rarely discussed elsewhere. It is hoped that this will draw new scholars to her work, including unlikely ones.

I myself am an improbable interlocutor of Strathern, given my primary work on Christianity, secularity and politics in Brazil. These are hardly Strathernian themes, yet my reading of Strathern has transformed the way I think about them. This transformation took time of course; I first read her work on the suggestion of my supervisor at Cambridge, Stephen Hugh-Jones, while I was conducting post-MPhil/pre-doctoral fieldwork in indigenous Northwest Amazonia. And so after long days spent with Hupde communities near the Tiquié River, every night for weeks I dutifully read *The Gender of the Gift*, holding it behind a candle stuck on the ground as I balanced in the hammock where I would later sleep. I didn't understand much of what I read at the time (nor did I realize that the reading arrangement was preposterous for such a book), but perhaps the flickering candlelight seared some of it into memory: insights kept returning in later years, even after I had to change my field site and project due to complications with research permits.

Or maybe my engagement with Strathern was presaged when she hired me to produce an archive of the grey literature and audio collected during her ESRC project with Erich Hirsch: Property, Transactions and Creations. Or perhaps it was also participating in the 'writing-up' PhD seminar when Strathern was at the helm commenting on our work in progress. Regardless of whether there was a specific catalyst behind my extended reflection on her work, I enjoyed the process of 'rediscovering' it so much that I wanted to prepare this book. I now hope that others will use it as a tool to accompany their reading of Strathern, as once the challenge to engage her scholarship is embraced, inspiration and delight will no doubt follow.

Introduction

Strathern's Redescription of Anthropology

Ashley Lebner

In 2007 a seminar was held at the Centre for Research in the Arts, Humanities and Social Sciences to discuss Marilyn Strathern's Huxley Memorial Lecture 'A Community of Critics' (2006), with the author there to answer questions. At one point, it was asked whether or not she was arguing that individual academic disciplines generate better critical debate than interdisciplinary work.[1] Strathern smiled, raised her eyebrows slightly and pulled subtly at the audience with her hands. '*I am trying to draw people into the conversation*', she said. Although the remark may have seemed offhand or even evasive, Strathern was in fact directing the audience to the centre of her text and her anthropology more generally: 'Critics find themselves *drawn* – precisely by their own interest – into other people's agendas . . . To argue with an idea is to be captured by it. In this kind of engagement, one can be captured more than once. This is where I see hope for interdisciplinary endeavour' (2006, 203 emphasis added). Thus Strathern was not so much discounting the value of interdisciplinarity as noting that the terms of any field or debate are learned through repeat encounters. What cultivates creative scholarly criticism, she states, whether within or between disciplines, is to be able to engage and re-engage ideas as well as 'to re-multiply, re-divide, the outcomes of any one particular argument' (Strathern 2006, 199).

It is fitting to begin this volume with an image of scholars being drawn in, re-engaged, remultiplied and redivided. Certainly *Redescribing Relations* is a product of all of the contributors' 'critical' re-engagements with Strathern's work, which no doubt have remultiplied and redivided our sense of what anthropology can do. Here, I add my reading of the essays that follow to my engagement with Strathern's work. I have come to see that if Strathern considers 'a discipline as no more or no less than the effort to describe, [and if] the genius of anthropology has always been its descriptive engagement with the fact of description, with how people generate accounts of themselves' (2005b, xii), then Strathern offers her own unique version of anthropology. This anthropology is built precisely around a principle akin to re-engagement and incorporates Strathern's understanding of critical conversation. It is accurate to call this principle 'redescription' – which I first tentatively noted in earlier work (Lebner and Deiringer 2008/9, 1, 2) – and Strathern's mode of redescription must be further explored to elucidate Strathern's overall project as well as the collective contribution of the essays in this volume.

Redescribing Relations draws some of Strathern's most committed readers into conversation in her honour – especially about ethnographic themes that her work has rarely engaged. The volume was conceived as a way for us all to express gratitude for the inspiration that she has variously brought to us through her writing, teaching and intellectual and personal generosity. The intent was also to deepen understandings of her work.[2] Indeed, Strathern's scholarship attracts the interest of an increasing number of scholars across the humanities and social sciences and yet she is regularly misunderstood, which inhibits or skews modes of engagement with her work. For example, she is often deemed one of anthropology's pre-eminent 'theorists'. Similarly, many scholars have reiterated how difficult it is to identify Strathern with one key issue or theme. This may all accord with a certain reading of her work; it is certainly the case that she has written about an astounding number of issues across the domains of kinship, gender, science, law, economy and bureaucracy. Yet she would also merely insist, as she has in a recent interview, that her project is concerned less with generating theory or concepts than with 'produc[ing] a good description' (Borič and Strathern 2010) – that her commitment is to getting the ethnography 'right' (see also Edwards and Petrović-Stěger 2011; Allard 2014; Street and Copeman 2014). In other words, Strathern's project couples a rejection of 'theory' with a singular aim – a singular aim that is of course a permanent task, as no description is ever perfect or final. And this is the most basic reason why 'redescription', in a word, captures her approach to anthropology.

Yet redescription in Strathern's work entails more than revisiting her own and others' arguments in order to re-form them. The very terms and forms of argumentation that she employs, how she writes by juxtaposing vignettes rather than enforcing terms of engagement, are expressions of her redescriptive aims, although this is rarely explored despite much discussion of her challenging writing. Redescription is also much more critical, even political, than is superficially implied by considering it the 'consistent re-formation of accounts'. Of course, it is critical in part because it reflects Strathern's redefinition of criticism, which was cited at the beginning. But it is also important to know that subtending this notion of criticism is a persistent attention to analytical language and how to shift it.

As Strathern is keenly aware, conventional concepts have played pernicious roles in state discourse, whether intended or not (Strathern 1996a; also Greenhouse, this volume) – and this is Strathern's political concern for anthropology. While it is true that she writes little about 'politics' as such, what critics miss when they see this as evidence that her work is apolitical (e.g. Josephides 1991) is that Strathern's elision is due not to a lack, but rather to deep reflection on politics – and anthropological politics in particular. As I discuss later in this introduction, the contributors to this volume are distinctly aware of Strathern's politics and their ethnographies are written with her politics in mind.

Yet before we can fully grasp the politics of Strathern's redescription, or how the contributions mobilize aspects of it, this introductory essay will elucidate a series of interconnected moves, albeit slowly, in turn. To start, it must be clear that rather than charting the repeated use of a 'concept', we must first grasp Strathern's redescription as *a series of relations*. This is not only because Strathern employs the term and its iterations (for example 'redescribing'), sparingly in her work.[3] More significantly, Strathern's anthropology does not *prioritize* the creation of 'concepts' to begin with.

'The invention of concepts' has long been identified with the work of philosophy (see especially Deleuze and Guattari 1994, which has since inspired a series of provocative anthropological reflections). Yet because Strathern is committed to articulating the distinctive contribution of anthropology and ethnography in particular, she remains wary, as we will see, of using common analytical categories – like 'society', 'individual', conventional 'comparison' and 'theory' more generally. In contrast, she never pushes very directly against the notion of the 'concept' – a difficult thing to do given the constraints of our scholarly languages – yet the significance of the series of 'relations' that give impetus to her analyses cannot be overlooked.

Thus while Strathern defines 'relations' as the conceptual and interpersonal connections/distinctions that sustain social life (Strathern 2005a, 9–14), it is important to stress that for Strathern every word matters: even if concepts can be relational, focusing anthropology on creating and taking care of concepts is a very different proposition than 'us[ing] relations to uncover relations' (ibid, vii). The latter, another of her definitions of anthropology, should be read as a response to the call for anthropologists to create concepts to begin with (the relation helps redescribe the concept). It is also an initial clue, explored more below, to why Strathern's work should not be assimilated to the ontological turn, even if she is sympathetic to the creativity of its proponents and to their concern with honouring difference in their descriptions.

Focusing on redescription in what follows, then, will help make visible how relations animate Strathern's anthropology. Although elaborated throughout her mature work, redescription was initially articulated in Strathern's (1988) *The Gender of the Gift* (henceforth GOG), a book that 'unwrites' her first book *Women in Between* (Viveiros de Castro, Strathern and Fausto, this volume; Strathern 1972). In a key subsection of the introduction to GOG titled 'Negativities: Redescribing Melanesian Society' (GOG, 11), she outlines the distinctive core of her contribution, going beyond her earlier critical mode of 'setting up negativities' (ibid.). Her negative critical mode precisely focused on how different concepts do not apply to the ethnography of Hagen, the primary site of her fieldwork in the Highlands of Papua New Guinea (see for example her classic early critiques of nature and culture, Strathern 1980; or of law and social control, Strathern 1985). Instead GOG engages the broader issue of scholarly language itself: 'Our own metaphors reflect a deeply rooted metaphysics with manifestations that surface in all kinds of analyses. The question is how to displace them most effectively' (GOG, 12). Beginning with the displacement of key concepts – in particular the displacement of society and individual – other analytical relations are elaborated in GOG and throughout her later work: from deploying analogy, to uncovering relations that defy scale. These relations, which can be so called because they rely on other terms to operate, are what constitute Strathern's redescription (of course itself a conceptual 're'lation), which enables a new mode of anthropological critique and politics.

Displacement, analogy, relations, politics – in what follows I explore how each of these relations contribute to the redescription(s) at the heart of Strathern's anthropology. By the end I hope it is clear how *displacement, analogy, relations* and *politics* are each implicated in, related to, the other. This is not to enforce the idea that one cannot engage aspects of Strathern's work, for in a sense this is what Strathern invites, as we will see. Nevertheless, my choice to focus on a certain integration in Strathern's thinking comes, on the one hand, from a sense that it is the best way to allow new readers a way 'in' – understanding Strathern's redescription can, I hope, provide insight into any of her arguments. On the other, while my primary aim is certainly not to 'answer' or 'correct' critics (I cite but few here, for clarity), my sense is that engagements with her work are often elaborated without taking into account her wider project, which is to effectively redescribe ethnographic writing, as well as

the anthropologist as author – even as person – with and through the relations that compose her. She thus creates a new ethnographic genre of sorts,
even though she does not envisage others necessarily reproducing it, given
their own relational entailments. If Strathern does not have a 'programme'
to reproduce, then, the first aim of this introduction is to show that there is
nevertheless 'consistency' to her work (Borič and Strathern 2010, 281)[4]: from
GOG onwards Strathern develops a remarkably coherent project that has
answers to most of the questions we might ask of it, including political questions. Whether one is satisfied with the answers is something that others may
ask again later – however, the first task is to properly understand.

The second aim of these pages is to frame this volume's hope: to draw
scholars, anthropologists and otherwise, into new conversations on a wide
variety of themes. To be sure, the contributors to this volume deftly show how
Strathern's anthropology can inspire ethnographic reflection beyond her
usual forms and terrains. As I discuss in the final section of this introduction,
each of the contributors deploy elements of Strathern's redescription – they
variously use relations to redescribe relations while reflecting on the politics
of knowledge – and produce original contributions to their ethnographic
fields as a result: from the state (Greenhouse), corporate design (Corsín
Jiménez) and indigenous worlds in the Americas (Kirsch and Viveiros de
Castro and Goldman) to conflict resolution (Navaro) and audit (Jensen and
Winthereik) in the Mediterranean and Northern Europe, respectively. Thus
as a whole, this volume illustrates how Strathern's project invites any scholar
to redescribe relations, which can offer them not only new understandings
but the critical, even 'political' perspectives that they might seek.

I: DISPLACEMENT

The displacement of concepts is where redescription begins. For Strathern, it
must start there because some Euro-American concepts can be so overpower-
ing they mar description. Anthropologists must therefore displace these concepts to 'create spaces that . . . exogenous analysis lack[s]' (GOG, 11). Yet the
act of displacement entails a series of other analytical moves, which emerge
in part from the concept(s) being displaced. This is especially the case with
regards to the main set of terms that Strathern displaces in GOG and all of
her subsequent work: society and its natural companion, the individual.

The displacement of society and individual is important to pause upon
because although there are other analytics that she displaces, and I mention more below, it is rarely noted just how central this displacement is
to Strathern's anthropology. Indeed, it is often assumed that displacing

society/individual is something that she pursued only in GOG. As a result, most discussions of her work do not acknowledge that the analytical creativity of her whole oeuvre starts with it; it undergirds her critiques, her choice to deploy analogy rather than (conventional) comparison (see below) – it subtends her search to redescribe relations generally. *The importance of the displacement of society and individual for all of her post-GOG scholarship cannot be stressed enough.*

As Strathern explains, displacing society and the individual is necessary, though not because they are poor translations of native concepts. In fact, Strathern maintains that translation is a 'fancy' (GOG, 29); one can never render others fully legible, as they 'are', in anthropological language. Anthropologists can only ever get closer to better descriptions by consistent vigilance after first addressing this perceived opposition between society and the individual, which is a particularly tenacious assumption: 'Society is seen to be what connects individuals to one another, the relationships between them. We thus conceive society as an ordering and classifying, and in this sense a unifying force' (GOG, 12). Inevitably, this force is seen as gathering and shaping unique individuals who can then modify this relation, although crucially, individuals are always 'imagined as conceptually distinct from the relations that bring them together' (GOG, 13). It is this persistent notion of society and the individual, of a whole composed of and encompassing its individualized parts, which Strathern will pick out in order to arrive at her first description of what she calls 'Melanesian sociality'. 'Melanesia', it should be said, is less a location than an ethnographic synthesis and thought experiment that explores the possibility of difference within the confines of Euro-American analytics (note that all of my future references to Melanesia are really to 'Melanesia'; see also Gell 1999).

Meanwhile 'sociality', or 'the creating and maintaining of relationships' (GOG, 13) allows for the exploration of Melanesia away from the shadows of what we might call 'society thinking', which is more persistent and ultimately less understood than the oft-discussed 'commodity thinking' – the assumption that individual persons are different from, and less alienable than, 'things'. Yet crucially, society thinking encompasses, even produces, commodity thinking, even if this is rarely acknowledged.[5]

Of course displacing society and the individual means no less than displacing the organizing concepts of modern anthropology. To start, 'society' was dominant in British social anthropology from its functionalist inception. It is true that classic social anthropology often enjoined practitioners not to 'reify' society; it also favoured the 'person' over the individual to emphasize 'how [the person] was already an element of a social relationship, already . . . a function of relating,' a relatum (Strathern 2005a, 41).[6]

It should be said that this precedence of relations is also why personhood is a vital concept for Strathern, and it is what makes her more indebted to classic social anthropology than to structuralism (see Viveiros de Castro and Fausto and Strathern, this volume; Allard 2014).[7]And yet, classic social anthropologists were still wedded to society: they were concerned with describing kinship *systems*[,] which made up a "complex unity" or more generally . . . *structure*[s], which constituted 'an arrangement of persons in institutionally controlled or defined relationships' (Radcliffe-Brown, cited in Strathern 2005a, 41). Indeed, although there was a certain reflexivity among social anthropologists about the problems that society and the individual created for ethnography, through 'systems' and 'structures' they were reinstalled nevertheless.

Strathern displaces society in view of its presence in subsequent models as well, which were perceived in their time as ways of transforming or modernizing (social) anthropology. In GOG, for example, Strathern engages feminism and by association the Marxist tradition it often draws upon. Marxism has long informed critical traditions because it unites the adjudicatory with the analytical: it theorizes the production of inequality while it exposes the class strategies that lead to domination and exploitation. Although feminism (or certain feminist 'lines') can be critical of Marxism for its androcentrism, it ultimately shares with Marxism an interest in depicting and fighting forms of inequality (albeit with specific reference to gender). Although undoubtedly sympathetic – Strathern is a feminist and was one of the first anthropologists to write specifically about women (Strathern 1972) – she is concerned about what these critical analytics might do to ethnography. Indeed, even if engaging with relationships, 'inequality' still conjures an overarching societal frame and its division by groups such as classes and genders, which are comprised in turn by 'individual' agents. 'Inequality' also ultimately renders our view of difference as always being ultimately hierarchical, *scaled* (Strathern 1987a, 1987b, 287).

Yet before Strathern likely knew that she would critique society, and 'inequality' as a conceptual product of it, she wrote this of feminist concerns: 'Notions such as male bias or the woman's point of view can be tremendously productive, and certainly alter the way we 'see' . . . Yet the sounds of our own industry should not deafen us to the point of forgetting that others are creative too' (Strathern 1981, 684). This is among the most pointed and direct critiques that Strathern has made of another anthropologist, or school of thought, in print.[8] Nevertheless, it marked the beginning of a continued awkwardness with feminism and other scholarly trends that bring Euro-American interests directly to bear on ethnography (Strathern 1987c). While her critical mode changed as she developed her redescriptive approach through the 1980s, her concern with making space for others' creativity has guided her efforts ever since.

Perhaps it is this prioritizing of ethnography that has led to a misrecognition of Strathern's politics among critics, even though her displacement of society had critical valence in light of the (ongoing) neoliberal revolution, epitomized by Thatcher's infamous 1987 phrase 'There is no such thing as society' (cited in Strathern 1996a, 53). I elaborate on this at greater length only in section IV because Strathern's 'politics', or critical interests for anthropology vis-à-vis power, is fully integrated with her redescriptive practice. Therefore, we must first attend to the analytical moves that comprise redescription itself.

Thus far, I have focused on the first of these moves, displacement, less to codify it as a concept in Strathern's repertoire than to shed light on one of her primary practices: first, the permanent removal of society/individual as concepts in her work[9] and, second, her more general tendency to avoid overdetermining Euro-American concepts, which are often connected to society in the first place. Indeed, since GOG, she has kept watch on how society haunts subsequent anthropological models and themes. To cite only a few examples, *Partial Connections* ([1991] 2004, henceforth PC), which I discuss more below, shows how a host of late 1980s attempts to retheorize the discipline once again reinstated society thinking – from the 'crisis in representation' and neo-Marxist globalization theories to comparative anthropology. That is, they reinstate society by *mobilizing images of a scale or an abstraction that transcends concrete individual instances* (e.g. the global/local or theory/datum), or they *describe how a whole becomes fragmented into parts* (e.g. the postmodern predicament).

Then, in *After Nature* (1992a, henceforth AN), which discusses English kinship before and after new reproductive technologies, Strathern shows that social constructionism similarly reinstates society insofar as societal/ collective/discursive forces and individual ones are seen to 'construct' one another. As an approach, constructionism thus remains as 'pluralist' and 'merographic' – and therefore as 'modern' – as those knowledge practices it claims to have left behind (and, therefore, as Corsín Jiménez [2015, 184] might agree, it developed its own mode of redescription).[10] Strathern later engages Science and Technology Studies (STS) and even Derrida in *Property, Substance and Effect* (ch. 1: I & II, Strathern 1999a, 1999b) to show how they smuggle society back in via the concept of infinity (STS' 'infinite networks' and Derrida's 'grammatological understanding of recurring equations' 1999b, 237).[11]

Strathern's (2000a) discussion of 'audit cultures' then suggests that her concern with society thinking is why she has never written much about 'ethics' (or 'morality'): "ethics, audit, policy – are the places to be looking these days if one is looking for society" (Strathern 2000b: 282; of course, under Durkheim's extended period of influence in anthropology, the place to look for society was 'morality' and vice versa). In other words, 'ethics' or 'morality' tend to conjure relations as being 'outside' and 'between' individuals and a transcendent collective – whether society, state, moral code etc. As such, for Strathern, 'ethics' and 'morality' are better approached as ethnographic objects (which are especially vibrant in Euro-America, as she shows in *Audit Cultures*), than deployed as cross-cultural analytical/comparative concepts. And yet, it is arguable that her work to extend society by focusing on relations extends the *study* of ethics and the anthropological *enactment* of ethics as well (Strathern 2012b; see also my discussion of Strathern's politics as guide, section IV).

Finally, as I have argued at more length elsewhere (Lebner 2017), for Strathern society thinking haunts recent discussions of ontology, insofar as the (individual and potentially individualizing) concept of ontology (and therefore the transcendent observer) is ultimately privileged over relations. Yet this remains her 'unconscious' critique of anthropological uses of ontology, while she foregrounds other concerns about the concept in her writing that I focus on here (see section III, especially note 15).

In sum, Strathern sheds consistent light on how 'society' is not only a term but a way of thinking that pervades our analytical approaches and clouds our ethnography with a Euro-American mathematic or idea of scale. (Put the other way around, it is rarely noted that Strathern's whole interest in, and *subversion* of, the idea of scale is due to how it haunts Euro-American analyses via society thinking: the hierarchy and encompassment evoked by the [bigger] society and [smaller] individuals). And this brings us to the problem of comparison.

II. COMPARISON, (AS) ANALOGY

Comparison is often considered a stable concept at the heart of Strathern's anthropology – even a central analytic – yet this is not quite the case. Indeed, few have explored how PC focuses precisely on the task of 'g[etting] rid of the problem of "comparison"' (PC, xxviii). Similarly, it is rarely noted that GOG already starts addressing this problem, whose central redescriptive aims are worth citing here as a guide:

> I displace what 'we' think society is by a set of different constructs, promoted in opposition in order to suggest an analogy with 'their' view. At the same time,

that very analogy grasped as a comparison, treating both sets of ideas as formulae for social action, then extends for us the original meaning of the concept. (GOG, 17)

Although this phrase encapsulates all of the analytical moves Strathern will make in order to arrive at her redescription of Melanesian society, it is also a general statement about how her displacement produces new conceptual relations – in particular analogy, which she *contrasts* with comparison. Strathern concedes that her analogy will be 'grasped' as comparison, yet she is clearly *distancing* herself from the latter and even arguably 'the concept' more generally – a term of course conventionally conceived to facilitate comparative study, and even the universalizing enterprise of (most) philosophy. The above suggests that with analogy, part of a different set of 'constructs', the meaning of society will not only be extended but so will comparison (and the 'concept' as well).

PC, a book centred on Strathern's approach to writing, is where she focuses on how the concept of comparison, conventionally conceived, is a product of the society thinking that she is trying to avoid. And certainly, critiquing comparison challenges anthropology as much as displacing society does – after all, comparison has been central to anthropology since the nineteenth century. Of course comparative practices have changed. Armchair evolutionists like Morgan, Tylor and Frazer took specific societal features 'out of context' to compare them (Strathern 1987d, 265). Then, early twentieth-century fieldworkers studied the structures of distinct societies with the hope that future comparisons could reveal universal social laws. Numerous subsequent projects retooled this aim towards the mid-twentieth century: neoevolutionist, structuralist and holocultural (represented by the Human Relations Area File; Gingrich and Fox 2002). Even beyond these more explicit comparative projects, and even when there was a sense that the comparative method was 'impossible', it was still often considered the 'only method in anthropology', as Evans-Pritchard once told Needham (1975, 365).[12] This abiding faith in comparison through the 1980s may be why Melanesianists among others continued to pursue comparison despite numerous problems[13]: what are the appropriate units of analysis for comparison? How are boundaries drawn? Strathern shows that the predominant solutions all rely on a familiar mathematic: 'individual instances' (societies, traits) are counted and evaluated by an 'entity' able to abstract and uncover, or produce a 'theory' about, the meaning of their similarity and difference. In other words, regardless of solutions given to punctual problems, conventional comparison – and indeed the concept of 'theory' itself versus 'data' – always reproduces 'society'.

Society: comparison :: sociality: analogy

Hence Strathern's interest in analogy. Yet in order to understand Strathern's analogical mode, it is necessary to first explore how Strathern replaces society with 'sociality'. Strathern generally does not seek to create neologisms to mark concepts, except sometimes when speaking about Euro-America (her coining of 'merographic relations' is a case in point).[14] Thus sociality, like many of Strathern's terms, is a colloquialism repurposed for redescription: if society is conventionally seen as a singular entity and 'context' for interaction, 'sociality' conveys how in Melanesia, a 'relational matrix' (Strathern 1996a, 53) generates and sustains persons in their everyday lives. More specifically, sociality in Melanesia *composes* persons; persons are singular entities, sometimes 'individually' conceived, but ultimately 'dividual' in the sense that they are 'the plural and composite site of the relationships that produced them' (ibid).

Significantly, this dividual is androgynous and constantly moves from one gendered state to another depending on the social circumstances – its internal differentiation is suppressed or 'cut' and the male or female aspect is drawn out in given interactions/exchanges (thus the gift is gendered in specific interactions too, as Melanesians do not distinguish between subject and object). The point is, the person isn't only 'one'; it is divided – and multiple relations are 'fractions of one' (Strathern 2011a, 93). It is for this reason that 'men' are not seen as 'controlling' 'women', even though gender imagery organizes much of Melanesian life. Similarly, although relations produce the person, this does not imply that the collectivity 'makes' persons into social beings; that would be to reinstall the hierarchical, vertical 'scale' of a transcendent society shaping the individual. Instead, Strathern endeavours to show how Melanesian persons are seen *analogously*: each person is equivalent – *on the same scale;* each contains the gendered relations/exchanges that made them; each must have certain relations supressed or cut in order to make others appear; each is a *not-quite-replication* (PC, xx) of the other. In short, the displacement of society and the discovery of Melanesian sociality reveal the fact that analogy, rather than comparison, better approximates the Melanesian mode of apprehending others.

Writing anthropology, ignoring scale

What Strathern then does with the discovery of analogical reason is striking: she applies it to her writing on both Melanesian and Euro-American material. This is more radical than it sounds: Strathern again reconceives – and

redescribes – the anthropological endeavour, much like the early twentieth-century anthropologists who invented a new genre, the monograph,
when they changed their conceptions of society and comparison (Strathern
1987d). The difference here is that unlike early anthropologists, who were
invoking a certain model of science premised in part on subjects/anthro-
pologists describing their objects/individual societies, Strathern develops
her own genre (although she has never put it this way). We might call this
genre analogical ethnography, which is modelled on her apprehension of
Melanesian knowledge practices.

Strathern elaborates these ideas in PC in dialogue with debates of the
time. Most notably, contributors to *Writing Culture* (Clifford and Marcus
1986; though also see Fabian 1983) had begun interrogating the modernist
conventions of ethnographic authorship in dialogue with Foucault. They
felt ethnography was facing a 'crisis in representation': it was no longer ten-
able for anthropologists to ignore power relations and to retain the authority to 'represent' the truths of timeless others, the objects of ethnography.
Instead, they called for a postmodern ethnography, one conceived as fiction
and written more experimentally against presumptions to objectivity, truth
and the ahistorical distinction between 'us' and 'them'. While for Strathern
many of these arguments were 'after the event' (Strathern 1987d) – feminists
had already been writing experimentally for a while – their desire to recon-
ceive the anthropologist and *therefore* anthropological writing had distinct
resonance with Strathern's redescriptive intent.

Nevertheless, their suggestions to replace the anthropological field-
worker with figures such as 'the traveller' and the 'cosmopolitan' in their own
ways reinstalled 'society' and 'the individual' and therefore 'comparison'
(PC, 7–16). Strathern's response was to offer the image of the cyborg instead,
which captures how the anthropologist is transformed by the analogical
practice of (the relations with) her Melanesian interlocutors. We should
also note that in Strathern's rendering, the cyborg is a much more complete response than postmodern ethnography to Foucault's (1989) critique
of 'anthropology' (anthropology broadly was conceived by Foucault as the
discourses geared to retain the sovereignty of the human subject – 'Man').

The cyborg was first made popular by Donna Haraway in a mani-
festo that is critical of a feminist politics searching for 'natural', essentialist
identities and argues for a 'partial' rather than a 'universal' perspective
(Haraway [1985] 1991, see also 1988). Resonating with these aims, if not the
language, Strathern deploys the cyborg to help redescribe the anthropological endeavour (' "Partial connections" ', after all, says no 'more or less than,
for example, the phrase 'writing anthropology' does'; PC, xxix). While not
a Melanesian image, Strathern sees the cyborg as uniquely able to perform

social/analytical work (almost) like a Melanesian person might: the cyborg does not 'observe *any scale,* it is neither singular nor plural, neither one nor many, a circuit of connections that joins parts that *cannot be compared* insofar as they are not isomorphic with one another' (PC, 54, my emphasis).

The cyborg is thus more than an 'individual' person – more than the anthropologist – because it is the anthropologist extended by its circuit of connections, which in Strathern's case includes Euro-American and Melanesian knowledge practices, as well as the technology of writing anthropology. Otherwise put, Strathern's writing does not entail the anthropologist writing *about* others, as the cyborg does not reinstall the view from individuals (or society). Rather, all other positions and capacities converge in the circuit to make 'connections without assumptions of comparability' (PC, 38).

While this implies that the cyborg retains relations with both benign and potentially pernicious forces (see especially Navaro, this volume) attention to this cyborgian operation also elucidates why Strathern retains a peculiar positionality in the text, which has been previously remarked upon as resting between a first-person and third-person description, whose 'individual' perspective is absent (see Viveiros de Castro and Goldman 2008/9 and this volume). In short, the networked cyborg replaces the individual author with the many relations it entails. And thus, 'Strathern' attempts to make other modes of personhood, agency and creativity visible thereby.

Strathern also offers a visual analogy to help readers see how the cyborg writes: the image of cantor's dust, a fractal image whose complexity (internal relations) is self-similar at every scale (i.e. the opposite of society).

On page 2 of the 'contents' section, Strathern presents the below fractal (see figure 1) as a 'synopsis' of the book. Of course, the chapters of PC itself are comprised by levels of paired sections, and the nonlinear argument emerges therefrom. Yet like the cyborg, the image also recalls Strathern's description of Melanesian sociality and personhood, whereby persons are recognized as analogous insofar as they are composed of pairs upon pairs of relations – each containing an equally complex 'sociality'. And yet, recall that one must make cuts in order to make specific sets of relations/persons visible or known. These cuts and self-similar relations are reflected in the below image, and Strathern thus communicates how her knowledge is produced: *by drawing analogies between sets of relations.* In distinct contrast to the linear-vertical form of argument that society thinking imposes on writing, the cyborg/fractal – only ever a *not-quite-replication* of the Melanesian person – makes it possible to think and write a different kind of anthropology.

Within and beyond PC, Strathern follows this model of writing: placing Melanesian vignettes (stories of relations) alongside Euro-American ones.

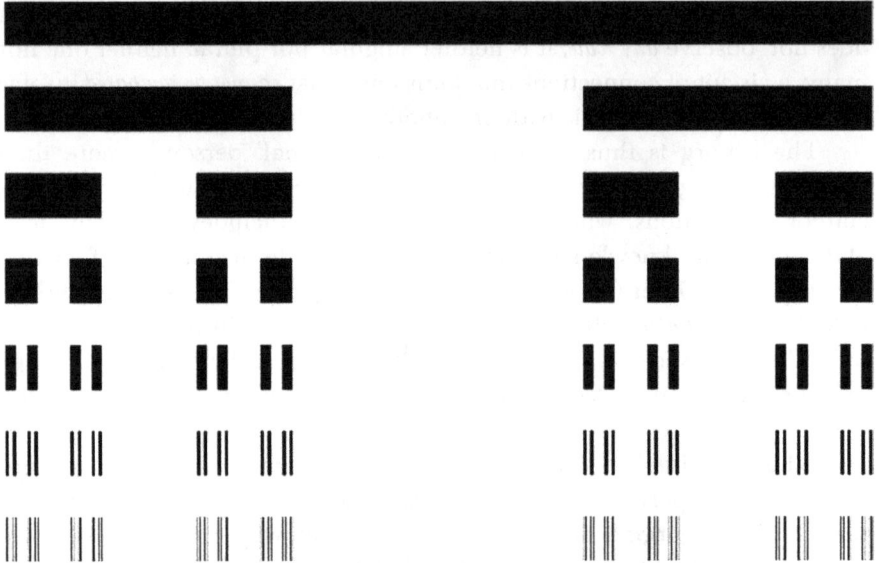

Figure 1. Cantor's Dust

The aim is not to compare, whether to evaluate their 'sameness' or 'difference' or to establish 'symmetry' (see Viveiros de Castro and Goldman, this volume, on the difference between Latourian symmetry and Strathern). Rather the goal is to elucidate one through the other, without aiming to 'abstract', produce a hierarchical or scaled view. We might think of Strathern as offering the experience of her ethnographic understanding to her readers, as opposed to merely knowledge or theory about it. That is, she demonstrates via form as well as content what it is like trying to see, write and understand the world as Melanesians might, with all the short-circuiting that is evidently entailed in making such connections.

Now, the cyborg and cantor's dust do not reappear in Strathern's later work, which is perhaps why there has been little elaboration in secondary literature on its role in her approach to writing and 'comparison' (Holbraad and Pedersen 2009; Hirsch 2014). This does not mean that the cyborg and fractal are not relevant to understanding her current practice; as she implies herself, different conversations will conceal the origins of certain thoughts (PC, 54). It is also an example of how not all of her analytic tools or insights remain prominent or evident. For example, despite her critique of comparison, she still does use the term on occasion in less critical ways (Strathern 1996b, 2003a, 2014b).

Yet this does not mean that she has abandoned her attempt to extend comparison. On the one hand, sometimes comparison is an appropriate term to use, especially when she is discussing or challenging 'theories' that abstract from their materials to greater or lesser extents (e.g. actor network theory and the idea of limitlessness [Strathern 1996b] or even anthropologists' descriptions of relations that do not escape conventional Euro-American modes [Strathern 2014b, 44]). On the other hand, it would seem that enough critical and descriptive work has now been done on her part to show the power of analogy – that 'comparison' has been successfully extended and is no longer a 'problem'. Indeed, as she says in her interview in this volume:

> Deconstruction, if it works well, is mobile; that is, it doesn't stay put. It's a temporal process, you open things up and then they close again, and you open them up, and they close again, so on and so forth. So I'm not at all embarrassed about having disposed of the concept in one context and using it in another.

And of course, she continues to draw people into her work by inviting them to reflect on the problems of description rather than discounting their interest in comparison. In her forward to an edited volume that cites her briefly as a key theorist of comparison, she playfully writes, 'Comparison is [anthropology's] game in at once the most serious and the most playful sense – not to be given away, but played. And with whom does one play but with this or that side?' While she doesn't elaborate there what the game is, she is clear about how to play it: 'begin with the problems' (Strathern 2002, xvii). In taking the problems of comparison very seriously, Strathern has come to see that the best way to extend comparison and anthropology itself is via analogy – a relation less haunted than comparison by the metaphysic of society. Indeed, with analogy she has learned that the only universally 'comparable' units are relations.

III. RELATIONS

If displacing society and extending comparison is what provides the basic conditions for redescription, what enacts it is the analogical study of relations or, simply put, studying the relations between relations. Yet for Strathern, relations – the conceptual and interpersonal connections and distinctions that sustain social life – are not only what anthropologists must describe. Rather, relations sustain anthropology as well. In other words relations, whose first principle is that they are free from the constraints of scale (Strathern 2005a, 63) operate everywhere; they are both 'anthropology's relation' or tool, as well as 'a tool, *tout court* for social living' (ibid., 7). If this sounds like a universalism, it nearly is. Relations are likely the only universal that Strathern would acknowledge, even if the relation has its own cultural contingency that was born from the social and intellectual ferment that was the scientific revolution, as we will see. An outline of Strathern's relational view in what follows will complete my discussion of the 'academic' side of Strathern's redescription. Then we can turn to her politics.

It is worth noting that Strathern's first explicit exposition of *The Relation* (1995) defied earlier criticism of her relational view of anthropology. Some years before, it had been argued that conceiving the relation as the grounding assumption of anthropology was too totalizing; it made it impossible to see beyond (Weiner 1993, 2001). Similarly inspired critiques emerged later, not all explicitly promoting (like Weiner did) the study of 'being' or 'ontology' as an alternative to relations. She mentions these briefly in the preface to *Kinship, Law and the Unexpected* (2005a; KLU), simply noting her agreement with many aspects of these critiques. She proclaims nevertheless:

> I can best serve the new radicalism by my own conservatism, and thus conserve what will then become an original position rather than consume new ones! So I endeavour to remain true to a point of view not because I defend it but because there is some mileage to be gained from specifying – precisely at this juncture – what is so interesting about it that it could become important to leave behind. (KLU, x)

Although Strathern here characteristically defers direct criticism, one can still read KLU, and her work on the relation before and since, as offering robust responses to questions about the centrality of relations in anthropological analysis. Indeed, she demonstrates that while anthropologists might wish to move beyond relations, it is likely still beyond anthropology to do so.

The legacy we have inherited from the scientific revolution, which was entwined with a social revolution, is why we are stuck with relations, as it were (at least for now). Strathern (1995, 2005a, 2014c) shows how the concept of the relation migrated from the scientific field into the sphere of kinship, undergoing a transformation therein, hence consolidating the connection between knowledge production and social relations. Prior to the seventeenth century the 'relation' as a term was used to refer to the field of logical relations. However as the scientific revolution got underway, which included new forms of association – embodied in burgeoning 'societies' (scientific and otherwise), 'relations' came to describe persons within the sphere of kinship and even beyond. *Why* it did so is more difficult to ascertain, but the very fact of it – and our continued use of 'relations' to refer to both conceptual and interpersonal activity – calls attention to the specific era in which anthropologists still participate. Ultimately, in pointing to the origins of anthropology's relational view, Strathern tells us that anthropology is still unable to escape the fact that conceptual and interpersonal relations are part of the production of knowledge itself. We can only *know anything* through this relational view.

This is not to say that science and anthropology rely on the same relations for their knowledge. Rather, Strathern contrasts 'anthropology's relation' to 'science's relation'. The latter deploys a different duplex, dividing knowledge into 'invented' and 'discovered' relations. Differences notwithstanding, anthropology's relationality developed under implicit and explicit influences of science. Implicitly, anthropology and the social sciences generally excelled at the 'discovery' aspect of science – an uncovering of relations already there, rather than the 'invention' of new relations (KLU, 39).

In contrast, an explicit influence of science on anthropology was the very idea that one could understand society through certain protocols and methods. One of these proposed methods was statistics, whereby data were quantitatively collected in order to seek correlations. Under this regime, data are 'understood as individual elements in the same way as persons may be thought of as individuals and society defined as the connections between them' (KLU, 38). Strathern notes how this imparted to anthropology many of the analytical problems associated with society thinking discussed above (see sections I & II). Indeed the view from science, what Haraway called the God trick (1988), can also be called the view from society.

Despite the vital role of science in the development of anthropology, Strathern is not arguing that the 'duplex' nature of anthropology's relation (its mobilization of conceptual and interpersonal relations) was created solely by the scientific revolution. Rather, the reliance on both conceptual and interpersonal relations is something she thinks one finds amongst people everywhere. However, where anthropology is concerned, the cultural and historical connection of anthropology's relation to the production of knowledge takes on particular significance. Its Euro-American provenance does not mean that it lacks general utility though; certainly, Strathern has shown us that our inevitably contingent analytics can still help us see 'others' and 'ourselves' better, as well as mitigate the differences between them – if we are diligent. Rather, it is the relation's relation to knowledge that indicates its usefulness for anthropology: in the disciplinary willingness to think relationally, to move between the conceptual and the interpersonal in producing knowledge about social life, 'anthropology arrives at a certain truth about sociality that could not be captured in any other way' (KLU, 8). In other words, without a relational view to produce our descriptions, we would not have as much knowledge of social life, quite literally. In fact, we might also say that without the relation to help us gain new perspectives, we would not be able to continually learn and to redescribe what we think we know.

It is important to note, finally, that Strathern's view of the relation should be distinguished from the current ontological turn, which at the time of my writing is often conflated (though the resonance of recent discussions with Weiner's earlier critique seems to be buried). This is not to say that Strathern does not recognize that certain practices are *ontological* (some ritual practice among Melanesians, for example, or the law), insofar as they constitute the phenomena in question rather than 'represent' it (as an *epistemological* practice might). Neither is it to say that she feels no affinity to the discussions being carried out by the scholars most affiliated with this turn – she does: they are similarly wary of how Euro-American descriptions might obscure the 'worlds' of the people they write about and this is ultimately why she comments on them.[15] Nonetheless, she affirms that anthropology's relation is an epistemological artefact. She also suggests that seeking another way to ground the anthropological endeavour amounts to ignoring the inevitable:

> For all that [the relation] allows one to ask about nonepistemic relations its limitation is (obviously) the form that it takes, [the relation, a duplex comprised by the conceptual and interpersonal]. For although [the relation] is good at elucidating the other side of things, especially in the case of societies outside the orbit of those developed by the Enlightenment and the scientific revolution, things indeed remain 'other', that is, *seen always in relation to the vantage point of the moment.* This is the trick of the Euro-American 'one world', and a final surprise that should be no surprise. What happens to the [relation as] duplex when anthropologists find they can count worlds in different ways is, precisely, nothing. In short, the relation will not disappear. (KLU, 91, my emphasis)

We should recall that part of the ontological turn entails the critique of epistemology as a Euro-American theory of knowledge, which tells us that there is 'one world' and many cultures (or construals) of the world. The suggestion is that if we displace epistemology we might find 'many worlds' or ontologies (in the case of the Amazonian worlds that Viveiros de Castro 1998 describes, there is one culture and many natures, for example). What Strathern is here referring to when she discusses the 'final surprise that should be no surprise' is that even when we find worlds outside the 'orbit of those developed by the Enlightenment', in the end these are always seen *in relation* to another world. In other words, even when we find different worlds, we cannot escape the *relation* between them and hence *epistemology.*

Strathern continues to consolidate this point in her recent writings. For example, despite attempts to develop an anthropology even 'beyond the human' (sometimes considered an attempt to move beyond relations, which are perceived as merely social), Strathern notes that relations continue to enable thinking everywhere. Indeed, in response to Haraway's (2003) call for a focus on human-animal relations, for example, Strathern playfully refocuses on the relation itself: she calls it our 'companion concept' (2014c, 8), ceding less to its conceptness than marking its consistent non/human relational work: relations certainly dog us, wherever and whatever we are.

Moreover, Strathern is increasingly clear about the consequences of focusing on the differences between worlds rather than attending to relations. She notes that if anthropologists do not acknowledge the importance of relations to being itself, we might lose the capacity to see transformation – including how relations can transform those who live ontological modes of being into the very 'others' who espouse epistemological modes of knowing – whether we would wish for it or not (e.g. KLU, 145–46; Strathern 2014a). She has thus come to call other anthropologists' acknowledgment of the social consequences of relations 'interventions' (2014a, 35) and she is conscious of her own need for intervention on this matter, an intervention in favour of ethnography as Corsín Jiménez might say (this volume). (Perhaps, moreover, she rewrites Foucault's own discussion of the 'procedures of intervention' that create the conditions for concept formation, while positing the relation as an always-already intervention before and beyond the 'concept').[16]

With her concern with intervention in mind, her invitation to those developing the concept of ontology comes into critical relief: 'Can one imagine a universe of scholars where this (caring for concepts) is not a primordial duty? . . . perhaps the locus of truth is found elsewhere than in concepts. That would put moral concern elsewhere too' (Strathern 2012, 403). Of course for these real or imagined elsewheres, Strathern is not denying the existence of concerns for how arguments are elaborated or how terms are used – what might be commonly called conceptual work. Nevertheless, she invites anthropologists to think about encounters and the relations that ensue – in particular how they relate to these other modes of description and how anthropologists might allow them to transform their own, rather than to begin from, and remain tied to, an individual concept. In other words, relations are not only 'thought'; they are enacted and ongoing and they have living and even moral valence – they are implicated in how persons are variously governed by 'themselves' and 'others'. In other words, relations, beyond concepts themselves, have implications for anthropology's 'politics'.

IV. IN SUM: THE POLITICS OF STRATHERN'S REDESCRIPTION

Strathern is not known for her overt debates of politics, anthropological or otherwise. One reason for this should be easily intuitable by now: 'politics', like society, is a weighty Euro-American concept that casts a long shadow. While many have variously critiqued the concepts of society, state and 'totalities' of all kinds, most have not abandoned 'politics'. In many ways, attention to politics remains the measure of a properly critical anthropology – and critical scholarship more generally. Yet Strathern might say that politics is all too readily written into our ethnographies, and if not handled carefully, politics might obscure rather than elucidate the relations that obtain therein. Indeed, the insistence on 'politics' may be reinscribing the very ('unequal') conditions of 'society' that 'politics' might be seeking to undo: after all, 'politics' is considered one of society's integral domains.

And yet, this does not mean that Strathern's anthropology does not have what could be grasped as a politics – and her work can certainly help elucidate it. First, Strathern's commitment to redescription is geared to extend not only the way we look at say, society, comparison and theory, but what counts as anthropological criticism and therefore politics as well. Second and most important, all of her work since GOG contests understandings that are implicated in modes of governance and policy, a sphere of the political that is shaped by our concepts after all. She also shows how anthropologists can enact a politics: through a long-term strategy of regular (ethnographic) redescription, which can prove just how variously relations sustain human life. This strategy includes disentangling anthropological practice from state discourse (see especially Greenhouse, this volume) and writing differently, beginning by attending to how anthropological and other knowledge is conditioned by specific relational arrangements. Significantly, as I discuss in the next section, the contributors to this volume all uniquely develop Strathern's insight into how the production of knowledge and the writing of anthropology is ultimately political.

Yet I begin with Strathern's refiguration of criticism, as it is the anthropological gateway to academic politics. If above I discussed her critical exegesis of 'society/individual' within predominant anthropological approaches, I should now add that this constitutes a critique of anthropological criticism as well – especially with regards to its common form and objects.

First, the conventional forms of anthropological criticism reflect the metaphysic of society: as with comparison, one plots data against an overarching theory in order to show the theory's truth or falsity. Strathern's redescription – her displacement of concepts and pursuit of analogical relations – obtains a more horizontal form of argument, which does not then abstract a transcendent theoretical truth per se; it is always embedded in her analogical narrative, which moves *through* her own and others' ethnographies. As discussed at the outset 'criticism in research is to re-multiply, re-divide, the outcomes of any one particular argument' (Strathern 2006, 199).

Second, her approach to criticism laterally interrogates how 'critical anthropology' is recognized by its objects in the first place. Let me emphasize that her aim is not to diminish common critical forms and political concerns. Not only is she sympathetic to them, but directly discounting other views would be contrary to her very definition of criticism above. Yet her approach to criticism contrasts quite a lot with, and is often seen as much less political than, a 'critical anthropology' that draws inspiration from the core of Marxist and Foucaultian traditions (different though they might otherwise be): to expose the use and abuse of power over time. In other words, it is assumed that critical anthropology should take the histories of political and economic exclusions, disciplines, struggles and violence as their object.

Strathern opens up what we might mean by critical anthropology: rather than training our descriptions directly on punctual struggles over power, her arguments convey a long-term political strategy for a discipline that occupies a particular place within the 'sciences'. If each science has a job to inform on the issues in which it has expertise, anthropology's role is to produce knowledge about relations. And anthropology is well poised to expose how relations can operate differently than power holders allow.

Strathern has offered critical insight into relations across an extraordinary range of themes. Yet to understand the political aspect of her interest in relations, it is helpful to start at the beginning again. Recall first that her redescription of Melanesian 'society' was written against the backdrop of the Thatcher (and Reagan) neoliberal transformation. The latter is of course captured by Thatcher's notorious declaration that I can now cite in full, 'There is no such thing as society. There are individual men and women and there are families' (cited in Strathern 1996a, 53). For Thatcher, doing away with the 'abstract' notion of society concretized the 'individual' and thus individualism – the sense that persons are autonomous, possessive, rational maximizers. Politically, this legitimated moves *against* social programs: 'You see what has happened. In one fell swoop Thatcherism could gather up all kinds of collectivities and organizations with a social presence and dump them. They no longer derive legitimacy from their *social* nature because society no longer exists' (ibid., 54, original italics). Ultimately, Strathern notes, 'Where the individual is produced "in opposition to" society, the move conceals social formations and power relations' (Strathern 1996a, 54). It cannot be forgotten that the conservative revolution is still in full swing. Nor should we neglect the fact, as she points out in a discussion of *After Nature* in her interview in this volume, that by 'looking at English kinship, one can find ideas and issues that in fact support these Thatcherite ideas'. Therefore, Strathern's call for an anthropology that does not take 'society' and the 'individual' as given and that foregrounds the importance of relations is not only promoting academic accuracy, it is also projecting a long-term political vision for the discipline as well. That is, the hope is to shift pluralistic society thinking, which is already changing, becoming 'postplural', though not only because of how (reproductive and genetic) technological transformations meet neoliberal effects (as Green, this volume, usefully reminds us).

Pluralism is also changing because it has been 'made explicit' as 'pluralist' by Strathern herself (AN, 7) and displaced as a mode of description. Yet clearly for Strathern, going beyond pluralism will take more 'contriving' (ibid., 4) – more writing and writing out still – and not only by her. How we will all redescribe things matters.

I have emphasized that Strathern's aim has been to arrive at better descriptions of not only Melanesia but Euro-America as well – and not simply as radically opposed social formations as some critics have claimed. To be sure, her redescription of Euro-America through Melanesian-cum-cyborgian anthropology allows her to see continuities through differences and to see how concepts pose political and legal challenges. In a discussion of the innovations of reproductive technologies, for example, she makes explicit the continuities amidst difference and change: 'Biotechnology has introduced into the domain of body management the kinds of separations, cuts and combinations that have always characterized relations between persons' (KLU, 30). If these 'cuts' recall Melanesian forms of relating, what makes Euro-Americans different comes down to language, 'the fact remains that Euro-Americans do not always talk about relations very clearly . . . [And] one reason for the shortage of relational idioms is the overdetermination of other idioms' (KLU, 30–31). This overdetermination of idioms makes it difficult to think or speak about, for example, the fact that mother and foetus are both separate and parts of one another at the same time. As a way to determine the priority of rights, debates continue apace on whether the foetus is independent of the mother or not. Strathern points out that mother and foetus must be separable in order for any relationship to obtain between them, but that does not mean that they are not still part of one another. Nevertheless, this understanding seems elusive; debates continue. *A relationship will never be a legal subject (as the individual is) in Euro-American law.* Strathern's broader point, however, is that amidst the universality of sociality, the different arrangements of social and conceptual relations have different effects. And some of these effects conspire, intentionally or not, to shape politics and knowledge.

Thus Strathern suggests that anthropologists should be alert not only to the past articulations of relations but also to their current rearrangements. Present forms of expression, even when they seem innocuous, can set dangerous programs in train. Strathern's discussion of audit is a case in point (Strathern 2000b). While audit seems to represent values that academics would champion, such as accountability and openness, when applied in the setting of higher education, for example, it is affecting *how* and perhaps ultimately *what* we know. The current proliferation of rituals of verification of 'good practice' and 'economic efficiency' are beginning to threaten the very open-ended enquiry that they claim to promote. And this has particular implications for anthropology and especially ethnography, which collects 'data' without knowing all of their immediate applications.

How can anthropologists respond to this threat to open-ended inquiry? (For respond they must, otherwise the 'response' will be imagined for them). Strathern suggests a 'political' stance, one which takes a position vis-à-vis policy (Strathern 2000b, 289–91): anthropologists must not only recognize the terms through which governmental rationalities promote themselves but be able to elaborate on the specific importance of ethnography as well. And yet, Strathern cautions, doing more or better ethnography of *policy* is not the answer per se. Rather, anthropologists should take care to distinguish themselves from the bureaucratic language that seeks to encompass them – bureaucracy, after all, has a peculiar capacity to absorb new, outside knowledge and turn it towards its own ends. Yet Bruun Jensen and Winthereik (this volume) show us that this seemingly pernicious absorption also offers some hope: as audit turns 'outside knowledge' into the 'inside,' it begins to implode, collapse under its own weight.

If Strathern's critical/political contributions seem most often applied to Euro-American knowledge practices, this is indeed the case. She has noted that her role is to criticize her own knowledge practices, rather than those of others (Viveiros de Castro and Fausto and Strathern, this volume). And yet, Euro-American knowledge practices have an inordinately powerful reach. They are crucial to attend to because they can affect how other societies come to organize themselves and even understand themselves politically. Strathern makes this clear in a recent piece, where she revisits a report of hers from the 1970s that she wishes she had written differently. In particular, she wishes she had written it without the concept of 'ethnicity', which she used to describe the different groups that had migrated to Port Moresby, the capital of Papua New Guinea.

Her wariness of ethnicity is due to how academic descriptions of 'ethnic' conflict in Papua New Guinea are converging with political/managerial descriptions thereof. It is not without consequence, she argues, to assert that what has 'always' been happening in Papua New Guinea is 'ethnic conflict', which assumes conflict grounded in perceived group differences and/or similarities. Indeed, the concept of ethnic conflict has perhaps come to constitute – maybe even drive? – the conflicts themselves. In light of this, Strathern redescribes her old forgotten report; she displaces the term 'ethnic' she used to describe different groups and now proposes that her interlocutors of the time saw each other by means of moral analogy, aware of the sociality that composed them all. In other words, 'There was not any common ground or viewpoint outside the entities being brought together, as one might imagine Euro-American appeals to *humanity* or *citizenship* lie outside' (Strathern 2011a, 96, my emphasis – she could have placed 'society' alongside 'humanity' and 'citizenship'). Today of course things may be different among migrants in Moresby; they might even see themselves in ethnic terms. But the question remains: how did conflicts there come to resemble 'ethnic' ones in the first place? There may be more than one answer to this question, certainly, but the suggestion is that persistent scholarly descriptions of 'ethnic conflict' have had an important role to play.

'If not a politics of [ethnic] identity, then what politics?' Strathern asks (2011b, 126), referring to a comment on this aforementioned piece by Pedersen (2011). She attributes the answer to him, yet it is really her own answer. It long has been. Strathern's own politics ultimately lies in revealing the 'inalienability of relations between, and thus the entanglement of persons with respect to, one another' (Strathern 2011b, 126). I emphasize that this does not mean that she sees relations as inherently 'good' (they can be divisive and violent after all). Relations, simply, are a permanent fact of life and anthropologists must work towards having this more comprehensively acknowledged in contrast to individualizing Euro-American politics. Similarly, for Strathern the mutual entanglement of persons does not mean either that that we are all fundamentally the same nor, for that matter, all fundamentally different.

Rather, there is unity in diversity. Strathern concedes that this might be a bit of a Euro-Americanism, 'but that is all right. There are many contexts in which that might be a good thing to do and one I have made my own indeed involves constantly returning to Melanesian materials' (Strathern 2011b, 124). Yet returning to Melanesian materials over and over again does not just mean viewing them in stark contrast to Euro-America in order to better understand the latter (as imagined by some commentators). Rather, listening closely to what others have to say – indeed *seeing* and *writing* with them – might make us more 'us' as well. All her work adds up, then, to a commitment at once anthropological and political: to move beyond our overdetermining analytical frames to practice writing as closely as possible – redescribing – with the perspective of others. She frames this as an invitation 'not just to imagine knowing about one thing through another, but to work through what it would be like in practice to write about Hagen migrants while writing about Corsica or the Darhad's Mongolia' (Strathern 2011b, 127).

In other words, she invites us not to replicate her redescriptive mode, but to practice an anthropology akin to hers, one that perennially rewrites what we think we know by enacting the particular sum of relations – the persons, places, various works and so on – we each encounter. Might any of us, one day, be able to parallel her? Perhaps not quite.

V. THIS VOLUME

Analogy, not-quite-replication only: this is indeed the point. Any anthropologist will only be able to write *with* Strathern while of course writing with all the other conceptual and interpersonal relations they contain within them (intentionally or not). This inevitable difference does not mean that others cannot enact their own redescriptions; as I noted at the outset, for Strathern, scholars are redescribing all the time (see also note 3).

However, I have shown that Strathern has her own unique techniques for redescription – her conceptual displacements and search for analogical/relational knowledge is recursive, attaining even the structure of her texts and her sense of authorship. Therefore developing a *Strathernian* redescription would entail questioning society and thinking relationally or analogically at least on some level of analysis. As noted at the outset, the essays collected here all offer their own kinds of Strathernian redescription, even as their ethnographies often begin far from her usual terrain. Their aim is to both honour and to inspire others to redescribe relations from wherever they write, with all of the political implications that this entails. This has certainly been my hope, too: as someone whose unlikely engagement with Strathern's work has been transformative (which I elaborate on in my acknowledgements), I know that her thinking can spur anthropological and political reflection in the most unexpected of ways.

Carol Greenhouse's 'The Scale(s) of Justice' reminds us that among the numerous impacts that Strathern's work has had on anthropology, what has been absorbed the least is how she studies the relations between relations in defiance of scale – what I have argued constitutes the core of Strathern's own mode of redescription. To demonstrate the critical vantage of a Strathernian approach, then, Greenhouse offers a redescription of the rise of US neoliberalism and the idea of the state itself. She focuses her ethnography on 1990s legislation: the failure of a major civil rights act and a new welfare reform law. She shows that these legislative developments supported neoliberal reform, enforcing an increased individualism and the occlusion of structural inequalities along the lines of race, for example.

Yet the reforms also reinforced the image of the state as transcending its citizens. In other words, with US ethnography Greenhouse shows what Strathern anticipates: not only that there are certain descriptive procedures that individualize, abstract and (re)scale entities, but also that the 'relationship' between the individual and the state is legislated, forged (in all senses of the word).

Alberto Corsín Jiménez similarly attends to the relations between relations with the aim of redescribing earlier work as well as the notions of analogy and symmetry – at least for a Euro-American context. His ethnography begins with the relocation of one of the world's largest oil companies to a new Latin American headquarters in Buenos Aires. Exploring the responses across different company departments to the 'paperless office' policy enforced for the new building, he finds that each department mobilizes specific and different 'equations' – arguments about the relationships between paper and the production of knowledge – as means to comply with and potentially modify expectations of paperlessness.

Thus, whereas he was once concerned with the analytical constraint of relationality for anthropology (Corsín Jiménez 2004), he now agrees that Euro-American knowledge is produced through relations – and through the 'exchange of equations' in particular, which he offers as a redescription of analogy for the Euro-American knowledge economy – a distinct epistemic form therein. In the process he questions the emerging disciplinary interest in symmetry, which he defines as equations between knowledges: should anthropology not instead, he asks, be seeking modes of redescription that 'breathe and transpire a certain "inadequacy" . . . that are not ad-equated'. In short, shouldn't anthropologists be crafting modes of redescription that do not mimic the equations between relations?

Stuart Kirsch's contribution also explores what the relations between relations can teach us – in particular how 'thinking across domains' can redescribe the practice of comparing indigenous rights. Whereas much scholarship has either compared different definitions of indigeneity, or has been critical of indigenous rights as a category, Kirsch begins with Strathern's riposte that one can analyze indigenous claims without devaluing their political purchase.

He then shows via comparison of Surinamese land struggles and US repatriation claims that distinct national contexts see the mobilizations of different domains of knowledge and practice to support rights claims. In Suriname, indigenous land claims mobilize the domain of 'freedom'. In the United States in contrast, claims surrounding Native American human remains invoke the domains of science, property and kinship – and often no single domain dominates the other in importance. Thus Kirsch's analysis not only develops Strathern's relational interests in domains of knowledge practices – particularly those of law, science and kinship – but sheds new light on how political claims are fashioned through modes of domaining more generally.

Then, in order to redescribe the technologies for peace she studied in northern Cyprus, Yael Navaro asks a Strathernian question: how do new technologies reimagine relations? She answers this by looking for the knowledge embedded in the artefact; indeed knowledge, as Strathern notes, always travels with the artefacts it makes, accumulating along its routes. Looking specifically at a computer program called Structured Dialogic Design Process (SDDP), which was developed to facilitate dialogue and reconciliation between Turkish and Greek Cypriots, she finds that it is a 'paradox in the making' insofar as it deploys a cybernetic organism or cyborg to accomplish a humanist project; cyborgs are reimagined as a way to mend human relations.

Of course at the core of this paradox is that military cybernetics was the crucible for technologies such as SDDP, while the latter's developers continue to assume that technology is by 'nature' peaceful. Thus Navaro is redescribing these 'pacifist devices' as not-quite-pacifist, while noting, as Strathern and indeed Haraway does, that cyborgs are never innocent, even as they develop their own particularities and paradoxes in given relational arrangements.

Casper Bruun Jensen and Brit Ross Winthereik then offer a redescription of audit's very power of description. They do so not only via ethnography of the Danish National Audit Office but through their research itself being drawn into what they call audit loops: recursive audit practices that occur across, outside and within organizational boundaries. In their case, their research looped between their writing and the audit office, which critiqued their findings and demanded modifications. This (participant) observation and analysis of audit loops tells us what comes after the audit explosion of the 1990s: an implosion of a particular kind.

Jensen and Winthereik go beyond an earlier prediction by Power (2000), who argued that after the audit explosion would come implosion, an internalization of audit practices becoming part of, as opposed to external to, organizations themselves. Instead, Jensen and Winthereik show not only that implosion entails increased internalization but that external and internal modes of monitoring begin to be indistinguishable – in a sense there remains nothing external left to relate to. This is what they mean by audit loop and how it consequently puts 'the *epistemology* and *form* of audit . . . under pressure'. Thus audit's seemingly ever-growing power of description, as identified by Strathern (2000a), is put into question, facing challenges from within and without.

Viveiros de Castro and Goldman's contribution then follows with comments on a few of Strathern's texts. Some of the issues they highlight of course appear in Strathern's wider work, and I have also touched on some of these themes above. Of particular interest to them, however, is her engagement with Amazonian perspectivism, especially how her discussion of Melanesian persons and relations can be described as an 'exchange of perspectives'. This exchange of perspectives is made possible not via different bodies (as it would be in Amazonian perspectivism, say) but by virtue of the relation, as they explain: 'The exchange of Melanesian perspectives is not an exchange of seen worlds; it is an exchange of relations between "giver" and "receiver"'. In other words, Melanesian perspectives (on relations) are created and made visible between 'social persons' because they are party to a relation in the first place.

Viveiros de Castro and Goldman ultimately characterize Strathern's writing itself as modelled on this Melanesian exchange of perspectives (eliding the Euro-American pluralist vision), and can stand as an analogy to what I have described here as Strathern's redescription of anthropology. Indeed, relations in Strathern's redescription as I have characterized it can also be grasped as exchange[17] – and the cyborg who writes anthropology, like the Melanesian person, is constituted by an exchange of perspectives.

Simply put, given that each contributor draws on Strathern to redescribe relations within their respective fields, there are certainly other Strathernian themes that appear across the essays (in particular a concern with scale and domaining and re-domaining). Yet what distinguishes this collection from others of its kind is precisely how the authors deploy such Strathernian insights to focus on how practices of (re)description generally are a source of knowledge and thus entwined with politics in the broadest sense: politics here referring less to state elections and parties than to forms of governance.

Certainly Greenhouse, Kirsch and Jensen and Winthereik present ethnographies more directly to do with the state and the entities that buttress it, and their collective insights are important for any scholar interested in law and bureaucracy in particular. If on the one hand Greenhouse and Kirsch show that the establishment of particular domains make certain political forms appear, Casper and Winthereik predict, on the other hand, a seemingly dangerous and immanent collapse of domains: one in which a state institution becomes no different from the outside it is supposed to evaluate – even ethnography being somewhat co-opted in the process as well.

Strathern has regularly cautioned against anthropology's absorption and even potential elimination by forces of governance (as well as flagging the co-optation of 'knowledge' more generally, Strathern 2000a, 2006). It is with this in mind that Corsín-Jiménez argues that anthropologists should avoid reproducing the 'exchange of equations' that governs the Euro-American mode of knowledge production. Indeed, he suggests that one might seek to contest this governance by writing against the oft-presumed symmetry between relations.

Navaro's account offers other vital suggestions for us still: namely, that we take care with the very idea of relationality itself, which like everything else can ultimately be co-opted and 'dehumanized' by emergent forms of governance seeking to 'protect' it. This is not to say that Navaro is promoting a more 'humane' or even 'human' form of conflict resolution *per se*. It is just that she crucially notes that in the context of such technologies for peace, 'relationality' becomes a technique to be acquired, a practice of 'dialogue' and 'communication' that is paradoxically deemed 'best managed' and 'made useful' through a post-human cyborg. Put otherwise, Navaro's piece also suggests that we should not only write to protect the right to 'useless'/'ungoverned' knowledge, but we should also care about the very ways that a codification of 'proper relationality' might be used as a way to discipline and govern relations themselves.

Finally, Viveiros de Castro and Goldman importantly remind us not to be governed too much by a concern with 'politics,' one of the 'overarching practico-theoretical modes of our society' (this volume). And yet, they also suggest that writing ethnography through an exchange of perspectives, as Strathern does, offers a more powerful anthropological politics than writing in favour of this or that struggle – and necessarily so. Indeed, 'Strathern wants to escape the alternative between "pluralist" or "liberal" relativism, on the one hand, and "imperialist" or "conservative" universalism, on the other. It is not necessary to choose between these two alternatives,' they say, 'another world is possible...'. In other words, it is by writing differently, as Strathern invites us to do, that anthropologists can contribute to the very political transformations that can in the long term be slowed by the recourse to 'politics' itself.

While I will let Sarah Green extend our perspectives on her own terms as a conclusion to this volume, some words on Strathern's afterword are appropriate. Certainly, in addition to being an exemplary redescription of the shifts in British bureaucracy through the twentieth century, it is also one of her most 'personal' essays. She conducts her analysis through the lens of the William Wyse Professorship, a post she held for over a decade at the University of Cambridge and was leaving at the time of her writing. 'The Disappearing of an Office' thus tells many stories, but most importantly for our purposes it brings Strathern's project home as it were: making visible while working within the changing conditions, limits and potentials of (anthropological) knowledge production and its politics. She does this of course by looking at one set of relations alongside another, here doubling down on redescription by illuminating bureaucracy through the self-revised perspective on Garia (Melanesian) ethnography by Meyer Fortes, a previous William Wyse Professor. Fortes was of course an Africanist at the forefront of the study of society in its heyday. No more needs to be said about Strathern's critique of society, but it echoes in Fortes's own redescription: he admits that his commitment to the study of structure (especially segmentary descent theory) left him unable to believe in the fluidity, even absence, of Garia social structure when it was first presented to him by Peter Lawrence in 1950. As a result of this scepticism, Lawrence only published his full view of the Garia over thirty years later in 1984, yet invited Fortes to write the foreword (Strathern 1992b). As Strathern (this volume) puts it, Fortes's 'handsome admission of a different perspective meant (indicated) that he was writing from a world that had already shifted'. Part of the shift she is referring to is an anthropological one, where the concepts of 'office' that Fortes had once championed, together with the concepts of 'role' and 'status', no longer held sway.

Yet this shift interests Strathern precisely because it elucidates a similar and more recent change within British bureaucracy in academia and beyond: the concept of public office and its related 'persona' has also begun to fade. In practice this means that post holders are ever more concerned with their own personal agendas than with representing their institutions, which was once the norm. This, Strathern notes, is a complex reconfiguration rather than a liberation per se. Yet the lesson she offers anthropologists here is less about how to proceed within bureaucracies (she speaks about this elsewhere, e.g. Strathern 2000a), than how to move on to the next redescription: 'how one might think anthropologically about any of these changes will be coloured by the comparisons one brings to mind' (Strathern, this volume). Indeed, in this characteristically recursive call to bring ethnography to bear on disciplinary practice and the anthropologists it produces, she invites us not only to continue discovering new relations but to keep redescribing – and reinventing – anthropology as well.

NOTES

1. The seminar was held on 21 May 2007 at CRASSH, the University of Cambridge. The question at issue was my own.
2. While the current volume draws some impetus from an earlier special issue (Deiringer and Lebner 2008/9), the aim was to extend and connect the par-

ticular discussions of bureaucracy, knowledge and anthropology (foregrounded in said volume) to general issues in Strathern's thinking on ethnography and politics.

3. Strathern also does not always use 'redescription' to refer to herself and she makes different kinds of arguments therefrom. In addition to using it to name what she is doing even in later parts of her work (e.g. Strathern 2011a; 2014b) she also sometimes uses it to critically note what others are doing with specific concepts – and perhaps should not be doing (e.g. Strathern 2003b).

4. Strathern associates having a programme with conceiving a somewhat totalitarian 'overall end' that others should follow (Borič and Strathern 2010, 281; see also Josephides, Rapport and Strathern 2015, 399).

5. Commodity thinking implies a set of assumptions about how individual persons are considered subjects that are different than things or objects; the former can act, own and alienate property, which they hold in their own persons and in things (though supposedly not in other persons). Much attention has been paid to Strathern's critique of commodity thinking; the interest in relativizing the distinction between subject and object is also found beyond anthropology, especially in the work of Bruno Latour. For this, and because Strathern's critique of society encompasses, includes and goes beyond the critique of commodity thinking, I focus on the former.

6. I thank Marilyn Strathern for the correction of the original citation.

7. It is true that Strathern's ethnographic synthesis of Melanesia resonates with Lévi-Straussian structuralism (particularly his work *Mythologiques*), insofar as cultural differences are rendered as versions of one another. Nevertheless, as she states in the interview in this volume, structuralism has served her more as a technique than a theory. Moreover, classic social anthropology had robust thinking on the relation as preceding terms, and she focuses in her writing on her social anthropological influences (e.g. Strathern 1995). This is another reason French readers should stop thinking that her anthropology is just another structuralism in disguise (adding to Allard 2014).

8. In this case she was responding to anthropologist Annette Weiner, who had accused Strathern of writing from a male point of view. See Strathern's interview with Viveiros de Castro and Fausto, this volume.

9. Society and the individual are spoken about as ethnographic objects, however, mostly via her ethnographies of England and the United Kingdom.

10. In AN, pluralism refers to the Euro-American idea that the world is composed of a 'plurality' of individual forms that can be bundled into groups: humans/individuals, animals, societies. Her idea of the 'merographic' relation captures other aspects of this pluralist view: that each of these forms can be described as parts of others, which serve as 'contexts' and therefore are never the same as the other (AN, 72–81). Both pluralism and merographic relations are ultimately related to society thinking; indeed, the concept of merographic connection, which is technically broader, is modelled on society thinking. She states that different forms of classification are 'given in the indigenous (English)

merographic connection between individual and society. One may switch perspectives from one entity to the other, so that the two perspectives seemingly encompass between them everything that might be said about social life' (AN, 76). I am aware that not all social constructionists may consider themselves postmodernist, but at the time of AN (1992), they were increasingly synonymous. AN is an attempt to specify the emerging 'postplural' epoch that is grounded less in the interrogation of truth than a recognition of the contingency of a pluralist grasp of reality. More recently Strathern has referred to this pluralism as 'perspectivalism', which continues to persist in some renderings of science and technology studies (not to be confused with perspectivism, see Strathern 2011a).

11. 'Society, in the twentieth-century Euro-American sense, is, as I have suggested, already evidence for such conceptualisations of infinity. [It] is held to contain diversity within it to be made up of countable/countless different subjects, each with their own view – whether those subjects are institutions, groups, categories or individual persons' (*Property, Substance and Effect*, 237).

12. Certainly, the journal articles of committed ethnographers trained around mid-century belied a certain sense of comparison/generalisation as a 'higher aim' in anthropology (e.g. Pitt-Rivers 1977).

13. Comparison in Melanesia seemed to promise an explanation of how societies could be connected, how and why they changed and even how they transformed from one 'kind' into another (Strathern 2004).

14. Commentators often misrecognize merographic relations as being a mode of thinking that she is promoting rather than critiquing; see note 10.

15. Although the 'ontological turn' includes a cross-disciplinary cohort of scholars, Strathern is primarily concerned with the anthropologists developing the concept of ontology (Viveiros de Castro 1998, 2011; Henare, Holbraad and Wastell 2007; Holbraad, Pedersen and Viveiros de Castro 2014; Holbraad and Pedersen forthcoming). Different ways of thinking about ontology within this growing group notwithstanding, they are not relevant for understanding Strathern's response. Indeed, she has been explicit enough about her concerns with the effects of *prioritizing* the development of 'concepts' generally and 'ontology' in particular, regardless of definition, and I discuss these issues below (see also the introduction and section II). Yet to these we might add another critique that can be deduced from her wider work (see also Lebner 2017): ontology privileges a *consummate* Euro-American philosophical concept (and a rather unitary one at that, thus evoking society, the individual and comparison) and assigns it to the task of ethnographic description. While she is fully aware that scholars cannot wholly escape their language, the engagement with such weighty concepts, especially ones that might conjure society thinking, is precisely what she has avoided in favour of defining anthropology's unique contribution.

16. It is worth noting that one of the three ways in which Foucault claims concepts are formed within specific discursive formations are through 'procedures of

intervention' (Foucault 1989, 65). These procedures may be of various kinds, including, for example, '*techniques of rewriting*' (ibid., original italics), which resonates with Strathern's redescription. Yet Foucault also notes that a system of conceptual formation is defined by the relations that constitute it, in particular how, 'for example, the ordering of descriptions or accounts is linked [related] to the techniques of rewriting' (ibid., 66). Thus the relation for Foucault is more than a concept – it is also what makes concepts possible, emerging between ordering and rewriting. (Moreover, Foucault's central concern with relations as constitutive of discourse often goes misrecognized, according to Dreyfus and Rabinow 1983, 63). Relations precede concepts too for Strathern, though as a result, the relation is where she trains her focus: her modes of rewriting or redescription move anthropology *beyond* the mere concept or discourse to the social consequences of relations – conceptual and interpersonal – that is her intervention.

17. See Gell's (1999) depiction of exchange as equivalent to relations in Melanesia; and also Strathern's discussion of her redescription of perspectivism (2011, 198).

REFERENCES

Allard, Olivier. 2014. 'Introduction: Marilyn Strathern et l'antropologie Française'. *Tracés* Hors Série: 167–73.

Borič, Dušan, and Marilyn Strathern. 2010. 'Arriving at a Good Description: Interview with Dame Professor Marilyn Strathern'. *Journal of Social Archaeology* 10(2): 280–96.

Clifford, James, and George Marcus, eds. 1986. *Writing Culture: The Poetics and Politics of Ethnography*. Berkeley: University of California Press.

Corsín Jiménez, Alberto. 2004. 'The Form of the Relation: Anthropology's Enchantment with the Algebraic Imagination'. Manchester: unpublished manuscript.

——. 2015. "The Capacity for Re-Description." In *Detachment: Essays on the Limits of Relational Thinking*. M. Candea, J. Cook, C. Trundle, and T. Yarrow, eds., 179-196. Manchester: Manchester University Press.

Deiringer, Sabine and Ashley Lebner (eds.). 2008/9. Special Issue of *Cambridge Anthropology: The William Wyse Professorship, the Organization of Knowledge and the Work of Marilyn Strathern* 28(3).

Deleuze, Gilles, and Félix Guattari. 1994. *What Is Philosophy?* Hugh Tomlinson and Graham Burchell, transl. New York: Columbia University Press.

Dreyfus, Hubert L., and Paul Rabinow. 1983. *Michel Foucault, beyond Structuralism and Hermeneutics*. Chicago: University of Chicago Press.

Edwards, Jeanette, and Maja Petrović-Stĕger. 2011. 'Introduction: On Recombinant Knowledge and Debts That Inspire'. In *Recasting Anthropological Knowledge:*

Inspiration and Social Science, edited by J. Edwards and M. Petrović-stĕger, 1–19. Cambridge: Cambridge University Press.

Fabian, Johannes. 1983. *Time and the Other: How Anthropology Makes Its Object.* New York: Columbia University Press.

Foucault, Michel. 1989. *The Archaeology of Knowledge.* Translated by A.S. Smith. London: Routledge.

Gell, Alfred. 1999. 'Strathernograms, or, the Semiotics of Mixed Metaphors'. In *The Art of Anthropology,* 29–75. Oxford: Berg.

Gingrich, Andre, and Richard G. Fox. 2002. *Anthropology, by Comparison.* London: Routledge.

Haraway, Donna. 1988. 'Situated Knowledges: The Science Question in Feminism and the Privilege of Partial Perspective'. *Feminist Studies* 14(3): 577–99.

———. 1991. 'A Cyborg Manifesto: Science, Technology, and Socialist Feminism in the Late Twentieth Century'. In *Simians, Cyborgs and Women: The Reinvention of Nature,* 149–81. New York: Routledge.

———. 2003. *The Companion Species Manifesto: Dogs, People, and Significant Otherness.* Chicago: Prickly Paradigm Press.

Henare, Amiria, Martin Holbraad, and Sari Wastell, Eds. 2007. *Thinking through Things: Theorizing Artefacts Ethnographically.* London: Routledge.

Hirsch, Eric. 2014. 'Melanesian Ethnography and the Comparative Project of Anthropology: Reflection on Strathern's Analogical Approach'. *Theory, Culture & Society* 31: 39–64.

Holbraad, Martin, and Morten Axel Pedersen. 2009. 'Planet M: The Intense Abstraction of Marilyn Strathern'. *Anthropological Theory* 9(4): 371–94.

———. Forthcoming. *The Ontological Turn: An Anthropological Exposition.* Cambridge: Cambridge University Press.

Holbraad, Martin, Morten Axel Pedersen, and Eduardo Viveiros de Castro. 2014. 'The Politics of Ontology: Anthropological Positions'. Theorizing the Contemporary, *Cultural Anthropology* website, January 13. http://culanth.org/fieldsights/462-the-politics-of-ontology-anthropological-positions.

Josephides, Lisette. 1991. 'Metaphors, Metathemes, and the Construction of Sociality: A Critique of the New Melanesian Ethnography'. *Man* 26(1): 145–61.

Josephides, Lisette, Nigel Rapport, and Marilyn Strathern. 2015. 'Dialogue'. In *Knowledge and Ethics in Anthropology: Obligations and Requirements,* 191-229. edited by Lisette Joesphides. London: Bloomsbury.

Lebner, Ashley. 2017. 'Interpreting Strathern's "Unconscious" Critique of Ontology'. Forthcoming in *Social Anthropology.*

———. 2016. 'La Redescription de l'anthropologie selon Marilyn Strathern'. Translated by Arianne Dorval. *L'Homme* 218(2): 117–50.

Lebner, Ashley, and Sabine Deiringer. 2008/9. 'Editors' Note'. Special Issue of *Cambridge Anthropology: The William Wyse Professorship, the Organization of Knowledge and the Work of Marilyn Strathern.* Sabine Deiringer and Ashley Lebner, eds. 28(3): 1–6.

Needham, Rodney. 1975. 'Polythetic Classification: Convergence and Consequences'. *Man* 10(3): 349–69.

Pedersen, Morten Axel. 2011. 'Non-Identity Politics'. *Common Knowledge* 17(1): 117–22.

Pitt-Rivers, Julian. 1977. 'The Kith and the Kin'. In *The Character of Kinship*, edited by Jack Goody, 89–106. Cambridge: Cambridge University Press.

Power, Michael. 2000. *The Audit Implosion: Regulating Risk from the Inside.* London: ICAEW.

Strathern, Marilyn. 1972. *Women in Between: Female Roles in a Male World: Mount Hagen, New Guinea.* London: Seminar Press.

———. 1980. 'No Nature, No Culture: The Hagen Case'. In *Nature, Culture and Gender,* edited by Carol. P. Maccormack and Marilyn Strathern, 174–222. Cambridge: Cambridge University Press.

———. 1981. 'Culture in a Netbag: The Manufacture of a Subdiscipline in Anthropology'. *Man* 16(4): 665–88.

———. 1985. 'Discovering Social Control'. *Journal of Law and Society* 12(2): 111–34.

———. 1987a. 'An Awkward Relationship: The Case of Feminism and Anthropology'. *Signs* 12(2): 276–92.

———. 1987b. 'Conclusion'. In *Dealing with Inequality: Analysing Gender Relations in Melanesia and Beyond,* edited by Marilyn Strathern, 255–77. Cambridge: University of Cambridge Press.

———. 1987c. 'Introduction'. In *Dealing with Inequality: Analysing Gender Relations in Melanesia and Beyond,* edited by M. Strathern, 1–33. Cambridge: University Press.

———. 1987d. 'Out of Context: The Persuasive Fictions of Anthropology' [with Comments and Reply]. *Current Anthropology* 28(3): 251–81.

———. 1988. *The Gender of the Gift.* Berkeley: University of California Press.

———. 1992a. *After Nature: English Kinship in the Late Twentieth Century.* Cambridge: Cambridge University Press.

———. 1992b. 'Parts and Wholes: Refiguring Relationships in a Postplural World'. In *Reproducing the Future: Anthropology, Kinship, and the New Reproductive Technologies,* 90–117. Manchester: University Press.

———. 1995. *The Relation: Issues in Complexity and Scale.* Cambridge: Prickly Pear Press.

———. 1996a. 'The Concept of Society is Theoretically Obsolete'. In *Key Debates in Anthropology,* edited by T. Ingold, 50–55. London: Routledge.

———. 1996b. 'Cutting the Network'. *The Journal of the Royal Anthropological Institute* 2(3): 517–35.

———. 1999a. 'The Ethnographic Effect I'. In *Property, Substance and Effect. Anthropological Essays on Persons and Things,* 1–28. London: Athlone Press.

———. 1999b. 'The Ethnographic Effect II'. In *Property, Substance and Effect. Anthropological Essays on Persons and Things,* 229–261. London: Athlone Press.

———. 2000a. *Audit Cultures: Anthropological Studies in Accountability, Ethics and the Academy,* edited by Marilyn Strathern. London: Routledge.

———. 2000b. 'Accountability . . . and Ethnography'. In *Audit Cultures: Anthropological Studies in Accountability, Ethics and the Academy,* edited by Marilyn Strathern, 279–97. London: Routledge.

———. 2000c. 'New Accountabilities: Anthropological Studies in Accountability, Ethics and the Academy'. In *Audit Cultures: Anthropological Studies in Accountability, Ethics and the Academy,* edited by Marilyn Strathern, 1–18. London: Routledge.

———. 2002. 'Foreword: Not Giving the Game Away'. In *Anthropology, by Comparison,* edited by Andre Gingrich and Richard G. Fox, xiii–xvii. London: Routledge.

———. 2003a. *Commons and Borderlands: Working Papers on Interdisciplinarity, Accountability and the Flow of Knowledge.* London: Sean Kingston Publishing.

———. 2003b. 'Endnote: Redescribing Society'. *Commons and Borderlands: Working Papers on Interdisciplinarity, Accountability and the Flow of Knowledge,* 87–102. London: Sean Kingston Publishing.

———. [1991] 2004. *Partial Connections.* Walnut Creek: Altamira Press.

———. 2005a. *Kinship, Law and the Unexpected: Relatives Are Always a Surprise.* Cambridge: Cambridge University Press.

———. 2005b. 'Prologue'. In *On the Order of Chaos: Social Anthropology and the Science of Chaos,* edited by Mark Mosko and Frederick H Damon, xii–xiv. New York: Berghahn.

———. 2006. 'A Community of Critics? Thoughts on New Knowledge'. *Journal of the Royal Anthropological Institute* 12(1): 191–209.

———. 2011a. 'Binary License'. *Common Knowledge* 17(1): 87–103.

———. 2011b. 'What Politics?' *Common Knowledge* 17(1): 123–27.

———. 2012. 'Response: A Comment on "the Ontological Turn' in Japanese Anthropology"'. *Hau: Journal of Ethnographic Theory* 2(2): 402–5.

———. 2014a. 'Anthropological Reasoning: Some Threads of Thought'. *Hau: Journal of Ethnographic Theory* 4(3): 23-37.

———. 2014b. 'Kinship as a Relation'. *L'Homme* 210(2): 43–61.

———. 2014c. 'Reading Relations Backwards'. *Journal of the Royal Anthropological Institute* NS (20): 3–19.

Street, Alice, and Jacob Copeman. 2014. 'Social Theory after Strathern: An Introduction'. *Theory and Society* 31(2/3): 7–37.

Viveiros de Castro, Eduardo. 1998. 'Cosmological Deixis and Amerindian Perspectivism'. *Journal of the Royal Anthropological Institute* 4(3): 469–88.

———. 2003. 'And.' After-dinner speech given at Anthropology and Science, the 5th Decennial Conference of the Association of Social Anthropologists of the UK and the Commonwealth'. In *Manchester Papers in Social Anthropology.* Manchester: Department of Social Anthropology, University of Manchester.

———. 2011. 'Zeno and the Art of Anthropology'. Translated by A. Walford. *Common Knowledge* 17(1): 128–45.

Viveiros de Castro, Eduardo, and Marcio Goldman. 2008/9. 'Slow Motions. Comments on a Few Texts by Marilyn Strathern'. Selections and Translation by Ashley Lebner. In Special Issue of *Cambridge Anthropology: Bureaucratic*

Knowledge Practices, the William Wyse Professorship and the Work of Marilyn Strathern, edited by Sabine Deiringer and Ashley Lebner. 28(3): 23–42.

Weiner, James. 1993. 'Anthropology Contra Heidegger Part II: The Limits of Relationship'. *Critique of Anthropology* 13(3): 285–301.

——. 2001. *Tree Leaf Talk: A Heideggerian Anthropology.* Oxford: Berg.

Ashley Lebner is Assistant Professor in the Department of Religion and Culture at Wilfrid Laurier University. She is currently completing her first monograph: *After Impossibility: Christianity, Marxism and Secularity on a Brazilian Amazonian Frontier.* Based on ethnography among landless workers in Amazonia, it explores the paradoxes animating Christian and secular formations and their implications for understandings of politics. She has published on the politics and cultures of friendship, secularity, science, and creationism, as well as on the history of anthropology. Lebner's new research explores struggles over science, Christianity, and secularity among Brazilian creationists and evolutionist scientists.

Chapter One

Within the Limits of a Certain Language

Interview with Marilyn Strathern

Eduardo Viveiros de Castro (EVC)
Carlos Fausto (CF)
Marilyn Strathern (MS)
Transcription by David Rodgers

EVC: Perhaps, Marilyn, we could start with a question concerning your career or intellectual trajectory. You were trained in one of the high places of classic, mainstream British social anthropology, but the impression that we have is that your work is distinctively different from this classic, say, accent of British social anthropology. We would like to know a bit about what made you make this set of theoretical decisions, so to speak, which lead you to what you have done.

MS: Well, of course as you know perfectly well, they weren't theoretical decisions; you're talking about outcomes from a whole series of different issues and I could probably only pick on one or two – but I suppose that means already that I do agree with your characterization, although you have to realize that anthropology in Britain in any case has changed and I'm not sure I'm so far from my colleagues now in Cambridge.[1]

   I'm not going to give you a rounded account; let me just pick on one or two things which crossed my mind as you were talking. One is that you realize that between 1960 and 1963 when I was an undergraduate in Cambridge, this was the highpoint of the contrapuntal debate between Edmund Leach and Meyer Fortes. We had two lecture rooms, one was called the North Lecture Room and one was called the South Lecture Room and they're sort of next to each other – and it was almost as though, so to speak, you could go to one and hear Edmund and you could go to the other to hear Meyer: not quite, because the time tabling wasn't done like that, but one got a very lively sense of debate. And that was the time at which Meyer was consolidating his *Kinship and the Social Order* (Fortes 1969); he was working up to his Morgan Lectures and so forth and he was really implementing his own paradigm. Edmund in the meanwhile had just written *Pul Eliya* and was regurgitating Lévi-Strauss, and he introduced us to some of Lévi-Strauss's thinkings via his own particular interest in taboo and all the rest of it. Edmund also led a fascinating undergraduate seminar on Malinowski, and this went the whole term on Malinowski's works and was most stimulating.

Now, whatever I want to say now sounds disloyal. I was very loyal to Meyer but I was thrilled by Edmund . . .

EVC: But there was an impression of students being divided into Fortesians and Leachians at that time?

MS: No, it was a gourmet feast. But personally, I suppose. And you might know that almost the first paper that Andrew Strathern and I wrote came out of a book edited by Edmund on dialectics and practical religion.

That was one thing. A second thing was I got married almost as soon as I finished being an undergraduate; I married that summer, before we went to Papua New Guinea . . . So the first fieldwork was in fact with a companion. Now, this sustained dialogue, debate . . . we agreed and we disagreed . . . I just wonder whether that might have been a factor, that there was debate in the background. However, the first book I wrote was blushingly orthodox, totally: *Women in Between* (1972) is an absolute product of orthodox Cambridge thinking. To look at that, you wouldn't see any signs of what was to come. And *The Gender of the Gift* (1988) of course unwrites *Women in Between*, in the same way as *After Nature* (1992) unwrites *Kinship at the Core* (1981b).

What *was* a deliberate theoretical choice, made by Andrew and myself, was to go to Papua New Guinea rather than Africa. I think the general presumption being that we would go to Africa because Andrew was Jack Goody's student and so on. But at that time the first ethnographers from the highlands had just appeared – Salisbury's and Marie Reay's work had just appeared – and this seemed like a breath of fresh air.

EVC: None of your teachers at the time in Cambridge were working in New Guinea?

MS: No. There was Reo Fortune but Reo had long since brushed his hands of anthropology. He was consumed by his diatribe against Malinowski;

the only subject he could lecture on was the fact that Malinowski had mistaken the number of wives that the paramount chief of Omarakana of the Trobriand Islands had.

MS: We decided to go to Papua New Guinea and initially we were going to go to the Orokaiva area, Mount Lamington.

Anyway there were problems, so we didn't go. Anyway, we decided on the highlands, so this was already a step to one side, so to speak. I'm trying to think of reasons why there might have been natural steps.

Now, I think you have to know a bit of personal history. We, Andrew and I, did fieldwork together. We broke off the fieldwork and went to Canberra for five months then we came back to New Guinea, then returned to England. I had a job in the museum there, Andrew wrote a doctoral dissertation and held a fellowship in Trinity College, Cambridge. Then in '69 he decided to go to Canberra, ANU [Australian National University], on a fellowship, and from '69 until '76 we were either in Australia or in Papua New Guinea; we moved to Papua New Guinea when he was offered the chair of anthropology at UPNG [University of Papua New Guinea]. Now, that absence from Cambridge I think was quite important. During that period of absence, feminist anthropology began. Now, this is actually relevant, because feminist anthropology keyed one into debates which weren't going to take anthropological paradigms at face value. They required a grounding in another set of issues. So I then began read-ing; in fact I wrote a book at that time that was never published on males and females, right way back, 1973.

EVC: *Women in Between* was published when?

MS: In 1972. I revised that in Canberra.

EVC: It was written when you were already away from Cambridge?

MS: It was my thesis, which was rewritten.

Feminist anthropology gave the kind of triangulation that you see in *The Gender of the Gift* – as I say right at the beginning – that there's anthro-pological theory and there's the ethnographic information and there's also feminist scholarship. I don't know how to phrase this. We all have doubts about how useful our work is; we all have doubts about who the audience is and whether what one is doing is of any worth, and I actually think that the depression and the doubt that goes with that is actually creative. Because it makes one listen. I think it makes one listen to other people. If you're very confident and all you can see is yourself, you're actually then a barrier, you're closed to communication. So being open to this other domain meant that I was always playing anthropological certainties against feminist uncertainties or vice versa. And I think that became quite important because the two points of anthropological theory

and ethnography, of course, just consume one another; I mean they can-
nibalize one another, so having a third point . . . Anyway, I'm just trying
to explain . . .

EVC: And how did you experience the feminist boom? What was your, say,
experience of this as a kind of major theoretical challenge? You experienced it as a major theoretical challenge or as a major political challenge
or as both?

MS: It was a theoretical challenge, because the politics seemed to be taken
care of in the sense that I had grown up always assuming that things to
do with women were of interest and significance. My mother was a pre-
feminist feminist. In the 1950s, she was an English teacher and she gave
adult education classes and she lectured on women and art, women in
history and so on, so I grew up taking these things for granted . . . and
when [second-wave] feminism came along, I took it for granted and it just
seemed to slip, so to speak, into what I was doing; but at the same time,
theoretically, quite clearly it opened up a lot of questions in anthropology.
But of course, I mean I always tell the story that it was Annette Weiner
who, in her book *Women of Value, Men of Renown* [1976], says there's been
nothing published on women in Papua New Guinea, except M. Strathern
– and what a pity because M. Strathern does so from a male point of view.
And that was the beginnings of having to rethink.

CF: And do you think she was right?

MS: No, of course not. But it took me from '76 when I read it to '81
when I gave the Malinowski Lecture 'Culture in a Netbag' [1981]. The
Malinowski Lecture was my answer, and it took me five years.

CF: . . . to digest it?

MS: I couldn't digest it; it was stuck in my throat. However, at that point the
feminism slipped in but, nonetheless, it was certainly a theoretical challenge, yes. Alright, I then returned and what had happened? Two things
had happened. First, structuralism had taken off in a major way, and if
you look at the Hugh-Jones' work, they are the products of a full-blown
structuralism being taught in Cambridge.

EVC: Mostly by whom? By Leach?

MS: By Leach, yes. Almost entirely, I would say. Alright, well then we
returned to England in '76; Andrew went to his chair in UCL [University
College London], but we lived in Cambridge and I became attached to
Girton College, although I didn't have a job at that time. Now, something else had happened: structuralism had happened, Marxism had happened, and this hit me. I could not understand, suddenly, where the focus
of interest was. Not so much in Cambridge because in fact there was no
one in the Cambridge Department of Anthropology – and this has been

one of the odd quirks of its history – that practiced as a Marxist anthropologist. But it was at University College, certainly, and the LSE, and in whatever one picked up and read, and it was in the air, and it was in social and political science and elsewhere in the university.

So, any sense that – how can I put it – one had done a job or a complete job was totally undermined by these further developments which just struck a chord, which seemed to be interesting and to some extent – although I didn't react at the time, it took some years – some of the things from *The Gender of the Gift* are the result of a not very deep but nonetheless strong sense that some issues that were being developed under that rubric of Marxist anthropology just had to be part of the general picture; so it was a question of filling in the gaps.

What I'm trying to show to you are all the points at which gaps and chasms have appeared because these require leaps.

EVC: You mentioned three major intellectual events which happened between the late '60s and early '70s, meaning feminist scholarship, Marxism and structuralism. Feminism hit you in Australia, right?

MS: Yes.

EVC: Marxism and structuralism when you were back in Cambridge?

MS: Yes, but with structuralism, the grounds had been laid by Edmund, but they were not fully fledged.

EVC: But of these three, say, paradigms, would you say that structuralism is the less visible, explicitly, in your work?

MS: [Pause] Yes, absolutely. I have never addressed those issues. Yes.

EVC: This is a provocation because I think you're a thoroughgoing structuralist, myself; I think that your work is – as Alfred Gell also thought – he wrote that you had lots of things in common with structuralism; although you have never used structuralist jargon etc., your work has a thoroughgoing structuralist inspiration. But, indeed, you do address Marxist and feminist questions directly, so they are obviously in the foreground of your writing, while structuralism is somehow muted as an explicit *source.*

MS: Yes, because it's a technique not a theory in what I do; it's a set of mental tricks. I have never done what Jimmy Weiner has done, for example, which is lay out the substance of particular texts and subject them to structuralist analysis; I have not done that.

CF: Don't you think that the whole emphasis on relations and not substances is a major point of structuralism?

MS: Yes, but it's there as an implicit tool. It's an irrefutable technique of apprehension that I've never subjected to the kind of critique that you'd want to subject it to if one were addressing this as a set of theories.

EVC: But then going back to your linear narrative . . .

MS: Okay. So, I was back in Cambridge in '76. It must have been about '78 that I then read *The Invention of Culture* by Roy Wagner [1981], and that was like a door opening. Not because I understood him – I think I must have understood about 10 percent – but because where I did understand, and especially where it applied to ethnography I was familiar with, the insights were absolutely stunning. So, those moments of comprehension were total. So, obviously I became intrigued as to how he reached those things and I began borrowing from him and, I suppose, the first evidence of that is in my contribution to *Nature, Culture, Gender* [1980], where I start referring to him explicitly.

EVC: But you were familiar with his former work, weren't you?

MS: *The Curse of Souw* [1967] I'd read and hadn't been able to finish. The embarrassing thing is, you do realize, he was writing *The Curse of Souw* when I was writing *Women in Between;* and I mean *The Curse of Souw* was twenty years down the line. It wasn't until much later I came to appreciate *The Curse of Souw* through this particular experience of reading *The Invention of Culture.*

EVC: But what was your Cambridge reception of Schneider's ideas, because Wagner was one of Schneider's most distinguished former students. It's interesting to know what was thought about American anthropology, especially that particular brand of American anthropology, the Schneiderian brand, which is the direct source of Wagner's work.

MS: Schneider was absolutely excoriated; I mean he was despised in Cambridge. He was the example of everything that was bad with American anthropology. And this was the time, of course, when Jack Goody was now in the ascendancy, and Schneider was trivialized away.

Anyway, Jack Goody then took on the mantle of this diatribe with Schneider. And it was partly mischievous, I suppose, of me to embrace Schneider at that point because that was the moment at which I was picking up Audrey Richards's stuff and doing the Elmdon work. The Annette Weiner episode had hurt me so much that I abandoned Melanesian things; I just couldn't bear to think about them, and I went off and did the Elmdon work. I was rather inspired by the thought of a cultural analysis. Of course, I have now worked through my culturalist phase, and I'm now back to social analysis, but at that point I was rather inspired by the thought of cultural analysis.

EVC: But you came across Schneider on kinship through reading Wagner or because you were about to embark on the Elmdon project?

MS: Because of the Elmdon project. I was searching for something in anthropology that I could use. And there was nothing. I couldn't use any of the stuff that the Cambridge people had produced – it just didn't speak to me

– but Schneider made a lot of sense, and of course the fact that Schneider had picked up as his core symbols culture, law and nature resonated with what had already interested me in the nature/culture question in the New Guinea context. So there was a crossover.

But it was definitely, I think, with a sense of mischief so to speak that I pursued Schneider – or rather, with a sense of freedom. You have to realize how peripheral I was at that point. Andrew had the job in London, I had little children, I was in Cambridge, had no employment, apart from a bye-fellowship in Girton and doing a bit of supervision, but didn't have an income. I was institutionally marginal. And this meant I could be myself, so to speak, or do what I wanted to do. So that was how Schneider became *involved* and was really quite an influence for quite a period.

EVC: And then you had this astonishing decade, no? From the late seventies . . .

. . . When you said, at that time you were engaging in, indulging in, cultural analysis, and then you moved back to social analysis; how do you phrase this movement back to social analysis? Where did it start? You would say that *Kinship at the Core* is a culturalist book? A Schneiderian book?

MS: Yes. Not until it had done its work; after *The Gender of the Gift,* I think I felt that I had thoroughly exploited that seam, as it were.

Well, I don't know what to say. I wonder if it's a little bit like the inventiveness that I think exists here in Brazil with you reading multiple languages, deriving things from multiple sources and perhaps feeling not metropolitan? I don't know.

I want to convey the role that a sense of inadequacy plays, because if you always think that somehow you haven't quite understood, then that puts you constantly in a position of embattlement, that there are things still to be understood. And I suppose what you referred to by that decade is that there were a whole lot of issues that I suddenly thought I needed to comprehend, which had I had a training in philosophy, I wouldn't even have dreamed of. And had I been actually doing the reading, other people would have done it for me, but I didn't do that reading; I was doing it for myself, so it's all very home-made. So, subject/object and nature/culture and what on earth relations of production are, and so forth, these things all seemed to me enormous intellectual obstacles that I needed to deal with.

CF: It seems that as you were telling your professional story that *The Gender of the Gift* was a major threshold in your career; also because, *as* you were saying, *you were* at that time marginal to any institutions. Then you were kind of institutionalized.

MS: Yes, although actually that had happened *a bit earlier*. The lectures I gave in Berkeley were in '84. I then returned to England and at that point it was going to be clear I was going to have to divorce Andrew Strathern, which I did. I didn't have a position, but then became a fellow of Trinity College and was subsequently invited to Manchester as the head of department. And in fact, the second version of *The Gender of the Gift* was written at Manchester. It's not insignificant that Roy Wagner came over as a visiting professor in Manchester for three months, a term, in '86, and he was quite an influence on the finishing of the book.

EVC: And when did you start, Marilyn, your work on modern Euro-American kinship? There's not exactly a direct connection between the Elmdon research and what you did, say, in *After Nature*. As you say, *After Nature* is an unwriting of *Kinship at the Core*. You told us how the unwriting of *Women in Between* happened – why and exactly how it happened. How did the unwriting of *Kinship at the Core* happen? And why?

MS: Okay, well this is something that I think I already talked about at Campinas. It began with a telephone call from someone who became a colleague, who said that there *was* going to be a discussion at the King's Fund think tank on egg donation. The issue *was* egg donation between sisters, which everybody portrays as a benign act of altruism. But this person said she had all sorts of anxieties because this in fact had introduced an obligation where an obligation never existed, and so forth. What would an anthropologist have to say about egg donation between sisters? This anthropologist had nothing to say, and this anthropologist knew of no anthropologist who would have anything to say either. I then began turning that over in my mind and thinking: what is my subject doing if at the end of the twentieth century in this context where it's been asked to comment on contemporary kinship practices, there's nobody who can say anything. And that really began *interesting me*. It then had alerted me to some of the issues in the new reproductive technologies. And then . . . just ten years on from reading Roy Wagner's book, I then read a book by Michelle Stanworth called *Reproductive Technologies* [1987], which was a collection of essays by mainly feminist writers, but not anthropologists – an early book. And that was about the time that I was thinking about the Morgan Lectures; I gave four Morgan Lectures. And it suddenly seemed here that here was a connection between my work on – or my interest in – issues to do with nature and culture, biology and society, and all the rest of it, and these contemporary debates. And it suddenly seemed to me that this presented me with a topic for the Morgan Lectures. And that was the basis of *After Nature*.

EVC: So *After Nature* and the Morgan Lectures *had* at least two strands: on one hand, say, American kinship, Wagner etc., and then from the other side, you had this demand for anthropology to have something to say about things like egg donation and new reproductive technologies etc. . . . So you somehow married the two projects? But you could have dealt with new reproductive technologies without bringing kinship in at all? Although now it seems obvious that those sort of things are related, the traditional kinship concerns of anthropology and new reproductive technologies, but come to think of it, there's no reason to connect the two things. You did it, but there's no particular reason. Of course, there is an obvious level where it can be connected, but not at the conceptual level at which you connected them. It was quite a momentous decision, I would say, to put these two things together.

MS: But it was so obvious from Schneider. Because Schneider had located law and nature – and what were these debates about? They were about social and biological *issues.*

CF: I think for *the* British, it is quite obvious that egg donation and new reproductive technologies are related to kinship. It's not from a contractualist view of kinship, from a French view of kinship.

EVC: Yes, but the good thing, the boon that new reproductive technologies represented for anthropology was that for the first time social anthropologists were disposed to take modern kinship seriously. Because the whole song was that kinship plays no role in modern society. That was the whole point.

MS: Exactly.

EVC: 'No, kinship is just an illusion, it's structural centrality, etc . . . ' That was the standard song. And even when Schneider proposed his model for American kinship, it was quite a sort of isolated voice saying, look, there's something more. Kinship is still part of Western cosmology; it is not something which is nonstructural; it is still central to Western cosmology.

MS: That's right.

EVC: But this was isolated, because it was American, because it was a symbolic anthropology, and he was not talking about society but about culture. You made culture mean society, right? How did you do this particular trick?

MS: I'm going to have to come back to that specific question. Can I go back to what you were talking about just a moment or two before that? Because you make me think now that actually, yes, there was an absolute parallel between that project in *After Nature* and *The Gender of the Gift*: in *The Gender of the Gift,* my intention had been let's take seriously the feminist claim that in talking about gender, we talk about society. What would a social theory of gender, therefore, look like? Which is what that book tries to be concerned with in the second part. Well, I'm doing in a sense the same in *After Nature,* which is exactly as you said. Let's take seriously *the question* . . . suppose kinship was central as it is elsewhere, what would it start looking like? And of course that's where I have to introduce my merographic *model,* because in relation to complex structures – *as* we know from French colleagues – you have to introduce nonkinship factors. And it was the realization that kinship was both 'kinship' *and* the nonkinship factors that I regarded as a sort of little breakthrough.

CF: So you think there's a completely different relationship with your data, let's say, in the case when you were working with Western society and when you were working with Melanesians?

MS: Yes. There was a polemic in *After Nature.* As a guest in Papua New Guinea, I felt I couldn't take issue with the material. I was at liberty to do what I damn well wanted to do in my own society.

CF: This *personal* relation with the data, how do you think this affects anthropological work?

MS: In my own case, I could be partisan. That is, I could take a partial view because I could expect my readership to fill in the rest. So I could simply be explicit; look, this is an account from a sort of middle-class person and so forth. Yes, because I was free, I felt free of that constraint.

There was also a political intention behind it. In Michelle Stanworth's book – you were talking about the confluence of influences on me at that point; there was a third thing – what jumped out of that collection of essays was the value being given to choice. And this, it seemed to me, was a political issue because Thatcher's government at that point was absolutely riding high on this image of customer choices: that you dispose of institutions, you recreate the individual as the choice maker, and – like many people – I was just very angry. And I formulated the question like this: how could a head of government make a statement such as there's no such thing as society? What has conspired to produce a head of government making a statement like that? It has to be all of us. That is, we are all in some way contributing to that statement. Where in English culture can I find a place where I can show the kinds of ideas that lead to a statement like that? Well, kinship is about as far removed from politics or government or whatever as you could possibly choose. If I can show that actually by looking at English kinship, one can find ideas and issues that in fact support these Thatcherite ideas, then I have shown how culture is society. That is, I have shown how in any particular domain, you will find what is replicated elsewhere in other domains – and if we want to understand

British society, we can do it through looking at English kinship. So that was my sort of mix. But the book's so diffuse you'd never guess that.

EVC: In the Manchester debate 'The Concept of Society Is Theoretically Obsolete,' someone put the question, if I can recall it well, that, okay you were attacking society in the name of culture, criticizing the concept of society but all the while keeping the concept of culture intact. And then you said, no, this could be applied to the concept of culture as well – this obviation analysis, let's say.

But at the same time, *while* in British social anthropology there was a thoroughgoing criticism of the concept of society, at the same time, if not a few years later, in American anthropology, a similar deconstruction of the concept of culture was beginning or was to begin. And it seems the very problems that British social anthropology has with society are exactly replicated in American anthropology. Sometimes you may have the impression that you can use one concept against the other, but if you put the two critiques together, what would be 'culturality', say, instead of sociality? Would such a thing as culturality exist? My question is, your work *The Gender of the Gift* is as much as *After Nature,* more than *After Nature,* a critique of the concept of society, right? There is a whole critique of the concept of society as utterly inapplicable to the Melanesian context.

MS: If you wish to understand the way they think, yes.

EVC: But then if someone comes with the American, modern critique of the concept of culture, wouldn't they say yes, but you're criticizing the concept of society in Melanesia in the name of Melanesian culture?

MS: Yes, that is absolutely right. Of course, my qualification just now was in terms of the way these people think; that is, society isn't an ingredient of their conceptual universes.

EVC: Is culture an ingredient of their conceptual universes?

MS: No, obviously it can't be either. Okay, this might sound like sidestepping. I think in answering you like this, actually, I'm answering your question as well. What are these terms for? I mean, they don't exist in themselves; we can't sit around the table and legislate as to what nature is or culture is, or the extent to which one dissolves in the other. These are concepts that, how can I put it . . . Deconstruction, if it works well, is mobile; that is, it doesn't stay put. It's a temporal process: you open things up and then they close again, and you open them up, and they close again, so on and so forth. So I'm not at all embarrassed about having disposed of the concept in one context and using it in another.

But you said, what would 'culturality' be? The problem, as I see it, with culture is not because we needed to deconstruct it internally but because it has been overused; it's the opposite: it's subject to giganticism, excess. It's used everywhere: the culture of car parking, the culture of tape-recording. So one of its characteristics is its ubiquity, the fact that it can have occurred at any moment. Well, I would salvage from that what I might call replication, that is, that what makes one set of configurations distinct from another is the extent to which certain conjunctions, relations, between forms reappear in order to make different domains familiar. So, for example, the notion that market relations are always distinct from nonmarket relations you can find in law, or you can find in families, or you can find in children's drawings or whatever.

EVC: This is a thing that plays a major role in your book *Reproducing the Future?*

MS: That's right.

EVC: This idea which cuts across all of the chapters.

MS: So I would say that the analogue to that generalized notion of sociality, if one were talking about culture, would be this notion of replication, and where you get to the limits of replication, where things cease to be replicable, where they cease to reappear, then you're in some other . . .

EVC: What you call in another context, forms which propagate.

MS: [Laughs] You show a knowledge of my work that is . . . Well, I feel I ought to give you a present. If I were a Hagener, I would kill a pig for you.

CF: Well, if you think so, I think we are even. But let me ask you: you were answering Eduardo, you were saying that you don't feel uncomfortable using a concept here and another one there in different senses because you think, after all, it is a kind of rhetorical strategy. And one of the things about *The Gender of the Gift* is that you were very explicit about fiction and rhetorical strategies, and so on. But what are the limits of this kind of rhetoric? Because as far as I understand your work, you're not a post-modernist; you're not saying all is representation of representations of representations, not this kind of vertigo. So what are the limits? – Because I think you're always in some sense using rhetorical strategies to make substantial claims about society, gender, sociality and the rest.

MS: Absolutely. There's two tests. One is the obvious one of resonance with ethnographic data; now that itself, of course, is a fiction because ethnographic data itself is produced and obviously it's produced in certain ways in order to answer the questions that you know you're going to ask; so it's to some extent a self-contained sounding board. That is why – this is the second kind of test – you will find me constantly going back to what other people have said, so that there's constant reference to other – not to other thinkers or theoreticians – but to other people who are trying to use similar ideas. So polemic is very important in my work and I think what I'm doing there – this isn't thought out, I'm trying to give an account now

– what I think I'm doing there is seeing how ideas have been digested by other people. That then gives me a moment of comment, so in other words I'm engaged with what Gregory says or Annette Weiner says or Battaglia says or Carrier says. I can be for or against; that's irrelevant. The point is all I've done is, so to speak, a half-turn from what somebody else has already thought. So what I'm actually claiming is that I belong to a community of thinkers who share a number of common suppositions, and I'm adding a twist to what other people have thought. And that's a rather Kuhnian thing to do, but I'm not . . . Do you understand what I'm saying?

CF: Yes, I do, but I think one of the things about your work and listening to you personally is that you are very conscious about rhetorical strategies and you use *them*. And when you were talking yesterday about account-ability, *you said*, well there are kinds of rhetorical strategies like irony and all that, to deal with that. So I was trying to understand what role rhetoric plays in your work. It sounds to me that it was a very conscious thing and elaborated.

MS: Well, part of it I'm afraid – and this doesn't put me in a very good light – part of it is being irresponsible; that is, I'm not claiming total responsibility for what I'm doing, I'm shrugging it off, I'm saying that's rhetoric – that's running away. One doesn't like to admit to that kind of thing. The second part, though, is perhaps the counterpart to the role that the notion of aesthetics plays in *The Gender of the Gift*, which is that things that live in culture, so to speak – or live in life – live because they have a particular form, and they persuade because they take a particular form. And I do actually think that it matters the form that things take, that it matters whether one starts off with relationships or whether one starts off with the notion of things as we were talking about earlier.

If I were a different kind of person, what I'd be telling you is that I have a theory here and the elements of my theory are A, B and C; and A means this, and B means this, and C means this, and I'm not dealing with X, Y and Z, and let's proceed from this theoretical base. That's just not the mode I operate from. What I'm saying instead – to whoever's listening – is that X and Y have posed this question this way, but there are other things to think about: let's change the form in which they're thinking. But because that is conscious, I'm not attributing to it any kind of absolute or essentialist status. I'm saying that is for the sake of argument.

EVC: Yes, I want an argument. Much of your theoretical effort has been to dismantle certain central theoretical oppositions, like say society and individual, culture and nature – precisely these two. On the other hand, many people have read *The Gender of the Gift* as erecting a major opposi-

tion between us and them. This is a recurrent theme now, centraliza-
tion, occidentalization, the gift and commodity dichotomy, etc. . . . And
you have answered this question on some occasions, precisely by saying,
now this is mostly a heuristic and rhetorical way of putting things. But
my point has to do with this: I suppose you have the feeling that the
Melanesians have something very distinctive, very different from our way
of thinking. I'm not asking you a question because I can't but agree with
you! That's the way I feel. But could you share with us some of your ideas
about these particular types of criticisms.

MS: Okay, yes, this has been a consistent problem with readers and critics:
gift and commodity, us and them and so forth. What you have to realize
is that us and them isn't male and female; in other words, were I coming
at it *from* a feminist perspective, I would be wanting to create a division
between male and female and say that we look at these things, one thing
from a masculinist point of view, another thing from a feminist point
of view – and what I'm actually inserting is an anthropological comment, that actually the divide between Melanesians and Euro-Americans
is greater. So the one is an answer to the other. But, of course, you solve a
problem and create new problems. So the problem I'm left with is that it
looks as though I'm endorsing this essentialism.

   You put your finger on it when you said that the difference is in
ways of thinking, which I would expand slightly and say it is in ways
of description. And I think that, perhaps – bizarre as though it might
sound – some of this recent thinking I've been forced to do in relation
to audit and so forth, whereas I was saying yesterday, audit trades in
descriptions and in self-descriptions and from your own comments on
epistemology, I think you, Eduardo, have helped me see the distinctiveness of our ways of knowledge making, which, of course, rests so centrally
on description. And I have intuitively, for a long time, thought that the
way we live, the way we live with ambiguities, with contradictions, with
being able to do several things at once, is so different from what we
require of descriptions – I mean, it's like the difference between riding
a bicycle and describing how to ride a bicycle: you wouldn't finish a
book describing how you actually get on a bike and keep there. It is in
the practices of description that these differences emerge, but we traffic
in descriptions and therefore, absolutely, I would stand by the fact that
we produce different descriptions of ourselves from the kinds of descriptions that Melanesians produce of themselves. This has nothing to do
with comprehension or cognitive structures or whether I can understand
a Melanesian or whether I can interact or behave or whatever. Those
things are not problematic. The issue comes the point at which one starts

producing accounts of the world. And I think something very similar happens in relation to the genders.

EVC: So this is not a universal versus relative issue at all? In the sense that you are not saying that ... Because what people are actually implying is that you are denying commonality of human nature between us and them, right?

MS: Yes, because what I'm saying is that where the difference is, is that their accounts of human nature are radically different from our accounts of human nature, but the point is we can only traffic in accounts. There's no way of sidestepping that difference. I mean, you can't say, well now we understand, it's just a matter of different accounts, let's get on with our commonalities, because at the moment we enter into communication, we do so through these self-descriptions. And I think one has to absolutely understand that.

EVC: Marilyn, I'd like to take up a particular concept which I think plays an absolutely central role in your work – and it probably has to do with that last question I was asking about, us and them, which is a concept of form – your notion of perspectives in your use of form. In a world dominated by processual concepts, you are almost isolated, one of the few voices that speak in favour of form and not in favour of process.

MS: Alright, there's a whole lot of concepts that I can't abide. Now that doesn't mean to say, going back to this contradiction thing, that I haven't used them myself, but in the abstract I can't abide them. It began way back with John Barnes; it began way back with the notion that if you didn't have clear-cut descent groups then somehow you were in a fluid position. And there was a whole language to do with fluidity and ambiguity that I couldn't stand because it seemed to me what the ethnographers were doing were not describing observed fluidities; they were simply being careless with language. That is, that they weren't using language with precision. So when people start saying, well, things are much more ambiguous, I want to *know* do they really mean ambiguous, do they really mean there's a choice between ways of going, or are they just saying things are vague and unresolved, in which case it's a failure of description. So that's one thing that irritates me no end.

That then became taken over by the notion of fragmentation, which is something else I can't abide; when people *say* the world is fragmented and all the contemporary jargon about ... You know, the sort of stuff that Clifford uses, again *this* irritates me because anybody who poses a notion of fragmentation poses a concept of wholeness and they aren't thinking it through; they're just escaping from having to make connections.

Now process belongs to that family of terms that I find irritating when they're used simply to escape from other ways of describing – which is one reason why in the paper I gave today I talked in a very cumbersome way of two trajectories and of doing two things at the same time, which seems to me more interesting and more fruitful than going the Geertzian mode of blurred genres and wading in shallow waters. I just don't like that imprecision. And it seems to me that to say that things are processual and so forth belongs to this set.

Form. Form, I suspect, is a black box. You may not agree with me, but for narratives or accounts to work, there have to be things that are unexplained. There have to be repositories like holes in the ground where you put things that aren't otherwise at work in what you write.

I suppose, if I don't want to unpack form, if I want to keep it as a black box, I suppose there is one strong sense in which I'm using it which is in relation to this concept of reification – which again I'm not sure if I've really thought through properly – but it's borne in on me by the kinds of judgements that people in New Guinea make as to whether things exist or not: Is someone healthy? Is this clan strong? What is that person thinking? What is the evidence that we have that things have happened? Well, the evidence that things have happened is how things now appear, and for things to appear, they have to take a particular form: the body has to appear in a particular way, or the number of men have to appear, or you have to have a dispute or you don't have a dispute. And this is your evidence; these are your things. And it struck me that this production of things is the counterpart ... well, didn't I say right at the beginning, maybe it's from another conversation.... Josephides's question, if the production of things in a capitalist economy conceals social relations, what then does the production of social relations conceal *if the not economy ... ?* It is symbolic form, the reification of things. And I understand things not in a substantial sense but in an aesthetic sense, that things are recognized by, and I use this term, form; their appearance, their qualities and attributes that are visible. That is what Hagen people *do not* theorize; they do not have an account of why things have forms, because the taking of form is their evidence. Evidence has to be nonnegotiable, or it doesn't work as evidence. So this is not an assumption of discourse. Whereas for us it is constantly; we're constantly investigating why things. All our taxonomies and botany and classification systems are about the specification of the nature of things. But these people don't do that because things are to them the evidence of people having acted.

CF: It's interesting – just a footnote – that the concept of sociality which you use and which we draw from your work many times in Amazonian ethnology – you could say that there are two ways of using it. One, *more phenomenological,* which is found in Joanna Overing's work, is to say sociality is a kind of experience of social relations or something like that. And we use it in, let's say, a more structural approach as forms of sociality: the word 'form' here is the main difference in Amazonian anthropology between a more structuralist approach to sociality and a more phenomenological approach to sociality.

EVC: This also has to do with something which I think in the Amazonian context. Since you are giving an interview in a context which is mostly composed of Amazonian ethnographers, it would be interesting if you could say something about what relation, if any, you see between your notion of sociality and notions of morality. Because in our context, in the Amazonian context, sociality has been strongly correlated with a certain moral conception of what social life is all about. And you say, if I'm not mistaken, in *The Gender of the Gift,* precisely that sociality has nothing to do with morality or something to that effect. A very short sentence, but very, very definite about that.

MS: Okay, those things go together. Yes, I would say I'm a formalist in your sense as far as relations are concerned. One reason why I like the word sociality is precisely because it is not the term sociability. Now sociability in English means the experience of community, empathy – and I said I didn't like these words – fragmentation, fluidity, processes. Well, there's another cluster of things I can't abide – I'm going to emerge as a very intolerant person! – another cluster of things I can't abide, and that is the sentimentalizing of the notion of relationality. Now, this comes partly from a feminist and a female sensitivity, because you must realize that feminists and women are supposed to be dumped at the sentimental end of social life. And whenever I talk about the word relations, people instantly assume, 'well, of course, she's a woman, she's bound to value relations,' and so forth, because they're reading into relations this peculiar construct which is derived, I think, from kinship, which is that relationships are somehow inherently of value. Now, something that Jack Goody taught years ago – I'm almost certain it was from him – something that always struck in my mind, is that warfare and so forth is as much a relationship as making peace. And that little rule of thumb, so to speak, has kept with me ever since.

We're dealing with a very persuasive set of constructs in Euro-American thought that I've not really seen described anywhere. Let me give you an example. Or maybe this isn't Euro-American thought; maybe it's just English. You must tell me. In English, I could say to you, Eduardo has a real personality. Now I'm using personality in two senses: I'm using personality in the sense that we all have personalities, but I'm also using personality in the sense that Eduardo has a strong personality. Now this occurs again and again and again in our language. And relations is a word exactly like this. I can say we have relations, and I mean both we have relations, of course, it's axiomatic, we belong to . . . this is a social context, we have relations in a formal sense, but I also mean that we have relations in an intensive socializing, sentimental sense: there's always this moral value. So I hate the sentimentalizing of relations, the reduction of reciprocity to altruism, for example. The reduction of sociality to sociability. All these moments when these terms become imbued – in these cases it happens to be positive overtones but, of course, if one talks about warfare or dispute they start becoming negative overtones. Now this is a problem that I see with the . . . It comes out of structural functionalism, it comes out of the notion that society is inherently solidary – and I think this is where Fortes, of course, puts his morality: the notion that it's a good thing to have relations, the notion that, therefore, disputes and warfare somehow fragment something. Now this, of course, was Lévi-Strauss's major contribution. And in fact if you look at the debate between Radcliffe-Brown and Lévi-Strauss, you see there the difference laid out very clearly. For example, in the use of the term alliance. When Radcliffe-Brown is talking about alliance – as in joking relationships – he means a relationship that can be both positive and negative between two entities that nonetheless carries a cohesive force, as though you had two entities being joined. And this of course is the primitive element in Euro. – I'm sorry, I keep calling it perhaps I should just call it middle-class English – English kinship thinking which Schneider understood, which is you have persons and they are related. And of course what Lévi-Strauss says is, no you have relations and entities are the products of relations, and that when he's using the term alliance, he's referring to a formal position of enchainment; he is not referring to what Radcliffe-Brown means in terms of solidarity and so forth. This is a major difference between the British and French views.

Now, long after Radcliffe-Brown and Lévi-Strauss more or less finished their debate, well, you see, it wasn't just a matter of debate, we are dealing with – this is where I want to borrow the term culture – cultural issues that are embedded in ways of managing relationships, in English constructs and all the rest of it. And the notion that relations somehow connect and somehow connecting is a positive activity endures; it's almost impossible to get rid of. If people tell me how to get rid of it. But does this make sense?

EVC: But this is a very interesting point because in my view of understanding it at least, of translating it, is that your concept of sociality is above all aesthetical. This other concept is above all ethical. So it's a problem of, say, pitting aesthetics against ethics, aesthetics in this wider, proper sense of form, social form . . .

MS: That's right because aesthetics is about the appropriateness of form. There is a propriety to the way things appear. And in fact, things don't appear unless there is some kind of will or intention, so to speak, which you can then act on and judge – and so it's judgmental. So, yes, aesthetics is a question of judgement.

CF: Just a last question. You have been in this comparative meeting on Amazonian and Melanesian gender relations, in Spain, the Wenner-Gren symposium[2]; what are your impressions about the possibility of comparison and the state of the compared things that were presented or suggested or alluded to at the conference?

MS: What emerged, I think, for all of us was the quite surprising extent to which we became interested in one another's ethnographies, because actually at many, many points, those ethnographies were joining, walking and speaking to one another. The most interesting difference, I suppose – and this is partly the point of the conference and certainly interesting for me – was the different role that gender constructs play and the visibility of this divide. And Eduardo and I have been talking about this often, off and on, since his visit in Cambridge.

What I have got from it, I suppose, is that the motivating instrument that creates boundaries for people – in your paper you talk about the need (in the context of reproduction and generation) the need to go outside in order to draw in what is exotic, which is familiarized and then, of course, re-estranged in order to be first absorbed and then killed and so forth. The motivating boundary that contributes to notions of reproduction – and I mean reproduction in the sense of procreative, fertile continuation of parent-child relations, generation and so forth – in Melanesia revolves around the difference between male and female, while in Amazonia we are dealing with possibly human enemies but otherwise with nonhuman spirits, animals and all the rest of it. This is a basically crude rendition. The fruitfulness of that to me is to realize that Melanesians are not dividing humans off from the nonhuman world, but they're making divisions between different kinds of humans and that the gender difference, so to speak, is crucial to this, that it creates a difference between paternal and maternal kin, and – borrowing now from Eduardo's interest in ontology – I can now formulate, I think, the fact that the way in which a person relates to their paternal kin puts them in a different state of being from the way in which they relate to maternal kin, that these are distinct worlds within which people are operating.

I don't think I've answered your question directly. The thing was that that conference, I think, was very generative. And I think everybody there was stimulated, but not in the ways that we were directed to be. The hope was that we might sit down and systematically compare item and item.

Can I ask a question back? Where would you see the future basis for critical anthropology? For critique?

EVC: I think the future of anthropology is that idea of Latour's of symmetrical anthropology; that's what you do.

MS: Yes.

EVC: That's precisely what you're doing, very few people do it because – this is the interesting thing – normally, traditionally, people used savages to teach moral lessons. It was basically either to make us proud of not being them or make us guilty of not being them anymore. And that was it. And then there was a moment where people who worked in so-called primitive societies and people who worked in so-called complex societies had nothing to say to one another

MS: There is a tremendous intolerance, actually, in Britain of anything that smacks of some kind of exotic or distant condition that can't be reduced to effects of colonization . . . European history, the expansion of the West, policy related and all the rest of it . . . which is actually really my quarrel with some contemporary anthropologists. I'm out of sympathy with the need to legitimate the interest of these things by showing they're contingent on the expansion of Europe in the Pacific or wherever. It's an ethical point.

EVC: This is narcissism, the worst form of narcissism.

MS: That's right. That then makes me exaggerate the differences. You know you asked right at the beginning about theoretical decisions. Here's a theoretical decision, and it's one that I've become conscious of in the issue of the new reproductive technologies because there, there is a whole lot of people who say, look, there's nothing new in this, we've always been doing this, the techniques have altered. And there are other people who say, oh my God, the world's coming to an end, it's cataclysmic. Well, I have taken the theoretical decision to belong to the second camp. Partly because I think it's more interesting, it's more entertaining, there's more juice for the mind; but seriously and politically, the first reaction – that is that there's nothing new here, we've always been used to this, we've always been doing this – is a profoundly conservative ethic that in fact encourages the most radical practice because it legitimates . . . you can do anything because you aren't doing anything new . . . therefore, whereas the second one which says, oh my God, the world's coming to an end, is of course absurd in that formula, but it does say, hang on a minute, stop, pause, what are we doing? And it is that moment of standing back and saying, my God, what's happening here? that I prefer. Well, the argument that says, look, everything is to be interpreted in terms of the history of colonization and Euro-American history, and you can only understand New Guineans as plantation labourers or whatever, and you're simply exoticizing – I belong to the other camp of very deliberately exaggerating the differences simply because it makes one pause, stand back . . .

EVC: Marilyn for a final comment about rights. I know that you have started to work more or less systematically to know the question of intellectual property rights, and you have a special interest in the notion of property but also especially in the notion of rights as a kind of language. I'm probably misconstruing what you haven't even started doing but . . . My feeling is that you're going to, I don't know why but I would imagine that you are going to . . . suppose that we stay with the gift-commodity distinction, this so comfortable distinction which I like a lot. Now, I would say that rights is the relational correlative of the commodity; the commodity is to the thing as right is to relation. Right is the type of relation, the only type or the model type of relation that you can have in a commodity situation.

MS: I am going to use this; this is very useful.

EVC: Right is the form that the relation takes in a commodity economy. What would be the equivalent of this ontological category of right in the gift economy? Could we develop a language equivalent? Could we present an alternative to the language of rights? Because my problem with the language of rights is that the language of rights inevitably implies the commodity horizon, let's say. The notion of rights is deeply embedded in the commodity horizon. There is only one right, after all: the right of property. Right follows; right is just the name of right of property. Now if you want to rephrase the whole notion of intellectual property, what could take the place of right as a particular reification of relations?

MS: Okay, rights is the relational correlate of commodities, so what are we looking for in the gift? We're looking for the substantial or the thing-like correlation of the gift? Is that what we're looking for? Is that where your emphasis is?

EVC: No, because I probably put the question wrongly, but, say, if you take the gift and the commodity as things, then you have . . .

CF: Two kinds of relations to these things.

EVC: Of course, gift is a relation, commodity is a relation, but commodity is a relation insofar as it embodies a certain number of rights.

MS: Okay, so we're taking gifts in a commodity sense, that is imagining a gift as a thing.

EVC: Absolutely.

CF: Commodity is to gift, as right is to what?

EVC: This was a commodity equation; you're absolutely right because I was defining gift in thingy terms of commodities, as it were, a thing just for the sake of the argument. Because we need a language to talk to politicians – and this language has to have a modicum, a minimum of reification. We have to present them with something similar to rights, if you see what I mean? We need some handle to grab the whole . . .

MS: Well, I must go away and think about this. Let me just work this through. The commodity rights presuppose a singular position, that is the definition of a singularity; whether we're dealing with one person or many doesn't matter. We're dealing with a state of singularity. The gift notion has to refer to the outcome of a relationship, the outcome of a difference; it can't be singularity. So it has to be something drawn from a procreative idiom, possibly a performative idiom like effect, but that won't do. Which is one reason I think I'm drawn to the intellectual property stuff because the intellectual property stuff is actually taking Euro-American thinkers way, way into fields that the language just doesn't cope with. These people are at the end of their conceptual tether.

NOTES

1. Interview date: 22 September 1998. This interview was first published in Portuguese in the journal *Mana*, 5(2): 157–75, 1999. The editor is grateful for the opportunity to publish it here in English for the first time.
2. This eventually became a book Gregor and Tuzin (2001).

REFERENCES

Gregor, Thomas, and Donald Tuzin. 2001. *Gender in Amazonia and Melanesia: And Exploration of the Comparative Method*. Berkeley: University of California Press.

Fortes, Meyer. 1969. *Kinship and the Social Order: The Legacy of Lewis Henry Morgan*. Chicago: Aldine Publishing.

Stanworth, Michelle, ed. 1987. *Reproductive Technologies: Gender, Motherhood, and Medicine*. Minneapolis: University of Minnesota Press.

Strathern, Marilyn. 1972. *Women in Between: Female Roles in a Male World: Mount Hagen, New Guinea*. London: Seminar Press.

——. 1980. 'No Nature, No Culture: The Hagen Case'. In *Nature, Culture and Gender*, edited by C.P. Maccormack and M. Strathern, 174–222. Cambridge: Cambridge University Press.

——. 1981a. 'Culture in a Netbag: The Manufacture of a Subdiscipline in Anthropology'. *Man* 16(4): 665–68.

——. 1981b. *Kinship at the Core: An Anthropology of Elmdon, a Village in North-West Essex in the Nineteen-Sixties.* Cambridge: Cambridge University Press.

——. 1988. *The Gender of the Gift.* Berkeley: University of California Press.

——. 1992. *After Nature: English Kinship in the Late Twentieth Century.* Cambridge: Cambridge University Press.

Wagner, Roy. 1967. *The Curse of Souw: Principles of Daribi Clan Definition and Alliance in New Guinea.* Chicago: University Press.

——. 1981. *The Invention of Culture.* Chicago: Chicago University Press.

Weiner, Annette B. 1976. *Women of Value, Men of Renown: New Perspectives in Trobriand Exchange.* Austin: University of Texas Press.

Marilyn Strathern had the good fortune to receive initial – and indelible – training in Papua New Guinea, which led to work, among other things, on kinship and gender relations. In the United Kingdom she subsequently became involved with anthropological approaches to the new reproductive technologies, intellectual property, audit cultures and interdisciplinarity. Now retired from the Cambridge Department of Social Anthropology, she is (honorary) life president of the Association of Social Anthropologists (ASA). Strathern is currently working on issues in the conceptualization of relations, some of which were sketched out in her 2005 book, *Kinship, Law and the Unexpected: Relatives Are Often a Surprise.*

Eduardo Viveiros de Castro is a Professor of Social Anthropology at the Museu Nacional, Federal University of Rio de Janeiro. He was Simón Bolívar Professor of Latin American Studies, Cambridge University (1997–98) and directeur de recherches at the Conseil national de recherche scientifique (1999–2001). His major publications are *From the Enemy's Point of View* (Chicago, 1992), *A Inconstância da Alma Selvagem* (São Paulo, 2002), *Cannibal Metaphysics* (Minneapolis, 2014) and *The Relative Native* (Chicago, 2015).

Carlos Fausto is an Associate Professor of Social Anthropology at the Museu Nacional, Federal University of Rio de Janeiro and senior researcher of the National Council for the Development of Science and Technology in Brazil. He has published *Os indios antes do Brasil* (2000), *Inimigos fiéis* (2001) and *Warfare and Shamanism in Amazonia* (2012). He has coedited *Time and Memory in Indigenous Amazonia* (2007), *L'Image rituelle* (2014), *Paroles en images* (2016) and *Ownership and Nurture* (2016). He is also the codirector of the feature film *The Hyperwomen* (2011).

Chapter Two

The Scale(s) of Justice

Carol J. Greenhouse

Marilyn Strathern's ethnographic work has been deeply influential in relation to current anthropological concerns with law, politics and bureaucracy, even though these were neither consistently in the foreground of her analytical concerns nor, nowadays, the contributions for which she is best known. Yet her work on disputing and the politics of law in the area of Mount Hagen was widely read by legal anthropologists as it came into print in the 1970s, and her subsequent projects of reflexive and comparative experimentation were prominent among the comparative and interpretive resources that enabled anthropologists to escape from subfield framings confined by older and more narrowly jural concerns and their corresponding theoretical tensions.[1] That this was the case suggests the power of her work to mobilize resources across lateral (even hidden) terrains.

Always ethnographically suspicious of anyone's claims to speak for others, Strathern has been keenly attentive to the mutual entanglements of anthropological practice and state discourse. Particularly in relation to personhood as a social fact not capturable by or reducible to the individual, Strathern attends to the protean qualities of persons and social relationality under different sorts of institutional regimes.

Strathern's publications on gender, dividuality, inequality, agency – framed around problems of feminist theory (especially at that time conceivable as a contradiction between universalism and relativism[2]) drew (and continue to draw) attention to the knowledge practices that constitute the person *in relation to other relations.* The relational person is at the convergence of two separate conversations – drawing together a figuration from classic social anthropology (a repertoire always nearby in Strathern's narratives of her own reasoning) and a proposition from feminist theory, registered as a comparative question about inequality. Her introduction to *Dealing in Inequality* states the problem this way:

> The present volume ... is non-adjudicatory in character, non-exclusive in method. Rather than foreshadowing a conclusion about the prevalence of sexual inequality ... , it draws attention to problems in anthropological prac- tice. To regard ourselves as dealing in inequality is to make an explicit stand in relation to the analytical activity which here defines us: how we make known to ourselves that inequalities exist. (1987, 2)

The critical valence of this body of work in the 1980s was inescap- able, since to reinstate the premise (if indirectly via Melanesian material) that persons grow each other through partnerships expressed as gifts and exchange (among other things) was not only to ironize the rising neoliberal- ism of the Reagan-Thatcher era ('there is no society, only individuals'[3]) but also to situate it centrally within a comparative ethnographic frame. That frame was built not of *likeness* but of *actual relations* of mutual asymmetrical responsibility.

The contrast between Melanesia on the one hand and Thatcher era Britain on the other opens a space for her scrutiny of anthropology's knowl- edge work as the third term that illuminates the others. Readers of *Patterns of Culture* (Benedict 1934) will recognize the literary method – here inverted to make anthropology's capacity for comparison the inseparable other side of its ethnographic richness and reflexive reach. The fullest statement of these always partial connections is spelled out in Strathern's *The Gender of the Gift* (1988), which came to U.S. readers just as the George H.W. Bush electoral campaign seemed poised to make the Reagan Revolution (including its recoil against elements of the civil rights legislation of the previous genera- tion) a mandate without a viable alternative.

For anthropologists in the United States interested in law at that time, the impact of Strathern's work was immediate – most visibly in three ways. First, her attention to the social conditions of knowledge production and exchange involving anthropologists' working relationships in the field and in the profession constructively broadened the conversation around the 'crisis of representation' in ethnography.[4]

Second, from this vantage point, one could move across distances and differences that local habit (and anthropologies otherwise) had led us to imagine as separate worlds – the one we live in as citizens and imagine we know deeply and the one where we work ethnographically and can imagine we know only problematically. Strathern cancels this divide by situating it within the middle of anthropology itself (how we make things known to ourselves), rather than between anthropology and its objects. For those of us who work on the United States as well as in it, this formulation was of the utmost importance – even a relief. I will come back to this point shortly.

A third area where the impact of her work was especially influential among anthropologists concerned with politics and law, and that was – is – her concept of the *dividual,* reclaiming partiality and partnership as the core of social life, and the vantage points from which knowledge practices are accessible as ethnographic objects. In this formulation – which could not have been more different than the free market individualism gathering force as common sense among the mediatized sectors of the public – anthropologists found a critical discourse of broad relevance and applied it well beyond the Melanesian social fields that were its original referent. These aspects of her contributions to the field are evident and ongoing, as is clear from her publications and a wide circuit of citation. Less prominent, I think, are the implications of her approach to comparison – as grounded in relations of relations – for anthropologists concerned with the state, and that is my focus in what follows.

In this article, I draw on Strathern's work to explore two major developments in the evolution of U.S. neoliberalism from partisan ideology (as it was during the Reagan administration in the 1980s) to bipartisan consensus (as it became under the Clinton administration in the 1990s).[5] I compare two legislative developments: the failure of a major civil rights act under presidential veto in 1990 and a welfare reform law that terminated entitlements that had been in place since the Roosevelt administration's New Deal. Both involve reworking of citizenship and security around the key terms of the rising movement for neoliberal reform. While Strathern's publications did not address these developments directly, her publications in this period – culminating in *The Gender of the Gift* – offered an ethnographic accounting of the incommensurability (read: nonuniversality) of cultural ideas about personhood and exchange.

Indeed, her work constitutes ethnography as an important critical counterweight at precisely the right juncture (against the discourse of relationality in the new political mainstream) and with the appropriate means (another discourse of relations). This is the context of my article, in which I take up the normalization of neoliberalism in the United States by examining highly public contests over these legislative initiatives from an ethnographic perspective. My material is drawn from congressional hearings over civil rights and social security, in the course of which the nature of private relationships became a volatile question with direct implications with respect to the legitimate scope of federal power.

THE STATE AS A PROBLEM OF SCALE

Since the late 1980s, the cultural turn in the ethnography of the state has rendered states primarily in their discursivity, that is, the ways they are imagined, read, spoken about and encountered in the instances where a state's agents actually appear.[6] If Margaret Thatcher could say that society does not exist, social theorists returned the compliment in their claim that 'the state' does not exist, its concreteness being an inference based on its moments of appearance through discourse. It is this *mutuality* of denial that I want to pursue through the self-proclaimed complementarity of their respective critical objects: the assertion of the state through a denial of its political communities against the assertion of political community through a denial of the state.

Thinking about the theoretical debate this way allows us to keep talking about states without defining them as a category or imagining them as a particular form of organization. And also since (from the vantage point of my own ethnographic concerns) this framing parallels the way federal legislative and judicial debates over rights in the 1990s and since unfold as contests over the relative and mutually implied powers of the federal government over nonstate institutions, notably businesses.

The convergence of the main U.S. political parties (though not necessarily the electorate) around neoliberal principles in the 1990s came about in part through these debates, which gave strong victories to those who argued for limiting the federal role in civil rights on the grounds that the problem of inequality was essentially a moral question rather than a legal one. Specifically, the winning position became one that claimed that the need for civil rights law had already been fulfilled. This framing was crucial, not only for legal reasons but also for the bipartisan political expedient of holding onto a reading of recent U.S. history that celebrated the civil rights struggle as a triumph of democracy – while reframing racial equality negatively as special rights antagonistic to the free market.

The triumphalism of that rendering was and is double edged: it defines the need for rights in terms of race (since the struggle was explicitly in racial terms) and defines it as past. How to claim equality in the present, then, becomes a serious gamble – since race is also not-race, and rights claims quickly morph into questions of state powers. Strathern's *Dealing with Inequality* is strikingly relevant to this conundrum, since – as in the historical moment that was the book's surround – the book opens with a meditation on the question of how to think *inequality* in the absence of conceptual categories state and society. Her terrain is Melanesia and other contexts where indigenous knowledge offers no parallels to these concepts; however, her solution to the problem is germane here, too, in her suggestion that the underlying question is not how people belong to these larger categories but how they imagine themselves in relationships of certain kinds.

She describes this as 'a cross-cultural problem' in their everyday 'living' (1987, 6–7) as well as the makings of a comparative ethnographic approach, as she explains in the volume introduction:

> One solution to this constructional issue in the building of relationships requires that things/persons also be conceptualized as standing for things/persons they are not. What is striking about many of the systems described in this book is not the immutability of gender, but its transactability. Contrasts between men and women become a vehicle for the creation of value: *for evaluating one set of powers by reference to another.* (1987, 7; original emphasis)

Once one accepts the premise that representation is not descriptive, thinking about inequality as a comparative problem of how relational categories function representationally obviates the aspects of state discourse that have always been most theoretically and methodologically tendentious for ethnographers – notably the construction of states as large-scale organizations and as arenas of membership. Strathern's suggestion sweeps away both of these problems, leaving us with the question of how relational categories function in the constitution of state powers of particular kinds. To borrow the exquisite pun from the end of the introduction of *The Gender of the Gift,* 'we need the discipline to hold the thought' (1988, 40). Let us turn to the first example:

REPRESENTATIONAL EQUALITY IN QUESTION

In 1990, the Democratic Congress was set for a major contest against the George H.W. Bush administration and the U.S. Supreme Court over civil rights. In a recent employment discrimination case, the Supreme Court had reversed a lower court's finding in a way that raised the bar for employment discrimination claims generally.[7] At issue was the standard by which an employer could be held to account for hiring practices that yielded *disparate impact,* a form of discrimination by which a universal criterion yields selective effects in terms of race, gender or other considerations not attributable to business necessity and barred by federal civil rights law.

The Supreme Court's ruling shifted the *burden of proof* (i.e. the responsibility for proving discrimination) in disparate impact cases to the plaintiff – that is, the unsuccessful candidate. Formerly, it had been the employers who were obliged to prove that their hiring practices were not discriminatory. In taking up employment discrimination, Senate Democrats made explicit their intention to block the effects of the Supreme Court's ruling with new legislation that would restore plaintiffs' access to law. The legislation was proposed as the Civil Rights Act of 1990, and the legislative process was an arena for major public debate over the meaning of equality.

In the ensuing debate, advocates and critics alike invoked the civil rights landmarks of the 1960s as their baseline reference.[8] But the rhetorical common ground belied deep disagreements over inequality as a province for law. For the bill's proponents, American history is a history of civil rights law and a history of ongoing need for federal remediation of racial inequality. For its critics, inequality is not the source of difference but the symptom of differences fundamentally beyond the scope of law. This was the position of Glenn Loury, a member of the faculty at Harvard's Kennedy School of Government and a leading witness for the opposition. Loury turned the question of responsibility and proportionality the other way, to ask why 'blacks . . . despite the long-term upward trend,' remain in poverty. His answer – in language that may sound dated and harsh to modern ears – outlined the symptoms of a social pathology that put inequality beyond the reach of civil rights legislation:

> The proportion of families headed by a single parent has risen dramatically among blacks during the same period in which individuals' earnings have improved. As well, the percentage of black children residing in households in which only one parent is present has risen sharply . . . More generally, the emergence of what some have called an 'urban underclass' has been noted in many of our cities . . . Unfortunately, these problems are unlikely to be mitigated by civil rights legislation, because they do not derive in any direct way from the practice of employment discrimination. (Ibid. 77)

Loury's position was already familiar from classic sociological accounts of the African American family. In the hearings over disparate impact in connection with the Civil Rights Act of 1990, the connection between race and inequality was reworked around the criterion of personal moral responsibility. Loury's argument about families compartmentalized race and class in two contradictory ways: For those who were upwardly mobile (those 'individuals' in a position to benefit from labour market gains) race is a personal characteristic, proof of the colour blindness of the market. For those others, the 'underclass', race and class remain fused by a collective cultural pathology that (the argument went) prevents people from taking advantage of their given opportunities. To overstate the position only slightly: if you are upwardly mobile we can help you through employment rights; if you are not it is not because of your race but because of your orientation to work and responsibility – so the law does not apply.

Thus settling the burden of proof on employers was – to critics of the bill – excessively and unnecessarily burdensome. Equality could not be achieved by adding to the law's antidiscrimination measures; indeed, critics argued, such measures could only hamper businesses' efforts to benefit everyone. Thus business was set in a privileged trade-off position relative to civil rights remedies. Congress passed the Civil Rights Act of 1990, but President George H.W. Bush vetoed it; a successor bill was passed into law and signed in 1991, without the burden of proof provision.

The burden of proof debate rewrote race positively as an individual's skin colour (i.e. of no determining value); it rewrote culture negatively as collective social pathology (i.e., associated causally with poverty and other social problems). As they emerged from the congressional debates of 1990 and 1991, these usages – deeply wound through U.S. history with racism and antiracism – had a complex afterlife. The defeat of racial equality claims as the basis for civil rights had major consequences in bringing to an end a federal politics of representation that the avatars of neoliberalism had so vehemently criticized as a burden on business and markets. Consequently, five years later, when a Democratic president faced a new Republican Congress fresh from its midterm electoral triumph, a bipartisan consensus – forged in the legislative context I have just described – looked again to the argument that had won in connection to the Civil Rights Act of 1990 and made new use of it.

The text of the Welfare Reform Act of 1996 opens with three pages of findings in support of a state's interest in marriage, on the grounds of defending vulnerable young women from predatory men. But they were premises more than findings (U.S. Congress 1996). The bill's proponents extensively and explicitly articulated a statistical correlation between welfare and teen pregnancy as the basis for eliminating welfare entitlements, and in spite of critics' challenges to that correlation, the bill went forward as a project cast explicitly as social engineering.

E PLURIBUS PLURUM

In the chapter on domination at the end of *The Gender of the Gift,* Strathern sums up some of the key points from the Melanesian side of her analysis: 'One body is by contrast conceptually unitary, whether in a singular or a plural form, and encompasses future relations within itself. But the conceptual equation between one and many hides a crucial sociological difference. The factor that is hidden is one of its terms, namely plurality itself' (1988, 327). At first this observation might seem to be specific to the material she has in view, but it is also suggestive of the way contemporary knowledge practices closer to home make individuality ambiguous through assessment and audit mechanisms.

In the hearings I have just described, the references to Americans were either singular (this person of colour, this welfare client) or plural (all of them), but only in the statistical sense. The individual – the person with rights – was never more than a figuration of a statistic; even the witnesses – sometimes as many as seventy in one day – were limited to just enough speech to make their representational claims performative and their appearance convincing as democratic participation. The connection between constructions (and corresponding performances) of personhood are here directly linked to the knowledge practices that – literally and figuratively – govern them; these mundane displacements of knowledge are both conventionally produced by and yield, experientially, the sense of scale (see Strathern 1992, 130–31).

But it is not just that the individual in these instances is limited to the figuration of the many. As Strathern insists, the 'conceptual equation between one and many' hides plurality within its terms. This formula is differently but equally apt in this case – in that the hearings constructed individuality only with respect to figurations of broader categories that are themselves plural. To explain: The history of racial domination and rights struggle before the state in the United States sustains a pervasive discourse that makes race trump other categories of social description. It is not biology that fixes race to individuals, in other words, but a thick history of legal and political struggles and stakes. The partisan struggles over rights legislation in the employment and welfare contexts that I have been discussing show something of how race functions in relation to these categories within the intragovernmental contest over liberalism.

In the context of such contests, we can see, for example, that the opponents of the Civil Rights Act of 1990 ultimately won by recasting race as an individual attribute and the problems of poverty as a collective cultural pathology. The opponents of welfare entitlements won by recasting poverty as the result of failed partnerships, that is, between abusive men and vulnerable women – as if it were happenstance that almost every example within the hearing room involved African American men and women. This option of re-presenting is available because (as Strathern notes in other contexts) the unitary body is always multiple: gender, race, ethnicity, income status – are elided as *culture* in this same mainstream discourse. As Strathern notes in a related context, 'culture is everywhere on hand' (1995, 3). Culture (in this sense) functions as the agglomeration of statistical categories (each with its own legal history) in relation to which an individual can be simultaneously classified.

The statistical layerings of officialized identity in these instances do not recognize a person's multiple commitments to communities of different kinds but are sedimentations of the prerequisites of federal power. Thus, those senators who sought to curtail the power of the courts over business practices claimed that taking race into account rendered the equal *un*equal – while claiming to defend the equality rights won by a previous generation. Those who sought to disembed the state from the social sector by ending welfare similarly suspended racial difference in favour of its reference – hidden in plain sight – to gender difference.

Paradoxically, perhaps, they did so while claiming to support the values of the New Deal – the Roosevelt administration's innovative expansion of federal powers during the Great Depression, as measures to support markets through regulation and to mitigate the effects of market failure through an entitlement program that provided children and the elderly with monthly subsistence payments, popularly known as 'social security'. The Welfare Reform Act of 1996 was technically a revision of the Social Security Act of 1937.

In the U.S., the public construction of culture as a protean omnipresence is an artefact of a neoliberal consensus whose zone of compromise is narrowly fixed to the limiting federal obligation. Accordingly, for advocates of neoliberal reform, there is a strong political incentive to reframe need negatively as dependency – shifting from economic discourse into moral discourse. In the debate over the civil rights bill, critics leveraged the moral discourse of responsibility explicitly against legal rights as the appropriate idiom of reform. In the welfare context, the discourse of responsibility was specifically and elaborately gendered – as the spectre of wastrel young men and victimized young women haunted the hearing rooms and the pages of transcripts.

The emphasis on marriage – explicitly in the welfare context – focused on an ideal in which men not only marry women and maintain stable relationships but also support their wives financially, relieving the state of this responsibility. This aspect of the testimony points beyond personal responsibility. It underscores the openness of the question of the value of labour and the gift within competing visions of capitalism and the extent to which capitalism defines key terms of social reproduction.

The proponents' insistence on an economy of the gift within marriage corresponds directly to the value they ascribe to the state's withdrawal from social programs. This correspondence is obviously gendered, but it must be racialized, too, since it is only via the legal history of racial equality claims that federal powers may come so close to private life in the name of liberalism.[9] *Family,* in other words, functions in multiple ways in the Welfare

Reform Act – eliding race in its reference to sexual reproduction, class in its reference to social reproduction and culture in its reference to learned values but, above all, in relation to the highly contentious legal and political contingencies of the state's interest in the spheres of private life.

In both of these legislative processes, the category *race* is predicated on the political limits of the federal government's constitutional powers, a context in which it never functions alone – even if those functions can be reworked as elements of individualized description. This does not make *race* or any other aspect of identity disappear; rather, it points to the stakes in social description, as actual persons become vulnerable to recomposition and erasure even from the middle of the field of citizenship, even at the moment of their recognition. That citizenship itself is categorically available for recomposition is a reminder of Polanyi's cautionary distinction between actual persons and the discourse of individuality and society derived from the fiction of the self-regulating market (1957 [1944], 42, 72ff.).

CONCLUSION: BUREAUCRACY AND THE RECURSIVITY OF SCALE

I am not suggesting we dismiss race and other social categories as constructions or epiphenomena of federal power or as essentialist expressions of state hegemony. Rather, the examples point to a critical connection between anthropology's knowledge practices (emphasizing the constructive sociability of persons through their relationships) and the politics of statistical manipulation in legal and judicial processes in specific historical contexts. This connection (between social construction and statistical deconstruction and recomposition) has implications for actual persons and their lives with others and also raises further issues. The federal processes in effect substitute identity categories for identities but only in ways that are already implicated in their narrow technical concerns with the nature and limits of their own powers in any specific circumstance. Thus identity categories serve only problematically as a repertoire of description for anthropologists or anyone else. The habit of seeing culture as a body of norms with individuals as adherents is relevant here, and, significantly, this is central to the critical concerns Strathern develops in *The Gender of the Gift*.[10] We might add that the habit of seeing the state as a large-scale organization, and individuals as its members, compounds the complexities of this issue, since the illusion of the state's scale (in this context) is sustained in part by the same sort of statistical prowess that I have pointed to here.

Strathern's impact on anthropology is such that the ethnographic practice she derives between Melanesia and the West is now widely accepted –
as if it stood for anthropology as a whole, as we know it. Here it is relevant to
note that anthropology enters her analysis not as a unitary discipline but as
a contingent comparative method – in *The Gender of the Gift* and related publications, a mediation between feminism's universalism and anthropology's
relativism. The critical force of her comparative method with respect to the
state is clearer if that critical mediation remains in the foreground. In *The
Gender of the Gift* and the other works I have especially drawn on here, the
state surfaces in her account implicitly, under the mutual transference she
finds between 'the West' and classic social anthropology, in their common
account of identity categories and their structural settings, as well as in the
critical address of feminism to the world at large. The ethnography she
invites us to envision is not that one but (as noted at the outset) a third term.

It is especially in relation to that third term that Strathern's comparative
method is so powerful for legal and political anthropology – in pre-empting
scale as the primary feature of the state and indeed drawing scalar claims
into an ethnographic framing as knowledge practices relatable to interests of
various kinds, as these were admitted (literally and figuratively) in the hearing room. For Weber, *economy* was the third term, holding apart – yet on the
same page – law and society, viewed inversely and respectively as the powers
of abstract propositions applied indifferently and the felt force of embodied
personal relations within actual political communities; this, he explains,
is how 'legitimate violence' enters the state (Weber 1954, 14, 343–348). It
is in the market, in real time, for Weber, that these varieties of power are
made socially (i.e. experientially) real – in the process blurring a distinction
we might wish could be kept bright between the bureaucratic rationality of
democracy and the practices of the absolute monarch in his 'star chamber'
(ibid., 356). Weber concludes that bureaucratic rationality – the core requirement of 'modern civilization' (ibid., 350) – cannot escape this ambiguity:

> Fully developed bureaucracy operates in a special sense 'sine ira ac studio'. Its
> peculiar character and with it its appropriateness for capitalism is the more
> fully actualized the more bureaucracy 'depersonalizes' itself, that is, the more
> completely it succeeds in achieving that condition which is acclaimed as its
> peculiar virtue, namely, the exclusion of love, hatred and every purely personal,
> especially irrational and incalculable, feeling from the execution of official
> tasks (Weber 1954, 351).

But this is not just a state of mind or a symbolic order; it is a self-reinforcing
process of depersonalization – the essence of the *large scale*. Weber continues
the passage:

In the place of the old-type ruler who is moved by sympathy, favour, grace and gratitude, modern culture requires for its sustaining external apparatus the emotionally detached, and hence rigorously 'professional', expert; and the more complicated and the more specialized it is, the more it needs him (Weber 1954, 351).

These passages clarify the situated stakes of Strathern's formulation of *ethnography* in our own era, marked by the depersonalization of the public in favour of proxy forms of sociability (consumption, taxation, profit, shareholder value, 'security'). Viewed ethnographically, *depersonalization* (as she demonstrates consistently) is not merely a misapprehension of or failure to regard the actual person but a substitution of one kind of knowledge for another, a denial of knowledge demands specific to the person – let alone *this* person. The actuality of the person is not simply disregarded, then; it does not arise. This is not first a problem of description (e.g. of how institutions 'construct' persons in one culture or another) but a problem of interpretation linking knowledges and their displacements. Seen through an ethnographic frame, as she makes clear, the incalculable and mutable plurality of relationships implied by personhood emerges in plain sight. In that light, real persons, in real time, will always loom larger than the so-called social forces we tend to associate with modernity. This connection between other worlds and our own is perhaps what makes anthropology – for some readers – arcane or difficult to grasp as useful knowledge; however, that difficulty only underscores the extent to which the 'applied maths' (Strathern 2005, 157) of membership account for the illusions of scale that make the state seem vast and elusive in theory and practice.

NOTES

1. Tensions evident in, for example, Collier (1975), Comaroff (1980), Comaroff and Roberts (1981), Fuller (1994), Roberts (1978), Starr and Collier (1989).
2. A framing referenced by Strathern in relation to her own interpretive and comparative project in Strathern (1988, x and chs. 1 and 2).
3. Margaret Thatcher, qtd. in Strathern (1992, 144).
4. The phrase is Marcus and Fischer's (1986), and the reference is to that same work and its long afterlives.
5. See Harvey (2005) and Aman (2004) for histories of neoliberalism from standpoints in social science and administrative law, respectively
6. In anthropology, strongly influenced by Abrams 1988, Corrigan and Sayer 1985, and Mitchell 1991 and Foucault 1991; for a contemporary review of these emergent developments, see Alonso 1994.

7. *Wards Cove Packing Co. v. Atonio,* 490 U.S. 642 (1989).
8. Transcripts of the hearings – and the source of quoted passages not other-wise cited in this section – are from U.S. House of Representatives (1996a, 1996b).
9. Kandaswamy (2008) examines the marriage incentive provisions in the 1996 Welfare Reform Act in relation to the Defense of Marriage Act, passed during that same congressional session and subsequent federal marriage incentive programs developed by the George W. Bush administration explicitly for the purpose of reducing dependence on welfare. Kandaswamy enquires into wel-fare reform from the standpoint of the debate on same-sex marriage and the vexed position of LGBTQ activists – divided among those who endorse mar-riage as a basis for claiming rights and those who oppose it as central to racial-ized inequalities, particularly in the welfare context. Subsequent U.S. Supreme Court decisions have now legalized same sex marriage, but the fundamental dilemma within liberalism with respect to privacy within marriage remains, as the political and legal debates over reproductive rights in the United States (predicated on the right to privacy) continue to rage. In relation to the liberty implications of the right to privacy, the legalization of same sex marriage may deflect the gendered association of privacy *within* marriage (i.e. its association with women's rights); however, in doing so, it asserts the liberty rights of the *couple.* The relevance, if any, of this discursive turn with respect to abortion law remains to be seen. Be that as it may, the legalization of same sex marriage has so far not altered the marriage provisions of welfare and other federal benefits – only their implementation.
10. Critical terms explicitly revisited in Strathern (1992, 4–6).

REFERENCES

Abrams, Phillip. 1988. 'Notes on the Difficulty of Studying the State'. *Journal of Historical Sociology* 1: 58–89.

Alonso, Anna-Maria. 1994. 'The Politics of Space, Time, and Substance: State Formation, Nationalism, and Ethnicity'. *Annual Review of Anthropology* 23: 379–405.

Aman, Alfred C., Jr. 2004. *The Democracy Deficit: Taming Globalization through Law Reform.* New York: New York University Press.

Benedict, Ruth. 1934. *Patterns of Culture.* Boston: Houghton Mifflin.

Collier, Jane F. 1975. 'Legal Processes'. *Annual Review of Anthropology* 4: 144–212.

Comaroff, John L., ed. 1980. *The Meaning of Marriage Payments.* London: Academic Press.

Comaroff, John L., and Simon Roberts. 1981. *Rules and Processes.* Chicago: University of Chicago Press.

Corrigan, Philip, and Derek Sayer. 1985. *The Great Arch.* Cambridge: Polity Press.

Foucault, Michel. 1991. 'Governmentality'. In *The Foucault Effect: Studies in Governmentality,* edited by Graham Burchell, Colin Gordon, and Peter Miller, 86–110. Chicago: University of Chicago Press.

Fuller, Chris. 1994. 'Legal Anthropology, Legal Pluralism, and Legal Thought'. *Anthropology Today* 10: 9–12.

Harvey, David. 2005. *A Brief History of Neoliberalism.* New York: Oxford University Press.

Kandaswamy, Priya. 2008. 'State Austerity and the Politics of Same-Sex Marriage in the U.S.'. *Sexualities* 11: 706–25.

Marcus, George E., and Michael Fischer. 1986. *Anthropology as Cultural Critique: An Experimental Moment in the Human Sciences.* Chicago: University of Chicago Press.

Mitchell, W.J.T. 1991. 'The Limits of the State: Beyond Statist Approaches and their Critics'. *American Political Science Review* 85: 77–96.

Polanyi, Karl. 1957 [1944]. *The Great Transformation.* Boston: Beacon Press.

Roberts, Simon. 1978. 'Do We Need an Anthropology of Law?' *Royal Anthropological Institute News* 25: 4.

Starr, J., and Jane F. Collier. 1989. 'Introduction'. In *History and Power in the Study of Law: New Directions in Legal Anthropology,* edited by J. Starr and Jane Collier. Ithaca: Cornell University Press.

Strathern, Marilyn. 1987. 'Introduction.' In *Dealing with Inequality: Analysing Gender Relations in Melanesia and Beyond,* edited by Marilyn Strathern, 1–32. Cambridge: Cambridge University Press.

——. 1988. *The Gender of the Gift: Problems with Women and Problems with Society in Melanesia.* Berkeley: University of California Press.

——. 1992. *After Nature: English Kinship in the Late Twentieth Century.* Cambridge: Cambridge University Press.

——. 1995. 'Foreword: Shifting Contexts'. In *Shifting Contexts: Transformations in Anthropological Knowledge,* edited by Marilyn Strathern, 1–11. London and New York: Routledge.

——. 2005. *Kinship, Law and the Unexpected: Relatives Are Always a Surprise.* Cambridge: Cambridge University Press.

Weber, Max. 1954. *Law in Economy and Society,* edited and translated by Max Rheinstein, translated by Edward Shils. New York: Simon and Schuster.

U.S. HOUSE OF REPRESENTATIVES

1996 Personal Responsibility and Work Opportunity Reconciliation Act of 1996. 104th Congress, 2nd session. H.R. 3734.

1996a Contract with America – Welfare Reform. Hearing before the Subcommittee on Human Resources of the Committee on Ways and Means. 104th Congress, 1st session, January 13, 20, 23, 27, 30, 1995. Part 1. Serial 104–43. Washington, DC: U.S. Government Printing Office.

1996b Contract with America – Welfare Reform. Hearing before the Subcommittee on Human Resources of the Committee on Ways and Means. 104th Congress, 1st session, February 2, 1995. Part 2. Serial 104–44. Washington, DC: U.S. Government Printing Office.

U.S. SENATE

1990 Civil Rights Act of 1990. 101st Congress, 2nd session. S. 2104.
1991 Civil Rights Act of 1991. 102nd Congress, 1st session. S. 1745.
1995 Welfare Reform Wrap-Up. Hearing before the Committee on Finance. 104th Congress, 1st session, April 27, 1995. Washington, DC: U.S. Government Printing Office.

UNITED STATES SUPREME COURT

Wards Cove Packing Co. v. Atonio, 490 U.S. 642 (1989).

Carol J. Greenhouse is Arthur W. Marks '19 Professor of Anthropology at Princeton University. A sociocultural anthropologist, her interests are in the ethnography of law and politics, especially as regards federal power in the United States. Recent publications include *The Paradox of Relevance,* on ethnography and citizenship in the United States and *Ethnographies of Neoliberalism.* Greenhouse has served as president of the American Ethnological Society, the Law & Society Association and the Association for Political and Legal Anthropology. She is a member of the American Philosophical Society and the American Academy of Arts and Sciences.

Chapter Three

Exchanging Equations
Anthropology as/beyond Symmetry

Alberto Corsín Jiménez

'What imaginative work do measurements do?' asks Marilyn Strathern in an essay on the imagination of scale in compensation payments and gift exchange in Melanesia (1999, 221). In the Papua New Guinea Highlands, exchanges of pigs and shells index the exchange of human capacities, which index in turn the exchange of body expenditure, such as body exertion and body loss over reproduction, land cultivation, pig rearing or caring for relatives. As Strathern puts it, 'what keeps one equation in place can only be other equations' (1999, 209).

Marilyn Strathern's contribution to anthropological and ethnographic theory is of course far ranging. There is little point and no avail in trying to pin it down to a singular moment or insight. But I think it is fair to say that a great deal of her theoretical impulse comes from her elucidation of the work of 'relations' as both sociological *and* analytical descriptors. Relationality is a form of knowledge, Strathern has long taught us, capable of making both the social and the analytical visible at once.[1]

In this chapter I would like to take inspiration from Strathern's writings and dwell on the relation as a theoretical object. I am inspired here by the citation with which I opened above. In this Melanesian vignette, the relational moment is inflected by what Strathern later in the same text calls 'measurement by ratio' (1999, 218). A ratio is simply a form of measurement in which 'part of the measurement is also what is being measured: one item valued in terms of another yields a ratio'. Significantly, measurement by ratio is a scale-independent activity. The scale is internalized in the relation between values: '[W]hat is held constant is not the values on the scale but a relation between values' (Strathern 1999, 205).

The internal relation between values makes such forms of measurement by ratio work as 'an equation or . . . an analogy' (Strathern 1999, 205). According to Strathern, certain economies of information operate under a form of ratio elicitation: ratios that elicit other ratios. Thus, for example, 'while the cost of houses will not in itself indicate the cost of food, the capacity to earn will tell us something about the capacity to spend – they are not the same activities at all, yet information on one also provides information on the other' (Strathern 1999, 205). Ratios elicit information that enables other ratios to come into being. The conversion of one ratio into another fares in this context as an analogical extension. In this context, then, it would seem that the cultural apparatus of analogy is fuelled by what we may call an epistemic regime of *exchanging equations*.

Although I am no Melanesian specialist, I would argue that Hageners do not of course exchange *equations*. The idiom is Strathern's analytical shorthand for an analogical economy of relations. Hageners exchange pigs that 'stand for' (embody) the food grown on clan lands, that stand for human bodily work and strength, that stand for kinship nurturance and relations, that stand for streaming entanglements of capacities. These are relational moments that are 'measured' in terms of, or 'equated' to, other relational moments. Thus, 'equation' is Strathern's choice of idiom for describing a cultural economy of relationality. It is an evocative descriptor that helps readers reimagine the theoretical conditions of social process.

In this chapter I want to take Strathern's provocative descriptor seriously and attempt to unpack it as an epistemic object. I shall introduce an ethnographic context in which social form is deliberately and consciously deployed as an *exchange of equations* – in which the 'equation' is not only a measured form of something else (another relational moment) but an epistemic form on its own terms and, therefore, in which social form is effected, bundled and put in circulation as streams of equations. What follows, then, is an attempt at writing an ethnography of a Regime of Exchanging Equations.[2]

A final interest of the chapter is to use the ethnography to ponder on what the exchange of equations might say about our own cultural economy of relations and information – that is, about the cultural epistemology of a Euro-American knowledge economy. As we will see, the logos-equation has been an engine of Western epistemology since antiquity, although social theory has rarely reckoned its own internal organization as one such building and stacking-up of equations. In the ethnography below, I hope to offer insights into one such building process.

Some of the questions that I want to pose upon making explicit such reckoning include the following: What does the knowledge economy have in store when 'exchanging equations' becomes its internal model of organization? What do analogy or indeed 'relations' look like when they work as equations within a Regime of Exchanging Equations? What might happen to anthropological theory if we were to substitute its canonical 'epistemological device' (Strathern 2014, 55), namely, the relation, for an alternative device: a relation of relations, that is, an equation? Placing the equation at the heart of anthropological knowledge suddenly complicates the discipline's own *symmetrical* project: the project of theorising its *ad-equation* to indigenous theories of knowledge. If the anthropological project is to produce relational accounts of other people's relationships – a relation of relations – should it not be considered itself, too, a project in the production of novel forms of equations?

The first equation I shall be talking about is a building. I am interested in how a building becomes an object of knowledge: how this object comes to be, what it does, and what it may take for granted. The ethnography that follows examines the cultural and epistemological resources employed in the building-up and summation of knowledge about a building: how knowledge grows, what engines are used in building it up into an epistemic object.

WHAT IS A BUILDING FOR?

The question was posed by a management consultant at a meeting with senior executives from one of the world's largest oil companies. 'A building', he proceeded, 'is a lever for change: a privilege, a unique event. Few people in a corporation's history have the opportunity to be part of a relocation to a new building'. 'A new building', he added soberly, 'offers us the opportunity to pause, reflect, and start anew'. A building is a source of hope, promise and wealth.

Some weeks earlier, at a meeting with senior clerks and general back office administrators, the same consultant had offered a rather different image of how employees might want to relate to the new building. Some of the clerks pointed out that the new building was looked at with suspicion by a large part of the workforce. There appeared to be a spell of uncertainty around the building. Thus, rather than in temporal terms (an event, an opportunity), such people seemed to relate to the building in spatial terms: a gigantic vacuum, an empty place, even a source of emptiness itself, for apparently there were rumours that in relocating to the new building some jobs would be shed.

These two vignettes are part of ethnographic work I carried out in 2007–2008 when I moved to Buenos Aires to collaborate with an international 'innovation consultancy' firm in designing the 'knowledge environment' of one of the world's largest oil company's new headquarters in Latin America. On arriving, I joined a team of ten people, including architects, engineers, geologists, public relations managers, information technology (IT) specialists, consultants and graphic designers, who were dedicated to the task of designing a new office environment for the company's new purpose-made 34-storey building. The plan was to relocate over 2,000 people from a variety of office locations in Buenos Aires to the company's new flagship building in the luxury harbour area of Puerto Madero.

The change of building was seen by management and consultants as an opportunity to restructure the company's 'workplace strategies', coming up with a blueprint for an 'ecology of new ways of working' that would promote knowledge and managerial transparency, teamwork, work flexibility and mobility and the reconciliation of professional and lifestyle values. The movement of people from a variety of offices to a central location was taken as an opportunity to shake up and lose old and antiquated work habits and practices – an opportunity for making work more dynamic and adaptive to change. The corporate strategy for the new building included a new spatial design, a new ecology of work practices and a new corporate culture. These were to be integrated and fleshed out in a year-long 'change management' programme to be rolled out to the company's workforce in the months prior to the move.

The design of the new building's knowledge environment was of course a complex project, and I cannot offer here a comprehensive description of all its facets. I shall limit myself to one aspect of this project: the design and implementation of a 'paperless office'.

The myth of the paperless office, as Abigail Sellen and Richard Harper call it (2003), partakes of the longer history of the making of corporate architecture in the immediate aftermath of World War II. Central in the history of such architecture are modernist experiments with spatial flexibility and 'modularity', where the spatial module epitomized the architectural equivalent to 'a unit of exchange passing through invisible [communicational and network] circuits' (Martin 2003, 6). As a unit within a network, the status of space in midcentury architectural discourse was equivalent to the status of information itself, or indeed of media in systems theory: an object or resource whose circulation was at once a communicative and an infrastructural event, a message and a medium. Informational resources thus understood fed back and contributed to their own sustenance as metastructures. They were self-organized. The organization of information followed the principles of cybernetics.

Throughout the 1950s and 1960s, the organizational architecture of cybernetics was mapped onto a preference for open environments and glass buildings (Martin 2003). Circular flows of information were mirrored on spatial flows and the movement of people. Spatial and informational exchanges converged, too, on a number of social tropes, such as 'collaboration', 'coordination' and 'interdisciplinarity'. Norbert Weiner's projects on weapons research and human-machine intelligence at the Rad Lab or Arthur Rosenblueth's physiological work at Harvard Medical School, for instance, were 'actively facilitated [by the] networking and entrepreneurship' of cybernetic rhetoric (Turner 2006, 25). The spaces of the 1950s interdisciplinary military-industrial laboratory became therefore a model for the organization of corporate knowledge at large. It is this tradition, then, of open, flexible and informationally resourceful spaces and spatial relations that informed the work of the 'new ecologies of workplace' consultants (Becker et al. 1992; Becker 2007).

LOWEST COMMON DENOMINATORS

As noted above, a fundamental aspect of the projection of the new building as a knowledge environment was the programme for a paperless office. When the programme was set in motion, however, the concept of a paperless office encountered a number of lines of resistance.

The first step in the design programme towards a paperless office was the implementation of a 'clear desk policy'. This required of employees to leave their desks clear of all papers, personal objects and removable storage media before they left the office every day. A central part of the consultants' philosophical approach to knowledge management, the clear desk policy was intended to maintain the appearance of a new working environment on a daily basis, to discourage the retention of unnecessary paper, to promote the storage of classified and sensitive documents and thus reduce the risk of unauthorized access to information, and in the long run to help promote mobile work by ensuring that shared workspaces would not become owned by individuals over time.

Some people at the oil company, however, felt that 'clear desk' and 'paperless' were not identical terms, and some further disambiguation was necessary. A communications manager, for example, concerned about her own role in designing a communications campaign for the programme, noted at a meeting that 'paperless' was often interpreted by people as 'deskless'. Not unreasonably, people feared that the promotion of mobility enabled by a paperless environment would in time encourage the 'depersonalization' of workspaces. And there was much anxiety over losing one's own personal workspace, for a variety of reasons, including losing one's capacity to 'personalize' (that is, decorate and furnish) one's workspace, but perhaps more importantly, the fear of not knowing where one would fit in a new work structure and workflow of information. The ultimate fear here was that in the new work environment some people's jobs might no longer be deemed necessary.

At the meeting the comment by the communications manager triggered a discussion on the convenience of paperless or clear desk as overarching design concepts. The discussion was put to an end, however, when a senior consultant observed that what was really at stake was neither paper or desks but 'a whole new way of working'. An IT manager seconded the observation, noting that it was 'crucial to keep the *global project* in view at all times'. Neither paper nor desks, nor indeed people, were of ultimate concern here, but the lowest common denominator of the project's global reach as a 'knowledge environment', or an 'ecology of new ways of working', as it is sometimes referred to in the management literature (Becker et al. 1992).

It was crucial, the senior consultant noted, that concerns about paper trails, archives or desks be reconceptualized in terms of spatial and knowledge flows. Thus a number of equations were set in place, as we will see shortly, in which the paper form was invested with an imaginary of spatial and epistemic immobility. Paper was seen as immobile and weighty, as were desks, archives and drawers. These were high denominators of knowledge that did not facilitate conversions and flows. An example often proffered by consultants concerned some people's idiosyncratic archiving of files: 'If a filing system is only known to the person who keeps the archive', they would say, 'then knowledge is fixed to that person and place. It cannot travel'. To have knowledge travel, they insisted, one has to start with knowledge as the lowest common denominator. Knowledge ought to be the basic or fundamental integer underlying other epistemic multiples.

If the invocation of a knowledge environment contributed to silencing doubts about people's own relationship to the project in one context, it was however of very little avail in other contexts. The many bifurcations that the implementation of a clear desk policy had been opening up called for the organization of a 'less-paper task force' (LPTF). The change of emphasis – from paperless to 'less-paper' – was a response to some of the anxieties that the imagery of a weightless office had provoked. The LPTF enlisted representatives from IT, human resources, facility management and communications as well as two management consultants. The LPTF was in charge of developing an actual corporate-wide operations programme for bringing into existence the paperless environment. In the context of LPTF discussion there was never any mention of a 'knowledge environment', and indeed its invocation as a lowest common denominator would have made no sense.

In its stead, what figured centrally in most LPTF meetings was the 'digitization' of information at a corporate level. Within the corporate intelligentsia of the LPTF, the weightlessness of a knowledge environment turned around the lightness of the digital rather than the absence of paper. For the LPTF, the lowest common denominator in the project turned out to be, not the global reach of knowledge management but the informational economy of digital bytes.

WEIGHT

Clear desks were the tip of a wider knowledge management programme that encompassed a new architecture of digital information storage and archiving, new ways of handling the paper legacy and an overall effort at generating cross-cutting and transversal organizational synergies. In this model, paper became a token and emblem of informational pollution. 'Information', consultants would argue, 'is free; what varies are the mediums (paper, digital) through which it travels.' Paper was therefore seen as a (superfluous) intermediary between information and efficiency. In its ideal form, pure information was paper-free. It was weightless.

Over the coming months, weight became indeed an arithmetic of cultural change. The focus on digitization led the LPTF to develop a three-fold strategy for streamlining paper processes, in printing, archiving and internal communications. The strategy was self-consciously articulated as a 'knowledge management' programme, which was in turn incorporated into the corporate-wide 'change management' programme that had been set in motion in preparation for the relocation. The programme established a set of 'short term wins' (STWs) that were devised to motivate and help employees visualize their own progress towards the less-paper office.

There were four such sets of STWs, which were represented in the shape of steps in a ladder. Each step was explained at a dedicated workshop. The first step was a call to consciousness: to becoming aware of how paper circulated through the office space. The second step was an introduction to classificatory practices and standards. The third step, an introduction to how to organize one's own personal files. The fourth and last workshop, finally, described the clear desk policy proper.

The company's senior managers were asked to select eight representatives from the various units and departments that would attend each of the four workshops. Following each workshop, attendants were then given a month to downstream the project to their departmental peers and colleagues and upstream back their comments and reactions to the next workshop. (The use of the idioms of downstream and upstream was a sympathetic nod to the oil industry. Upstream refers to those areas of business concerned with the extraction of oil; downstream refers to the business of servicing and marketing final products.) The whole STWs programme thus stretched over approximately six months.

Central to the various step changes envisaged in the STWs ladder was the place of paper as a mediator of cultural change. Paper became the focal epistemic object of change as a cultural programme: it centralized people's reflexive orientations towards, as well as their new practices and habits of, knowledge making. Thus, at the workshops employees were asked to think about the role that paper played in their everyday work routines; to think twice every time they printed something; to think about the kinds of paper files they stored and archived; to think about the types of documents they copied or asked for duplicates; to pause for thought before printing out an email. People were asked to use paper as a film through which to make work processes transparent to themselves. This would help them better conceptualize the structure of the information they were dealing with and therefore make better judgements as to whether the ideal format for its output ought to be digital or paper based, people or machine related.

Although it was acknowledged that different units and departments were likely to have different work processes, a number of recommendations were made for general use and adoption. Paper trails, for instance, ought to be classified into 'closed' or 'alive': the former indicating work processes that were unlikely to produce further documentation; the latter referring to processes that were still producing red tape. People were also encouraged to ascribe different temporalities and spatialities to different kinds of paperwork. Thus one should try to distinguish those documents that should necessarily stay with oneself in the office from those documents that, although necessary and important, could be sent out to third-party archivists for filing.

Further recommendations included appointing a 'less-paper coordinator' in every department. This person ought to find a suitable time when every member of the department would leave his or her immediate tasks aside and dedicate 'around one hour' to go through his or her paperwork, deciding what should stay and what should be thrown away. It was generally agreed that a good time to do this would be on a Friday after lunch, when the loom of the weekend could help invest in the activity 'a certain festive mood'. Resorting to a convivial and festive mood soon became a standard practice. At a meeting of the LPTF, for example, it was reported how a less-paper coordinator had improvised a less-paper breakfast in her department. On a Friday morning she had arrived at work with freshly baked croissants and biscuits. She encouraged her colleagues to join her in taking a break from their routines and use the 'social breakfast' to start sorting out paper files. The event was a success and was quickly identified by the LPTF as a best practice. Friday breakfasts became a standard practice across the organization.

The success of such less-paper boutades was measured in terms of the amount of paper thus disposed. It was established that every department would weigh the amount of paper and cardboard thrown away on a weekly basis. The clearance was also incentivized: the earnings derived from selling the paper and cardboard thrown away were given to a local children's hospital. Within six months some 23.5 tonnes of paper and 3 tonnes of cardboard had been thrown away across the corporation. Another paper disposal experiment much publicized involved the firm's corporate directors.

Over a month a team of people in the Facility Management Department calculated the amount and cost of newspaper clips printed for use by the corporate directorate and then decided that the latter would receive an electronic, rather than a paper-based, file of press clips. The savings amounted to some 30,976 pages worth of clips. A number of equations and equivalences were quickly put together. All that paper weighed some 160 kilograms; it was worth some \$700, including the cost of copying, and it occupied $0{,}22\text{m}^3$, or the equivalent of six boxes and two packs of paper.

EXCHANGING EQUATIONS

Of course, the STWs and less-paper programmes did not go unchallenged. All kinds of problems arose. Lawyers complained that the distinction between 'closed' and 'alive' paperwork was utterly meaningless to them. Documentation long archived and forgotten could suddenly acquire fundamental relevance, should it become, for example, the centrepiece of a legal case. Indeed, such was their concern about the naturalization of paper as an epistemic object – an object about whose knowledge qualities one could speak in general and for all – that they successfully argued for and obtained a special treatment for their paperwork. Legal documents were denaturalized as paper objects.

Central to the reclassification of paperwork as legal objects was the question of time. Legal objects have an indefinite temporality: they may remain archived for years before they are summoned as evidence in a legal court. The temporality of the legal object is therefore different from the temporality of the ordinary paper document. Everyday paperwork has a short lifespan: it dies and is 'buried' in the archive within days. Certain legal documents, on the other hand, remain alive well beyond their move to the archive. Indeed, their being buried in the archive, lawyers argued, is not evidence of their death. Their potential to resurrect at any time was mobilized as an argument by the legal department to keep control of their own archiving and storage. It was in these terms that some lawyers spoke of their archives as an equivalent to accountants' cash banks: 'It's our documentary treasure, our patrimony', they would say.

The ontological distinctiveness of the legal document vis-à-vis ordinary paperwork was further established by some additional criteria. In particular, there were three aspects of legal work that lawyers thought required special consideration when designing the new building's knowledge environment. On the one hand, the archival temporality of the legal document was supplemented and enhanced by lawyers' obsession with photocopies. Running starkly against the grain of the whole less-paper programme, lawyers called for an expansion of the photocopying capacities at the new building: they wanted more and more powerful photocopying machines.

It was common of lawyers to complain of employees' general ignorance of the diligences of legal process. 'People just don't realize', they would often say, 'that the documents they work with on a daily basis could well become the centrepiece of a judicial process in the future'. 'We need to figure out a way to teach people from different departments', they would tell consultants, 'which documents are the key legal documents in each case'. Theirs was a call, then, for an awareness of the inherent proliferation of legal documents: their capacities for generating more paperwork in the future but also, more importantly, their own proliferative qualities as self-replicable forms. For it was paramount that one kept copies of all documents because of all documents' dormant capacities as generative of judicial process. Legal copies helped hoard in the present the proliferousness of documents in the future – thence lawyers' demands for more photocopying machines.

The idiosyncratic character of legal knowledge was expressed, too, in their robust defence for a 'legal library'. This also ran counter to the design of the knowledge environment that architects and consultants were arguing for. A document-based space, enclosed and guarded from passers-by, represented the exact antithetical image of what consultants had been preaching all along. But for lawyers the library was a fundamental place of study and learning. This was the place where they came to when they had to prepare for a case hearing. For lawyers, the process of documentation was not about paperwork but about study, consultation and legal practice. The library was not a paper space but an intellectual space. Perhaps management consultants thought that a paper-free environment was conducive to the production of knowledge – not for lawyers, however, for whom the bookish endowment of the library was fundamental for the production of robust legal knowledge.

The library was employed also to illustrate what some lawyers called the 'nonlinearity' of legal work. If the knowledge economy of the paperless office was epitomized by a linguistic space of frictionless communication, where mobile workers bumped into each other and smoothly interchanged units of verbal knowledge, lawyers insisted on the importance of preserving a cultural space for 'invisible' and 'silent' work. A senior legal director put it thus:

> I don't read off a computer screen. I cannot annotate a computer screen; I cannot reference and cross-reference marginalia on a computer screen. The practice of law is the practice of corrections. We write and rewrite texts. We produce layers upon layers upon layers of text. This is not a linear process. I do not start working on some case early in the morning, make progress with it throughout the day, in anticipation of its closure in the evening. Legal knowledge does not progress linearly. I may be working on up to fifty cases at once. We move forward one day only to take various steps back the following day. We take a book out of the library one day only to realize that we should have in fact been reading something completely different by the evening. Our culture of work is characterized by unpredictability. If you do not make room for such unpredictability, if you do not account for it, you'll be blind to the enormous 'hidden costs' of legal practice. If a lawyer is not allowed to work in silence, you have no idea what the scale of such hidden costs may rise to.

The most intriguing and remarkable of lawyers' hesitant relationship to the new building, however, came in the form of their demands for paper shredders and shredding equipment for heavy office use. The terms of the request challenged the knowledge-paper equation that organized much of the consultants' programme. On the one hand, the request for paper shredders was initially welcomed by consultants. It was seen as an endorsement of the general call for liberating the office environment of paper weight.

However, this enthusiasm was quickly curtailed on two fronts. It soon became obvious that the paper-shredding equipment lawyers were asking for would immobilize, rather than liberate, office space. The type of shredder bailers the lawyers had asked for were far larger than anything consultants or interior design architects could have envisaged. Their accommodation would require on the part of architects an expansion of the floor space originally allocated to the legal department in the new building. Moreover, it also turned out that bailers required specific materials, such as shredding bags and oil, which would require additional storage space.

Second, the focus on paper shredding brought attention to the distinct temporality of legal documents, and indeed of paper itself as an epistemic unit. A less-paper office environment, consultants argued, opened up new spaces of interaction, mobility and exchange. It would enable, they insisted, a focus on *work processes* rather than *work outputs*. If documents were digitized, one could access them from any and everywhere in the building. A favourite example of consultants put it like this:

> Imagine you are on your way to get a coffee from the refectory downstairs. At the lift you run into Peter, who works in accounting. You two have long been after each other but never quite found the time or place to meet (meeting rooms are always booked weeks in advance). You need to check some numbers against Peter's accounting records. Because the accounting department has digitized the latter, however, and Peter is therefore no longer dependent on having his physical files close to hand, your casual encounter turns suddenly into a work encounter. Peter brings out his Palm, logs into the department's server, opens and downloads the relevant file, and subsequently emails it to you. The *process* of casually bumping into Peter turns into a *knowledge exchange.*

When the LPTF and the team of management consultants met with lawyers, however, the description of knowledge's processual qualities encountered a certain friction. Sure, they understood that people may bump into each other and walk away with new information. They may even walk away with an *electronic copy* of a file. But there are files and *files*, copies and *copies*. For not all copies weigh the same. Legal copies carry an additional epistemic weight: the burden of legal proof. That is why the shredding equipment was of central importance to the legal department. One can only make knowledge disappear if you can make paper disappear. It is paper that is epistemically consequential. You may exchange knowledge in a casual encounter, but that has no serious epistemic consequences. The real objectual qualities of knowledge, for lawyers, resided in its ontological qualities as a paper-object.

Altogether, then, to all the talk of open-plan offices, transparency and the spatial flow of people and knowledge, lawyers counterposed the importance of 'sealed' environments, of ontological circumscriptions to the epistemic consequentiality of knowledge. They went as far as to suggest that, should the architects not be in a position to accommodate their spatial and archival requirements, it would be preferable for them not to move to the new building. Theirs was truly a claim for the *separation* of powers between the law and the rest of social forms.

The question of the temporality of paper documents was soon to emerge as a concern for employees everywhere, not just lawyers and legal clerks.

Although seldom expressed with the assertiveness of lawyers, consultants' sets of equations between knowledge, paper and processes were often challenged on a diversity of grounds. An explanation commonly given, for example, was that people held on to paper copies of all information because they did not want to find themselves empty-handed when their bosses came around asking for copies of paperwork. Paper mediates the relation that people have to information through the relationships they have to other people (and to their bosses in particular) – and paper archives embody the structure of all such personal relationships.

Consultants would reply that a central (ideally digital) archiving system would help take responsibility away from people and distribute it equally among everyone: information would no longer be 'owned' by an individual but would be publicly available in and accessible through the system. Bosses would not need to go around asking for information because this would be available for them to access it directly. Individuals would therefore be spared the embarrassment and shame of not knowing or not having a particular piece of information when asked by their bosses. Relations (to information) and relationships (to people) would be kept apart. Notwithstanding, on being told about the alleged shamelessness and relational purity of information, some employees grinned and murmured 'Bosses *boss* – that's their job. They do not relate to information. Theirs is a relationship to knowledge through people'.

A novel inflection on the question of the temporality of paperwork was offered by the fiscal and internal auditing department. The department held some 400 kilograms worth of insurance-related paperwork and customer guarantees, located in a room-sized fireproof archive. Not only should these archives not be moved outside the new building, the auditors insisted, but it was imperative that the standards of the archival system itself, including the rights of access and consultation of such documentation, be kept distinct from those used elsewhere in the organization.

This had to do for the most part with issues of confidentiality: the files contained information that was most definitely not for general use. But a number of auditors, including some of the departments' most senior members, noted on a number of occasions that this archive 'contained the company's historical heritage'. These, they argued, were historical documents that required certain conditions for their preservation or, at the very least (not being archivists or historians themselves, they pointed out), a certain awareness of their patrimonial importance. Across the organization, on the other hand, the historicity of paperwork was not something often reflected upon, and indeed, although there was a certain sense of pride about the company's 'national, historic character', there were few occasions on which people reflected on the historicity of their own practices. Interestingly, however, the appeal by the auditors to the 'historic and heritage qualities' of their archive was something that left consultants disarmed and to which they offered no resistance at all in their general call for downsizing paper spaces. The economy of history, in this context, overpowered the economy of knowledge.

METROLOGY

When consultants launched the STWs programme, they invited participants from every department to take photographs of the spatial layouts and the archiving and storage spaces in their units. Further, a management consultant took a tour of the organization, measuring 'linear metres of shelf space' in every department. The idea behind the photographs and the measurement was that, upon concluding the STWs programme, a second set of measurements and photographs would be taken with a view to obtain 'motivational evidence' of the improvements made in every department. It was hoped, or rather, firmly believed by consultants, that the second round of photographs would display neatly ordered and tidy spaces, work desks devoid of paper columns, empty shelf spaces and perhaps even a reduction in archival drawers and cabinets.

When consultants returned to the departments to take the second round of photographs, they confronted, however, a rather different scenario. Some departments simply did not understand the purpose behind measuring 'linear metres of shelf space'. Of all departments it was the engineers that expressed their bewilderment with most eloquence:

> We thought you wanted us to get rid of paper. We just don't get why you have decided to measure our capacity to bin paper in 'organizational' rather than 'volumetric' terms. Where and how we decide to file our paper records is our business. It says nothing about our capacity to throw away rubbish, let alone our capacity to streamline our work processes. If you want to measure the former, you should employ a metric such as 'cubic metres of waste', not 'linear metres of shelf space'. The latter simply says nothing about waste disposal, nor, moreover, about the organization of knowledge.

Perhaps daunted by the engineers very own professional capacity at thinking metrologically, the consultants opted not to challenge their argumentation. Not surprisingly, then, when the time came to tabulate comparatively how the different departments had done throughout the STWs programme, the engineers offered their own 'metric': they had piled up two boxes worth of paper and cardboard, which they had duly sent to the children's hospital.

Engineers were not alone, however, in concocting their own metrological imagination. When the team of consultants toured the organization in search of data on paper wastage, they encountered a diversity of numerical outputs. Some departments had indeed opted for 'boxes' as the numerical denominator of their paper output. In fact, most of such departments spoke of such boxes as 'hospital boxes', in allusion to the children's hospital which had been publicly announced as the recipient of the earnings of the recycling programme. Such 'socialization' of the wastage programme was interesting because neither consultants nor the LPTF had ever suggested 'boxes' as a metric of wastage. The original call was to weigh the amount of paper disposed. However, with one exception (marketing), no department handed in weighted numbers of paper waste. In its stead, most departments handed in the 'socialized' versions which were the charity boxes.

But even the metrology of charity boxes was differently put together by different departments. Some departments produced daily numbers for their boxed output. Others, perhaps less committed to the programme, aggregated their output into total outputs (say, ten boxes over the whole six-month programme). Others distinguished between 'hospital boxes' and 'external boxes'. The latter were boxes of paper destined to the external archive: an archive subcontracted to a specialized archivist company. The status of such material was ambiguous. On the one hand, sending paperwork to an external archive was in compliance with the requirements of the less-paper programme: paper was indeed made to disappear from the local office environment.

But it was doubtful that in doing so a department had accomplished a reorganization of its work processes. If anything, the relocation seemed rather to duplicate the costs of managing information and knowledge unnecessarily: now there was a waiting time associated with retrieving information (the time it took for the subcontractor to retrieve the file and transport it back to one's desk), as well as the fee associated with such service. Last, some departments opted for producing their own 'measurements by ratio', such as indicating the percentage of reduction in paper space. One department thus reported that they had reduced their paper stock by 95 percent, a figure not only a little unrealistic but altogether incomprehensible, because there had been no prior indication of what their point of departure was. 'You may see loads of paper around us', they thus explained to the consultants, 'but this is only 5 percent of what there used to be' – a wonderful example of the use of exchanging equations for epistemic self-sufficiency.

WHAT IS PAPER FOR?

Hirokazu Miyazaki has recently written on how different documentary practices are deployed to make the temporality of the present available to participants in a social event (2006). He looks at participants in Fijian gift exchange mortuary rituals, in which the anticipation of reciprocation elucidates a sociology of hope and promise.

Miyazaki's ethnographic analysis centres on two documents: a matrix used to record gifts received during the mortuary exchange and a second document written as a report for overseas clansmen that summarized the scale and success of the event. The matrix had a simple format: rows where gift givers were named and four columns for each of the four types of gifts. The process of filling in the matrix, Miyazaki tells us, replicated the temporality of hope and expectation that gift receivers invested the ritual with. Every empty cell in the matrix pointed to a moment of exchange to come: 'On the document, a moment of hopeful anticipation was made visible repeatedly in the grid and stretched over the entire period of mortuary exchange event' (Miyazaki 2006, 214).

Unlike the matrix, the summary report invoked a different temporality. In providing a retrospective account of the ritual, the report 'described the *outcome,* not the process, of the successful execution of the mortuary exchange' (Miyazaki 2006, 218, emphasis in the original). But the document's very own prospective travelling overseas gestured, too, towards a temporal extension of the exchange of greetings and thanks that characterized the ritual encounter. Thus, although the report had a different temporal format than the matrix, in its own internal replication of the mortuary exchange it helped make the ritual present available in ways not unlike the matrix's own processual recording of it. As documentary practices, both the matrix and the report thus contributed to the replication of the ritual present as a placeholder for sociological knowledge.

Echoing the vernacular Fijian description of giving and receiving gifts as an act of 'attending on' (*veiqaravi*) each other, Miyazaki recalls that the report sent to the overseas clan was 'part of the hosting clan's own "attendance" on its fellow clansmen' (Miyazaki 2006, 207, 219). I would like to suggest, however, that a corollary to the carrying of attendance to outside parties was the report's *attestation* of satisfactory exchanges. What was being carried forward for the *attention* of the overseas clan was the *attestation* of a successful ritual encounter. Attendance/attention and attest are the two sides of what Miyazaki calls the replicative structure of presencing.

The matrix and the report that Miyazaki dwells on are paper forms. Miyazaki notes in passing that the matrix was 'produced in part with the use of a word processor', which was relatively uncommon at the time for 'other clans drew such tables by hand on a school notebook' (Miyazaki 2006, 210). Notwithstanding, the matrix circulated in paper form, and it is the annotated paper form that replicates the temporality of the ritual exchange. The report, too, circulated in paper form. The materiality of the paper form thus enabled the documentation of presencing as a replicative structure. The cultural work of prospection and retrospection, attention and attestation, which both the matrix and the report enacted, was facilitated in important ways by the materiality of the paper form.

In this sense, the investment of the paper form with replicative capabilities is not unlike the temporal investments that lawyers credited legal documents with. On the one hand, lawyers insisted on treating their documents as ontologically different from ordinary paperwork. Legal documents inhabited a temporality of their own. They were suspended in their own temporal condition: buried in the archive, yet dormant, in tension, in a condition of permanent alertness. A legal document could activate itself at any time. Importantly, the dormancy of the legal document was inherent to its paper form. Thus, the legal archive or the legal library institutionalize such cultures of paper dormancy. They are spaces of attestation: they attest to time's very own *durée*.

But legal libraries, of course, are also spaces of attendance. Lawyers attend libraries in preparation for court hearings; the library's legal corpus 'attends' to its visitors. There they search for papers that may be brought to, or distract, people's attention. Lawyers' obsession with copies and photocopying is an index of a culture of preparedness and attentiveness, in which the paper form is the ultimate pre-emptive and anticipatory technology. As Annelise Riles has put it, 'Moments of document creation anticipate future moments in which documents will be received, circulated, instrumentalized, and taken apart again' (Riles 2006, 18). No paper, no reproduction, no legal agency.

Not only lawyers but also accountants and auditors saw too in the paper form an enabling technology. The auditors' fireproof archive was thought to house the organization's historical consciousness. Here was another space of paper dormancy whose value, albeit unclear and not necessarily prospective in the way legal documents were said to be, was felt to be important. The archive embodied a patrimony endowed with unbeknownst temporal value. Paper, then, seemed to enable certain modalities of residence in time and in the temporalities of agency.

If for Miyazaki the replicative function of documenting gift exchanges offered participants in Fijian mortuary rituals a modality of access to the temporality of the event's present, I would like to suggest here an alternative function and operation of temporal apprehension. Namely, in its oscillation between dormancy and agency, historicity and anticipation, attestation and attendance, the paper form seemed to function as a *prototype* of a temporal culture of organizational knowledge. The paper form indexed both to its own continuity as an inscriptive and legal artefact, as well as to its discontinuity and future suspension as an archival object. It signalled both a *type* of institutional practice and a *proto*-organizational form.

ARCHITECTURAL OPTICS OF VOLUMES

The idea that a piece of paper could function as a prototype of organizational self-knowledge was alien to management consultants. At the risk of oversimplification, we may say that one of the aims of the 'less-paper' programme was to introduce and make known a cultural imagination in which paper was emptied of its epistemic productivity. A piece of paper was *not* a form of knowledge. If one were looking for knowledge, we should look for it elsewhere: in relational exchanges, in work processes, in spatial distributions. Never in a piece of paper.

When management consultants emptied paper of epistemic consequentiality, they were of course shifting the latter to other domains, in particular, to space itself as a cultural economy. For consultants, the building of a knowledge environment revolved fundamentally around a conceptualization of space as a mobile and flexible resource. A common way in which consultants framed such an economy of space was, simply, to ask for the number of uses that a given spatial resource (a meeting room, a desk, storage space or a filing cabinet) could be put to. The economy of knowledge was thus calculated in terms of occupational and mobility ratios: How many uses can a room be put to? How many people can take productive residence in a space?

Such an economy of knowledge had of course little use for paper. Paper is bulky, immobile, physical. It acts as a gravitational pull for space, for it constrains alternative spatial uses. Thus, when in the course of the STWs programme, management consultants invited people to reconsider their work culture and processes, the question they offered as a prompt was 'What is paper for?' In the last instance they encouraged people to measure the epistemic consequentiality of their documentary practices in terms of the following: Where does a piece of paper take residence? Who and how many times is it retrieved? Where does it travel to? How many times does it need to be reproduced? How long does it remain alive? When is it likely to die? These are questions that retrace the spatial itinerary of a paper document.

They locate the paper in a spatial economy of relations. The paper form is therefore conceptualized as one kind or another of a spatial ratio.

Consultants modelled the circulation of knowledge on space as a circulatory asset. There was a certain rationality to this practice, for the craft of the consultants' expertise was to work upon and around an otherwise apparently immobile and fixed object: the architectural form of a given building. The consultants' magician trick was to make their clients believe they could bring to life and animate what looked like an immobile and rigid object. They argued for a separation of spatiality and space. Theirs was the craft of disambiguating spatial uses from architectural form. Space was therefore consultants' lowest common denominator. It was their model for, and function of, organizational knowledge.

There is of course an ancient tradition that models the workings of epistemology on the forms of space, the articulation of spatial relations in particular. In this tradition, how to think about space has become an epitome of how to think about knowledge. Michel Serres, for example, has described the 'instauration of the moment of representation' by philosophy as an instauration brought about by the use of 'a perspectival geometry, of an architectural optics of volumes' (Serres 1982, 92). According to Serres, the internal configuration of space as a geometrical object is the epistemic engine fuelling the philosophical logos.

Serres' argument builds on the tale of Thales' measurement of the height of the great pyramid. Thales accomplishes this feat by placing a post in the sand. As the sun sets, the triangular shadows cast by the pyramid and post are then compared. In so doing, Thales invents 'the notion of a model' (Serres 1982, 86):

> By comparing the shadow of the pyramid with that of a reference post and his own shadow, Thales expressed the invariance of similar forms over changes of scale. His theorem therefore consists of the infinite progression or reduction of size while preserving the same ratio. From the colossal, the pyramid, to the small, a post or body, decreasing in size *ad infinitum*, the theorem states a logos or identical relation, the invariance of the same form, be it on a giant or a small scale, and vice versa. Height and strength are suddenly scorned, smallness demands respect, all scales and hierarchies are demolished, now derisory since each step repeats the same logos or relation without any changes! (Serres 1995, 78)

Steven Brown, who has commented on the originality of Serres's oeuvre for social theory at large, glosses Serres's analysis thus:

> Here truly is the 'Greek miracle' – one man dominates a mighty pyramid. In this 'theatre of measurement' invented through the simple act of placing a

peg in the sand, it is as though everything changed place. The weak human overcomes ancient hewn stone, the mobile sun produces immobile geometric forms ... There is an interaction or communication between two diverse part-ners (Thales, Pyramid) which involves a switching or exchanging of properties (weak/strong, mortal/durable). (Brown 2005, 220)

The world's intelligibility, then, holds itself together in this account as a set of volumetric equations. An ontological exchange of equations – between weak/strong, mortal/durable, colossal/infinitesimal, human/nonhuman – allows Thales and the Western philosophical mindset thereafter to imagine the organization of knowledge as a calculus of ratios, the world, in other words, as a regime of exchanging equations.

THE POINT OF VIEW OF THE EQUATION

When lawyers or accountants expressed their resistance to and scepticism of the consultants' programme, it was common for the latter to offer a coun-terargument by 'occupying' the formers' point of view. The occupation of the 'enemy's point of view' was articulated in two steps. First, consultants would nod in approbation and voice their sympathy: 'I understand your point of view', they would say. Then, they would proceed to 'expand' the point of view by globalizing its epistemic grounds. This was done by the operation, noted above, of 'lowering' its common denominator. This opera-tion was as much a body as a cognitive effort. A narrative much favoured by consultants in this regard was the 'judo combat'. One of the consultancy's top managers offered the narrative to me on a number of occasions as a 'technique' I ought to learn:

> Think of clients as your judo opponents. You cannot defeat them by force or simple aggression. On the contrary, you need to use *their* aggression to your advantage. Their strength is also their weakness. You need to move swiftly and elegantly, re-appropriating their ideas as your own; the sluggishness and stubbornness of their bodily movements ought to be what energizes your own movements.

Thus, for example, when lawyers' protested about employees in other departments and divisions not being aware of the legal purchase of the documents they worked with, consultants rushed to agree and point out that what was in effect needed was a 'legalization' of the global flow of informa-tion in the company. 'If only we could have a global strategy for defining the legal qualities of information', they observed, 'there would be no need to worry about this or that paper. We could do without paper altogether, for all information, indeed the very vehicular structure of informational flow itself, would be defined in accordance with legal requirements'. The point of view of the law was thus expanded to become identical with the point of view of organizational self-knowledge. Legal knowledge and organizational knowledge 'met' in the common denominator of global informational transparency. They were equated in the point of view of knowledge management. Therefore, the point of view of the equation became the point of view for all subsequent forms of managing knowledge.

In a recent synthesis of his theory of Amerindian multinaturalist ontology, Eduardo Viveiros de Castro has coined the image of 'exchanging perspectives' as a shorthand for describing the transformative dynamic through which bodies undergo processes of subjectification or objectification. As Viveiros de Castro puts it, such 'bodily metamorphosis [are] the Amerindian counterpart to the European theme of spiritual conversion' (2004, 476). The transformation of the body, Viveiros de Castro tells us, actuates a process of epistemic transformation: when bodies change, knowledge undergoes exchange too. The production of knowledge, to use a Eurocentric formula, obtains thus through processes of predation:

> At the risk of falling into allegorical excess, I would even venture to say that, in Amazonian cosmologies, the generic attributive proposition is a cannibal proposition. The copula of all synthetic a priori judgments, in a universe articulated by a 'logic of sensory qualities,' is carnivorous copulation . . . [where] the self is the gift of the other. (2004, 480)

Whereas the *exchange of perspectives* offers a model for the transformation-cum-predation of knowledge in the Amerindian context, it is the *exchange of equations* that fuels epistemic productivity in the Euro-American tradition.

Elsewhere, Viveiros de Castro and Goldman have observed, 'Exchange and perspective are trans-epistemological notions inasmuch as they establish a continuity between the object of description and the description itself. In sum, the process of anthropological description is, itself, a process of the exchange of perspectives' (Viveiros de Castro and Goldman 2008/2009, 31 see also this volume). If an exchange of perspectives in the Amerindian context demands a transformation of the bodies of knowledge, then, as Viveiros de Castro holds, what is ultimately at stake here are the ontological spaces wherein such bodies reside. One can only exchange knowledge if one's ontological ground changes – if we move from one ontology to another. Thus it is that the theory of Amerindian multinaturalism must be read as a call for 'richer ontologies' and for putting 'epistemological questions to rest' (Viveiros de Castro 2004, 484). Nevertheless, insofar as anthropological knowledge works to move in and out of ontology and epistemology through exercises in comparative description, ours is therefore a trans-epistemological project.

IN THE PRESENCE OF EQUATIONS

The trans-epistemological purchase of anthropological knowledge, suggests Viveiros de Castro, may reside in anthropologists' efforts at 'symmetrizing' (across, within) different epistemic cultures:

> If an anthropologist that studies Melanesia aims at a type of understanding of Melanesians that is predicated in the taking utterly seriously what they say, this does not mean that such an aim must be pursued in the same way and with the same means as when we work with scientists [Viveiros de Castro is alluding here to Latour's work]. Because the points of departure are asymmetrical, and the operation of symmetrization does not mean to suppose that everything 'is the same thing'. Symmetrization means choosing the right procedures, which may be the very opposite of those employed in a 'Melanesian-type', so that the *process* is symmetrical, producing a certain epistemic *dis*continuity vis-à-vis the interlocutors. Latour seems to have little interest in what the scientists *say* about what they are *doing*. (Viveiros de Castro and Goldman, 2008/2009, 37, see also this volume)

The status of the symmetrical in contemporary social theory is certainly worth a pause, and I would like to bring the chapter to a close with some reflections on 'symmetry' as a descriptor for the type of work that theory does.

When lawyers spoke of their legal archive as a 'cash bank', their 'treasury and patrimony', they were invoking an imagery of wealth and liquidity, of flow and storage. The archive was mobilized as a repository where legal paperwork would accumulate dust, but also as a place where it might accrue fiduciary and pecuniary value. The archive would therefore 'seem both to carry the flow *and to stop it*'. The phrase is Marilyn Strathern's, who is referring to indigenous descriptions of Highland (Hageners) brides as repositories themselves: 'as the repository of nurture from her kin which she contains, a bride is also a "store" or "bank" of the wealth due her kin in return' (Strathern 1996, 518, 517, emphasis in the original).

There are of course significant differences in Hageners' and lawyers' resort to the image of the repository as a deposit of wealth and relations. For one, in the Hagener case it is the person of the bride that sources the flow of wealth. As Strathern notes, this is likely to run counter to Euro-American conceptions of the person, who like to keep their 'persons' separate from what may be owned as 'property', if only because it 'was a hard-won project of their modernism' (Strathern 1996, 518). Exploring what happens when we press forms of modernist knowledge against their 'others' is in fact one of Strathern's aim in that very piece: how and on what terms can we try to symmetrize bodies of knowledge hitherto kept separate? What role does the symmetrical play when imagining how an analysis carries out its own analytical work?

A form that symmetrization takes in actor-network theory, Strathern observes, is 'summation'. If our analytical stance invites us to look for concatenations between different kinds of elements, then 'a network is as long as its different elements can be enumerated. This presupposes a summation; that is enumeration coming to rest in an identifiable object (the sum)' (Strathern 1996, 523). The sum holds the network together as a self-proliferative object. The network grows in additive fashion.

Thus, although enumerating elements is no doubt part of what the analyst does to help keep the fiction of the limitless network in place, in actual fact the figure of summation is exogenous to the network itself. We may say that the sum is placed in an *external* rather than an *internal* relation to the network. Summation is not something the network itself does. Someone has to do the sums for the network.

Now in this 'doing the sums for the network' what emerges as internally consistent is the very process of summation. We sum, and we sum, and we sum. With every sum we *build up* the network into an epistemic form. As Strathern notes, enumeration comes to rest in the identifiable object of the 'sum'. So if there is a symmetry at play here, it is a symmetry that is inscribed in the very process of 'building-up', of summation: to build up a network is to deploy symmetry as an internal engine of epistemic combustion. To sum is to symmetrize.

Although there are no doubt good reasons for social theory's recent enthusiastic deployment of symmetry, most notably for warranting symmetrical status to different ontologies (Henare et al. 2007), I wonder whether this has not been carried out at the expense of a close examination of *symmetry's very own internal organization* as an epistemic object. In this chapter I have offered one such attempt at unbundling the epistemic interiorities of symmetry: an ethnography of how the building-up of 'knowledge' is equated with the imagination of a building, and of modular space in particular, as an epistemic form: an ethnography of equations.

Let me make very clear that I am not concerned here with arguing for epistemology versus ontology. The distinction seems sterile to me. If anything, this is an argument for *ethnography:* where symmetry turns out to be an indigenous category for knowledge reckoning. Take for example consultants' and lawyers' projects at symmetrizing their own bodies of organizational knowledge. Here the symmetrical emerged indeed as a fundamental epistemic operator. The process of lowering the common denominator of mutual understanding was of course an attempt by consultants to symmetrize or level the playing field of knowledge.

They did this by using symmetry itself as the interpretative space in which to 'stop', 'rest' or 'cut' further interpretations (Strathern 1996, 522)[3] – thus their insistence on symmetrizing all knowledge processes and forms: into boxes, linear metres of shelf space, weight or even, if necessary, the 'legalization' of all informational flows. As the judo combat narrative put it, they translated heavyweight bodies of knowledge into lightweight techniques: 'one man dominates a mighty pyramid', in the terms in which Steve Brown translated Serres' 'theatre of measurement'. Thus the different 'sizes' of knowledge were made to disappear into consultants' own choice of symmetrical ratios and in particular volumetric and spatial ratios, the cultural epistemology of an 'architectural optics of volumes'.

Lawyers, however, seemed little concerned with sizes or ratios. They could not care less if their archives, libraries and shredders occupied far more space than was prudent or than had been assigned to them in the new building. With David Dery (1998) we may want to call their documentary culture, a 'papereality', for it was the paper form of knowledge that best condensed the temporal flights that most preoccupied them. For lawyers the paper form was a prototype of organizational knowledge: what the organization might lead to and how it ought to be conceptualized today. Between the proto and the type, the flow and the storage, the legal archive offered a place for knowledge to rest: where papers lay dormant, awaiting, perhaps, some future resurrection. The prototype of legal knowledge thus occupied an unstable zone *between* symmetrical equations.

The auditors' fireproof archive dwelled, too, in such an asymmetrical space. Its invocation of historicity and historical knowledge left consultants unable to effect equivalent conversions. They were left without equations. Not so with engineers, whose call for using 'cubic metres of waste' as opposed to 'linear metres of shelf space' was a little disarming initially but allowed consultants to set up a regime of exchanging equations.

The regime of exchanging equations that management consultants strove to set up was far from omniscient and comprehensive. It left many people indifferent; it provoked suspicion and offence among others; it was tweaked and modified by yet further people. And yet it remained the template with and against which people organized their social relationships of 'knowledge management'. They managed knowledge of others and of themselves through the exchange of ratios and equations: a spatial ratio of paper occupation was equated to a spatial ratio of desk occupation, which was equated to a spatial ratio of people occupation. Paperless was equated to jobless. Equations were set up that would hold in place and make significant other equations. Knowledge circulated as an internal stream of equations.

In the symmetrization between legal, auditing, management and perhaps even anthropological knowledge, the equation therefore became the engine that allowed trans-epistemological operations. It offered a modality of description in which part of what was being described (legal or financial or engineering cultural practices) was internalized in the register of description itself.[4] The equation became the internal engine of description.

Of course there was a lot of descriptive and imaginative work that the exchange of equations did not accomplish. Lawyers preferred, for example, the image of latency and potentiality, of the prototypical features of the legal document, to convey impressions of epistemic consequentiality. Notwithstanding, what I believe is particularly interesting is the very invocation of prototyping (by lawyers and auditors, among others) when pressed to symmetrize their knowledge practices. The epistemic culture of law took its defining features *against* a symmetrizing enterprise. One wonders, in this context, where anthropological knowledge itself might lie – before, in between or against the trans-epistemological purchase of symmetrical equations? Perhaps the task of ethnography is more modest, after all, such as finding ways for redescription that breathe and transpire a certain 'inadequacy', that is, that are not *ad-equate*, where the entanglement of capacities and social forms does not mirror an exchange of equations.

NOTES

1. Eduardo Viveiros de Castro and Marcio Goldman (2008/2009, 24) thus note that 'Strathernian anthropology is the most sophisticated theory of the relation that our discipline has produced since Lévi-Strauss's structuralism'.
2. The equations I shall be talking about are epistemic objects: they are self-consciously produced by participants in this regime as objects of knowledge. Once thus manufactured, these equations enter into a system of exchange. The system is of course itself formatted and performed by the transactional register of equations. There is no system proper outside and prior to the circulation of equations.
3. It is worth noting how in her account of how the process of interpretation requires of moments of stoppage or 'cut' to be rendered useful, Strathern resorts to a legal example herself: 'Thus the force of "law" cuts into a limitless expanse of "justice", reducing it and rendering expressible, creating in the legal judgment

a manipulable object of use; justice is operationalized so as to produce social effects' (Strathern 1996, 522).
4. Per Strathern's definition of 'measurement by ratio' cited in the opening of the chapter, where 'part of the measurement is also what is being measured: one item valued in terms of another yields a ratio' (Strathern 1999, 205).

REFERENCES

Becker, Franklin D. 2007. 'The Ecology of Knowledge Networks'. *California Management Review* 49: 1–20.

Becker, Franklin D., Andrew J. Rappaport, and William R. Sims. 1992. *Evolving Workplace Strategies: Investigations into the Ecology of New Ways of Working*. Ithaca: Cornell University International Facility Management Program.

Brown, Steven D. 2005. 'The Theatre of Measurement: Michel Serres'. *The Sociological Review* 53: 215–27.

Dery, David. 1998. '"Papereality" and Learning in Bureaucratic Organizations'. *Administration & Society* 29: 677–89.

Henare, Amiria, Martin Holbraad, and Sari Wastell. 2007. *Thinking through Things: Theorising Artefacts in Ethnographic Perspective*. London and New York: Routledge.

Martin, Reinhold. 2003. *The Organizational Complex: Architecture, Media, and Corporate Space*. Cambridge, MA and London: MIT Press.

Miyazaki, Hirokazu. 2006. 'Documenting the Present'. In *Documents: Artifacts of Modern Knowledge,* edited by Annelise Riles, 206–25. Ann Arbor: University of Michigan Press.

Riles, Annelise. 2006. 'Introduction: In Response'. In *Documents: Artifacts of Modern Knowledge,* edited by Annelise Riles, 1–38. Ann Arbor: University of Michigan Press.

Sellen, Abigail J., and Richard Harper. 2003. *The Myth of the Paperless Office*. Cambridge, MA: MIT Press.

Serres, Michel. 1982. 'Mathematics and Philosophy: What Thales Saw . . .' In *Hermes: Literature, Science, Philosophy,* edited by Josue V. Harari and David F. Bell, 84–97. Baltimore: John Hopkins University Press.

———. 1995. 'Gnomon: The Beginning of Geometry in Greece'. In *A History of Scientific Thought: Elements of a History of Science,* edited by Michel Serres, 73–123. Oxford: Blackwell.

Strathern, Marilyn. 1996. 'Cutting the Network'. *Journal of the Royal Anthropological Institute* 2: 517–35.

———. 1999. *Property, Substance and Effect: Anthropological Essays on Persons and Things*. London and New Brunswick: Athlone Press.

———. 2014. 'Kinship as a Relation'. *L'Homme* 210(2): 43–61.

Turner, Fred. 2006. *From Counterculture to Cyberculture: Stewart Brand, the Whole Earth Network, and the Rise of Digital Utopianism*. Chicago: University of Chicago Press.

Viveiros de Castro, Eduardo. 2004. 'Exchanging Perspectives: The Transformation of Objects into Subjects in Amerindian Ontologies'. *Common Knowledge* 10: 463–84.
Viveiros de Castro, Eduardo and Marcio Goldman. 2008/2009. "Slow motions. Comments on a Few Texts by Marilyn Strathern.' *Cambridge Anthropology* 28 (3): 23-42

Alberto Corsín Jiménez is Associate Professor in Social Anthropology at the Spanish National Research Council in Madrid. He has an interest in the organization of ethnography and anthropological knowledge as descriptive and theoretical forms. He is the author of *An Anthropological Trompe L'Oeil for a Common World* (Berghahn, 2013), in which description is placed at perpendicular angles vis-à-vis emerging forms of global public knowledge. He is also the editor of several edited collections, most recently *Prototyping Cultures: Art, Science and Politics in Beta* (Routledge, 2017). His current work examines the rise of an urban commons movement and the development of open-source urban hardware projects by architects, artists and engineers.

Chapter Four

Thinking across Domains

Structures of Debate in Indigenous Rights Claims

Stuart Kirsch

Over the past decade or so, anthropologists have found the definitional debates associated with indigenous rights to be vexing. Drawing on his work in Indonesia, John R. Bowen (2000) recommends sinking the category of indigeneity rights altogether because the exclusive criterion of 'firstness' disenfranchises other marginalized peoples facing comparable political and economic challenges. Drawing on Stuart Hall's concept of articulation, Tania Murray Li (2000) shows how some groups in Indonesia mobilize under the banner of indigenous rights, while others for whom the category seems equally or even more apposite remain indifferent to its attraction.

Other anthropologists acknowledge the appropriateness of the category in the settler states of Australia, New Zealand and the Americas, while pointing to problems in its application in Africa and Asia (McIntosh 2002). Adam Kuper (2003) criticizes all references to indigeneity, arguing that they uncritically recycle troubling tropes from the colonial era, including the categories of native and primitive. Similar concerns have been raised about the deleterious consequences of indigenous politics in north-eastern India (Shah 2010), northern Mexico (Muehlmann 2013) and Paraguay (Bessire 2014).

But once concepts like indigeneity have entered the public domain, they are not so easy to recall them. Moreover, some of the critiques of indigeneity may be too narrowly framed. In contrast to definitions that emphasize a single trait, such as prior occupation, it is possible to see indigeneity as a category based on family resemblance rather than a fixed set of attributes (Colchester 2002, 24; see also Niezen 2003; Rosengren 2002). Perhaps the closest analogue to the way indigenous politics operates may be the description of nations as imagined communities (Anderson 1991). Variation in the size, history and ethnic composition of nations is not seen to undermine their political and legal legitimacy.

The critique of indigenous rights also raises concerns similar to those expressed by Marilyn Strathern (1998, 217), who in a related context warns against the hasty deconstruction of political claims operating in the 'world of already existing inequalities, where ... it is hard to make one's voice heard'. Nonetheless, Strathern acknowledges that there is ample scope for anthropologists to analyze how such claims are mobilized and deployed without comprising their political power.[1]

Another focus of comparison for the study of indigenous rights is political recognition. In the absence of specific treaty rights, federal recognition in the United States is contingent on political continuity despite the historical challenges posed by discrimination and the pressure to assimilate (Clifford 1988). Genealogy remains an integral component of this process despite its reliance on racialized references to blood quantums (Fayard 2011; Simpson 2014). In contrast to the American emphasis on self-governance and descent, legal recognition in Australia requires demonstration of the continuity of native laws and customs, ignoring long histories of forced relocation, culture loss and intercultural relations (Povinelli 2002; Merlan 2009).[2]

Recognition in Brazil relies on problematic assumptions about authenticity (Ramos 1988). In Mexico, language is often the primary identifier of indigenous peoples (Speed 2008, 94; Muehlmann 2013, 146), although article 2 of the Mexican constitution specifies that they must be descendants of the people who occupied the territory at the time of colonization, and they must have preserved their own social, economic and cultural institutions (Muehlmann 2013, 14). Some of these requirements have been changing as a result of the adoption of the UN Declaration of the Rights of Indigenous Peoples in 2007, which emphasizes self-ascription over state-controlled processes of recognition.

However, it is possible to compare claims about indigenous rights on other grounds, bypassing definitional quagmires and state policy. Another axis for comparison is the way indigenous rights claims invoke conceptual domains prevalent in the larger societies into which they are incorporated. My use of the concept of domains follows Marilyn Strathern's (1992a, 1992b) innovative studies of kinship and new reproductive technologies. In

After Nature, she shows how English kinship categories make reference to the domains of nature, family and gender (Strathern 1992a).

In *Reproducing the Future,* she argues, 'If culture consists in established ways of bringing ideas from different domains together, then new combinations – deliberate or not – will not just extend the meanings of domains so juxtaposed; one may expect a ricochet effect, that shifts of emphasis, dissolutions, and anticipations will bounce off one area of life onto another' (Strathern 1992b, 3). However, Strathern also acknowledges that there are limits to these developments, that culture 'has its constraints and its effects on how people act, react and conceptualize what is going on around them: It is the way people imagine things really are' (ibid.). These works draw our attention to the significance of interactions between domains for understanding how political claims are made.

The question of structural relations between domains is especially relevant for indigenous rights claims. The invocation of overarching domains is in keeping with both James F. Weiner's (2006, 23) argument that indigeneity is 'always and already' relational and Francesca Merlan's (1998) emphasis on intercultural relations. In order to examine structural differences in how these domains are referenced, this chapter compares discourse on indigenous rights in two contexts. The first case comes from research on indigenous land rights in Suriname. These claims invoke the multivalent domain of freedom, which is simultaneously a shared concern among the members of the state and the basis of claims to difference. The second case is concerned with a dispute over the disposition of Native American human remains in the collections of the archaeology museum at the university where I teach. The participants in these debates invoke the domains of science, property and kinship to support or contest the repatriation of Native American remains.

Comparing the two cases is particularly instructive given the differences in the way that overarching domains are invoked in relation to indigenous rights. In claims about land rights in Suriname, the shared domain of freedom may conceal differences between indigenous claimants and other members of the state. In contrast, in the case of repatriation debates in the United States, strong political claims assert the primacy of one domain over the others. However, in other contexts in the United States, the domains of science, property and kinship have heterarchical relations rather than hierarchical relations organized by a fixed ranking system.[3] In both examples, indigenous rights claims make reference to domains that are broadly shared. But whereas land claims in Suriname make reference to a single, shared domain, the contestants in debates about repatriation in the United States assign differential weight to competing domains. The structural differences in how these domains are invoked suggest an alternative framework for comparing indigenous rights.

These comparisons are also intended to pay homage to Marilyn Strathern's strategy of creatively deploying unexpected juxtapositions. Whether by drawing on analysis of exchange in Mt. Hagen to show how social relations are truncated in Euro-American property claims, which she describes as 'cutting the network' (Strathern 1996), or by invoking Melanesian conceptions of the person to raise questions about the legal status of frozen embryos in the United States (Strathern 1999), Strathern offers fresh and illuminating perspectives on a range of important issues. These innovative thought experiments yield valuable results and expand the possibilities for anthropological research. By comparing the structural differences in how indigenous rights claims invoke larger conceptual domains, this paper is similarly intended to shed light on how political claims are fashioned and mobilized.

FREEDOM AND LAND RIGHTS IN SURINAME

The first case examines how the domain of freedom is invoked by indigenous land claims in Suriname.[4] In 2009, the Lokono (Arawak) and Kaliña (Carib) peoples filed a complaint with the Inter-American Commission on Human Rights against the Republic of Suriname.[5] The complaint challenges the state's refusal to recognize indigenous land rights despite its legal obligations to do so. Their territory in the lower Marowijne region has been progressively reduced and degraded by logging, mining and the granting of individual titles to third parties in four of the eight villages.

Three nature reserves have been established in the indigenous territory without their consent, one of which has become a major industrial zone. The Wane Hills bauxite mine, which until recently operated in the Wane Kreek nature reserve, has ravaged the landscape, transforming rain forest into barren red earth. A decade of restoration efforts amount to scattered plots of stunted trees. Mining company roads through the nature reserve have attracted legal and illegal loggers, and the removal of the bauxite layer has spurred extraction of underlying kaolin deposits. Until recently, Wane Kreek was the most important hunting and fishing grounds for the Amerindian communities living in the lower Marowijne region in East Suriname.

These developments have affected local subsistence practices, preventing the Lokono and Kaliña from feeding their families by hunting, fishing and horticulture. Consequently, they have become more dependent on the monetary economy. As one person told me, 'Before it was okay if you didn't have money, but now we need money [to survive]'. He explained that participation in the cash economy is fine for those members of the community who possess the skills required to earn a living wage but that others are unsuccessful. Even though they share food among themselves when they hunt and fish in the rain forest, they do not redistribute the wages earned through employment. This has resulted in new forms of structural inequality.

The encroachment on the territories of the Lokono and the Kaliña and the exploitation of their resources also compromises their ability to convey many of their important cultural practices to the members of future generations. For example, some of the practical skills associated with subsistence production are no longer regularly taught by fathers to their sons and mothers to their daughters: 'In some families, there are no elders to teach them these things. And even to get the materials needed ... you can no longer find them locally because of logging, but have to travel long distances'.

However, new markets for Amerindian products including cassava bread and beer (*kasiri*), agricultural produce, and wild fruits have recently emerged in the town of St. Laurent du Maroni, which is located in French Guiana across the river from Albina. Participation in these markets provides the Lokono and Kaliña with an opportunity to improve their standard of living by using local knowledge and skills for food production. But the long-term viability of these practices remains at risk due to continued environmental degradation from mining and logging.

The Surinamese legal scholar Ellen-Rose Kambel (2002, 148–53) identifies three discourses employed by the Lokono and Kaliña when challenging the state's refusal to recognize indigenous land rights: (1) the argument that land cannot be owned, which appears to be an older discourse that is rarely invoked given its incompatibility with contemporary political objectives; (2) the reference to historical precedent, that they were the original inhabitants of the land and therefore have the right to exclude others; and (3) the importance of land rights for preserving their freedom. Kambel (2002, 154) notes that only the first two rationales for indigenous land rights have previously been invoked in national debates.

However, it is the link between land rights and freedom that emerged most emphatically in my discussions with the Lokono and Kaliña in the lower Marowijne region. This corresponds with anthropologist Joana Overing's (1986, 151) observation that 'Amerindians of the South American rain forest, and particularly of the Guianas, place a strong value upon the freedom of the person, have an aversion to political tyranny, and demonstrate concern over the ambiguous relations between personal freedom and both socio-political right and constraint' (ibid.; references omitted).

I first became acquainted with indigenous concerns about freedom in Suriname while examining BHP Billiton's plans for a new bauxite mine in the Bakhuis Mountains in west Suriname (Goodland 2009). Initially, the Lokono communities living closest to the proposed mine site were enchanted by the prospect of economic development. Although the Lokono I spoke with recognized that modern mines provide relatively few jobs, they hoped the project would have a multiplier effect on local businesses. Their desire for economic opportunity echoes Amartya Sen's (1999) argument that the goal of development is to enhance human freedom, including a people's ability to collectively shape their own destiny.[6]

However, their views differed from Georg Simmel's (1978) observations about the relationship between money and modernity. Simmel describes how the universal form of value created by money is a vehicle for realizing new forms of the self that are freed from prior attachment to particular people, places and things. Thus the attraction of money has generally been taken to signify the negation of tradition, which is replaced by the modern project of self-realization (Maclean 1994). But when I interviewed young men about their desires for the future, their answers always included living in their villages: they did not dream of the bright lights of the city but wanted economic opportunities that would allow them to stay home. They did not view money as the path to individualization and modernity but as the means to remain traditional (see Sahlins 1999).

The women I spoke with in west Suriname also invoked the discourse of freedom in relation to money, albeit differently from the men. Women had their own reasons for supporting the mining project. What concerned them the most were recent economic changes that gave privileged men access to money through wage labour. They explained that traditional gender roles were complementary: in their gardens, men cleared the forest and wove the *matapi* squeezers for processing cassava, their primary staple crop, while women planted, weeded, harvested and prepared the root crop for consumption. Each gender needed the other's labour.

In contrast, women now find themselves dependent on their husbands for money and object to their loss of autonomy. For them, regaining their freedom requires access to their own source of income. They saw potential development opportunities associated with the mine as the means to earn the money required to overcome their recent dependence on their husbands. In contrast to Simmel (1978), Lokono women seek financial independence in order to reclaim their autonomy and ensure that they can provide for their families. Access to money becomes the means to achieve traditional values, to re-establish the interdependence of women and men and to fulfil their responsibilities to their children.[7]

In focus groups and interviews with the Lokono and Kaliña people of the lower Marowijne region, the most striking element of discussions about land rights was also their invocation of freedom. People told me that they only feel free on their own land, where they are able to do as they please. Without land rights, they emphasized, one is not truly free, because 'anyone can show up with a piece of paper and say they own our land'. Many people described freedom in terms of the ability to hunt and fish in the rain forest.

When I asked the young men about their future, they told me they wanted to stay on their land because 'We love this place. We want our own place where we can live. We like to be free'. Today, however, they are 'not free enough [because] other people are coming into our territory'. When describing the nature reserve established in their territory, they expressed their criticism in terms of the resulting constraints on their freedom: 'Before we were free to go there, but now someone is imposing rules on us'. Many people also brought up stories about 'no trespassing' signs on indigenous land alienated from its rightful owners.

When the Lokono and Kaliña spoke to me about freedom, they also mentioned the freedom to be indigenous, to possess their own culture and follow their own way of life. Kambel (2002) notes that the Lokono and Kaliña are familiar with the provisions of the UN Declaration on the Rights of Indigenous Peoples, including the 'collective right to live in freedom, peace and security as distinct peoples' and the ability to express 'indigenous cultural diversity' without prejudice. In this sense, the freedom to be indigenous implies the right to determine and reproduce important cultural values (see Kirsch 2001).

The concept of freedom also has broad historical resonance in Suriname, a Dutch colony from 1667 until 1975. Most of the inhabitants of Suriname are the descendants of slaves or indentured labourers. Creoles comprise 32 per cent of the population and are the strongest political faction; the Maroons, descendants of escaped slaves who settled in the rain forest of Suriname, constitute another 10 per cent of the population.[8] The largest group of people in the country is composed of the descendants of Hindi-speaking Indians who moved to Suriname as indentured labourers after the abolition of slavery; they comprise 37 per cent of the population. Another 10 per cent of the population is made up of the descendants of indentured labourers from Java. Given the historical significance of forced and coerced labour in Suriname, freedom is a powerful unifying discourse among its citizens, including the Amerindian communities, which comprise between 1.5 and 2.0 per cent of the country's population.[9]

In these examples from Suriname, freedom is a multivalent concept that simultaneously references traditional ideas about persons, gender and social relations; the freedom to hunt and fish in the rain forest; the UN Declaration on the Rights of Indigenous Peoples, which supports the freedom to be indigenous; and freedom in a recently independent country composed largely of the descendants of slaves and indentured labourers. The significance of freedom resonates across social divides in Suriname even as it is invoked in support of indigenous land rights, which have historically been opposed by the state. The multivocality of freedom means that differences in how the domain is invoked may be partially concealed by these shared meanings.

REPATRIATION DEBATES IN THE UNITED STATES

The second case is concerned with debates about the repatriation of Native American human remains, which invoke the domains of science, property and kinship. Although I draw on examples from debates at my university, I leave aside the specifics of the conflict to focus on the claims made by different parties: the archaeologists, who emphasized the scientific value of the artefacts in their collections; the university administration, which focused on its legal responsibility as the owner of the collections; and the Native American community on campus and in the surrounding area, which stressed kinship relations. All of the participants in these debates made strong claims that asserted the dominance of one domain over the others despite their heterarchical relations in other contexts. Rather than examine claims made by individuals, I focus on the structural relationships between these domains.

I begin with science, which offers the primary rationale for the maintenance of existing archaeological collections. In its modern form, science combines knowledge production with particular social roles or professions. Scientific knowledge production is based on a relatively homogeneous social process in which participation is restricted and hierarchical. Science and society are treated as separate and independent domains (Nowotny et al. 2001). The normative status of this model is evident in criticism of how the science of global climate change has become politicized. Scientists value the pursuit of knowledge above most other values and support the principle of open access to information. This is also a core tenet of liberal, democratic societies. As the Russian physicist and political dissident Andrei Sakharov (1968) observed, a society that impedes the free exchange of ideas is doomed to failure. The contemporary academy is modelled on these understandings of science and how it should be practiced.

However, recent discussions of the relationship between science and society point to a transformation in how scientific knowledge is produced

(Nowotny et al. 2001; Ziman 2000). Knowledge production is increasingly dispersed across a variety of institutions and settings. It is more heterogeneous, socially accountable and reflexive. An example is the way museums and communities undertake collaborations neither could complete on their own. This entails mutual recognition of complementary forms of expertise. Science and society are no longer treated as separate domains; Nowotny et al. (2001) argue that such arrangements produce more socially robust forms of science.

Rules and practices that restrict access to scientific information are seen to contradict the central values of liberal society. However, values associated with other domains regularly override this principle. For example, under certain conditions property rights trump access to information. We make exceptions to rules concerning open access to facilitate commerce: authors copyright their work and scientists patent their inventions for limited periods of time. These protections are intended to stimulate innovation and reward the investment of resources. They represent a compromise between the ideals of open access and information sharing and the desire to promote creativity (Lessig 2001; M. Rose 1993).

Similarly, the academy and the archive have not always fulfilled the ideal of open access. For example, Native Hawaiians once had difficulty in gaining access to the major repository of mele, the poetic verses that accompany hula performances (Stillman 2009). More generally, historians of science and empire have documented the relationship between scientific knowledge production and exclusionary practices of racism, colonialism and imperialism (Pratt 1992).

The second domain referenced by debates about repatriation is property. This is also a foundational concept of liberal society and, in the form of private property, the cornerstone of capitalism. The ownership of property is closely associated with the prevailing form of modern personhood, the possessive individual (Macpherson 1964; Radin 1993). However, there are legal limits on ownership (Kirsch 2004; C. Rose 1994; Sax 2001). An important example of restrictions on property rights was established by the Thirteenth Amendment to the US Constitution, which abolished slavery; the law no longer recognizes property interests in human bodies. People are still 'viewed as having control over their bodies and bodily integrity, but not as the result of the laws of property' (Greely 1998, 488).

Consequently, scientists who propose to carry out research on human tissue or DNA must obtain the permission of their subjects (Rabinow 1996). Individuals regularly agree to participate in clinical research in the altruistic hope that such studies will lead to scientific breakthroughs that will benefit others; the critical issue is consent. A recent legal settlement addresses these issues. From 1990 to 1994, the Havasupai Indians granted scientists at Arizona State University permission to use their DNA for research on diabetes. However, the scientists later used the DNA samples for projects unrelated to Havasupai health concerns. The university's decision to settle with the Havasupai plaintiffs who objected to these new studies is considered significant because it suggests that the 'rights of the research subjects can be violated when they are not fully informed about how their DNA might be used' (Harmon 2010).

Anthropologists have studied property since the beginning of the discipline (e.g., Maine 1986; Malinowski 1935). Whereas Euro-American law emphasizes private property, the dominant form of ownership in other societies may be collective. However, most societies recognize a variety of individual and collective property rights, as Malinowski (1935, 380) argued in relation to Trobriand Islanders. Colonial history may be characterized in part by the inability or refusal of the colonizers to recognize indigenous property rights (McLaren et al. 2005; Pocock 1992). These debates continue today, as indigenous peoples struggle to make collective claims to cultural property through legal systems that privilege individual rights (Brown 2003; Coombe 1998; Hirsch and Strathern 2004). More generally, contemporary understandings of property are being challenged by the implications of new technologies, including whether and how to assign ownership of genes (Pálsson 2007), human embryos (Strathern 1999) and pollution (Kirsch 2004).

A brief aside regarding the domain of human rights is warranted here, as the participants in repatriation debates also frame their arguments in these terms (see Trope and Echo-Hawk 2000, 140). These principles articulate the fundamental rights of all human beings. However, legal systems generally lag behind the recognition of human rights, making them difficult to enforce. Consequently human rights claims often remain aspirational (see Goodale 2009). An important component of human rights claims is that legal standing is not required to make a claim; one can object to the desecration of a cemetery, for example, regardless of whether one has relatives buried there. Native American Graves Protection and Repatriation Act (NAGPRA) regulations were originally presented as a response to human rights concerns, even though the legislation is written in the language of property rights.

The third domain invoked by repatriation debates is kinship. Although Americans say that blood is thicker than water (Schneider 1980, 49), anthropologists recognize that kinship claims are more than just blood: they are also social relations (Carsten 2003). Kinship relations may also be legal relationships; the responsibilities of parents are defined by law as well as matters of proper conduct and affect. It is not a coincidence that many of

the founders of the anthropological study of kinship were lawyers by training, including John F. McLennan (1865) and Lewis Henry Morgan (1870).

The courts are also increasingly called upon to adjudicate kinship disputes in the era of DNA testing (Strathern 1999, 2005). For example, the
courts have been asked to determine whether someone who acted as a social
father to a child by making child support payments is legally obligated to
continue those payments even when paternity tests indicate that he is not
the biological father (Strathern 1999, 74). The affirmative response follows
a social rather than exclusively biological view of kinship relations. In this
case, the social definition of kinship trumps scientific information about
genetic relationships.

Although kinship and the law are closely intertwined, the prevailing
assumption is that in family matters, the courts should defer to kin except
under extenuating circumstances (Strathern 2005, 16). This is most clearly
seen in the restraint exercised by the state with regard to interference with
the parental care of children. One instance in which this principle was
ignored was the placement of Native American children into boarding
schools, separating them from their family members and preventing them
from speaking their own languages; these interventions were subsequently
addressed by the Indian Child Welfare Act of 1978 (Smith 2005).

Possession is commonly said to be nine-tenths of the law, but anthropologists observe that kinship dominates ownership through inheritance
and succession. Kinship guides many forms of property distribution, including real property in land and things as well as titles, social roles and, in
some cases, occupational status. But kinship and ownership belong to different domains. A husband and wife have certain legal rights vis-à-vis one
another, but this does not include ownership. Kinship is better understood
in terms of responsibility: I may or may not be my brother's keeper, but
I am certainly not his owner. To invoke ownership with respect to kin is
a category error. Similarly, many Native Americans reject the invocation
of property rights with respect to human remains, which they view as kin
rather than property.

Kinship claims regarding the disposition of human remains might be
compared to how people take responsibility for relatives who are unable
to communicate their intentions because they are minors or adults com-
promised by illness. In the United States, the next of kin have the right to
arrange for the burial of the deceased (Greely 1998, 488). In the context of
repatriation, many Native Americans also see themselves as protecting the
interests of their kin. These may be more than secular duties, however, as
caring for one's ancestors is often understood as a religious obligation. The
extended care and concern with which such responsibilities towards human

remains are discharged is well documented for many other societies as well (e.g., Feeley-Harnik 1991; Richards 2010).

Societies vary in how broadly they define the scope of kinship relations. Nuclear families in the United States often maintain relatively shallow genealogies. In other societies, however, even remote ancestors may be regarded as members of one's family; there is no parting of the ways with kin at death. In some cases, such as with Trobriand Islanders, the members of future generations are already members of one's lineage (A. Weiner 1976). But it would be a mistake to treat these differences as oppositions. Americans can and do recognize lengthy genealogies, especially when they are associated with property and privilege, which explains why a Ford still runs Ford Motor Company. Kinship relations are always subject to telescoping and collapse for various purposes; such flexibility is one of the hallmarks of kinship rather than an anomaly.

Given the racialized history of kinship in the United States (Dominguez 1986), it is not surprising that Native American claims about kinship and relatedness may be retrospectively extended beyond contemporary tribal boundaries in claims regarding the disposition of culturally unaffiliated human remains.[10] Nor can these identifications be separated from the historical contexts in which native peoples have lost land, cultural knowledge and, in many cases, their languages through historical policies and practices of genocide, dispossession and forced assimilation (Fine-Dare 2002).

Shared histories of oppression have become de facto components of indigenous identity in many contexts (Niezen 2003). Repatriation is important to Native Americans both in terms of the proper treatment of their relatives (writ large) and as partial reparation for past injustices (Fine-Dare 2002; Mihesuah 2000). Gaining federal recognition, reclaiming tribal lands, revitalizing endangered languages and repatriating the remains of fellow Native Americans are political responses to the colonial legacy with which Native Americans continue to struggle (Riding In 2000).

As I have indicated, the participants in these debates regularly make reference to all of these domains. The pursuit of knowledge and understanding is not limited to scientific research by students and professors. All members of the state seek protection of their property under the law. Everyone values their families and kin. North Americans also regularly invoke more than one of these domains at a time to establish priorities and settle disputes. These interactions must be carefully negotiated, as there is no stable hierarchy of values through which claims to the primacy of one domain over the others can be made. Given their heterarchical relations, invoking principles from multiple domains may result in complex and even controversial interactions, as when scientific knowledge about wetlands affects how landowners are permitted to make use of private property or when estate taxes must be paid on an inheritance.

However, the participants in debates concerning repatriation often restrict their claims to a single domain. As scientists, archaeologists may treat human remains primarily in terms of the research questions they can help to answer. Universities and museums may view the same human remains primarily in terms of property rights governing their disposition, including compliance with the provisions of NAGPRA. Native Americans tend to view these human remains as ancestors and kin to whom they have important and even sacred responsibilities, although they also value repatriation as a political act of decolonization. The participants in these debates may be looking at the same material remains but seeing something entirely different (Henare et al. 2006).

There are, however, other ways to think about these issues. Archaeologists increasingly draw on collaborative models of science when working with Native American communities and vice versa (Colwell-Chanthaphonh and Ferguson 2008; Thomas 2000). Universities and museums are actively seeking to improve relations with Native Americans and other minority populations. New rules concerning the disposition of culturally unaffiliated human remains may help to resolve some of the outstanding claims (US Government 2010), but given their emphasis on property rights, they cannot be expected to solve all of the problems. For example, some archaeologists feel that the new regulations do not sufficiently value knowledge or research about the past (Sinopoli 2010).

CONCLUSION

This chapter examines the ways in which indigenous rights claims draw on domains that are often shared by the other members of the societies into which they are incorporated. It suggests that the invocation of difference is only one element of indigenous rights claims, whether Native American understandings of kinship and sacred responsibilities towards ancestral remains or the different registers of freedom, including the freedom to hunt and fish in the rain forest and women's desires to avoid dependence on their husbands for the Lokono and Kaliña in Suriname. It is also significant that the domains invoked by these indigenous rights claims in these two countries are very different, suggesting the importance of the social, historical and cultural context to how such claims are formulated.

Perhaps most interesting from a comparative perspective, however, are the structural differences in how these domains are invoked. In the North

American example, arguments about the disposition of Native American human remains by both indigenous groups and their critics make hierarchical claims about the relationship between domains, asserting that one domain trumps the others. This contrasts with the way that these domains are heterarchically organized in other contexts. Rather than argue across domains as in North America, the Lokono and Kaliña articulate their concerns by invoking a single, shared domain.

To some extent these choices may reflect the political positions of these communities and the contexts in which the claims are being made, with Native Americans in the United States being more willing to challenge how repatriation has been framed and interpreted by other parties. In contrast, for the Amerindian communities in Suriname, direct confrontation with the state may be less efficacious and even more risky than concealing the differences between them by invoking the multivocal domain of freedom.

In both cases, however, the domains invoked by these indigenous rights claims cross social boundaries. Attention to these structural relations, including how and why such claims are made, suggests a new way to compare indigenous rights. It also sheds light on the way political claims are fashioned, especially how references to shared domains can provide the basis for claims to difference.

NOTES

This discussion of repatriation debates in the United States previously appeared in *Museum Anthropology* (Kirsch 2011) and is included here with the permission of the American Anthropological Association. The discussion of freedom in Suriname appeared as part of a comparative chapter on the juridification of indigenous politics (Kirsch 2012) and is included here with the permission of Cambridge University Press. I thank Ashley Lebner, Sabine Deiringer and the reviewers for their constructive suggestions on earlier drafts of this paper. I would also like to acknowledge Marilyn Strathern's inspiration and intellectual generosity.

1. The political debate seems to have been resolved by the passage of the UN Declaration on the Rights of Indigenous Peoples in 2007. Legal scholars have also expressed confidence in the utility of the concept (Anaya 2004; Barsh 1994; Gilbert 2006; MacKay 2013–2014).
2. This requirement was expressed in the following terms during the Yorta Yorta case: if the "normative system has not existed through that period, the rights and interests which owe their existence to that system will have ceased to exist" (*Yorta Yorta v Victoria* 2002 194 A.L.R. 538, cited in Bulkan 2008, 224).

3. A classic example of heterarchy is the children's game of paper, scissors, rocks, in which paper covers rock (thus defeating it), but scissors cuts paper and rocks break scissors. There is dominance without hierarchy.

4. This research was conducted at the behest of the Association of Village Leaders in Suriname (VIDS) and the Forest People's Programme for submission to the Inter-American Court of Human Rights (Kirsch 2015).

5. In its landmark judgement of *Saramaka People v. Suriname* (2007, 2008), the Inter-American Court of Human Rights "expanded the scope of protection for groups seeking to protect ancestral land and resources, moving for the first time beyond indigenous peoples to extend protection to other tribal groups," namely the Saramaka Maroons who escaped from slavery during the seventeenth and eighteenth centuries to establish largely autonomous communities in the rain forest (Shelton 2008, 168; see also Price 2011).

6. However, Chakrabarty (2000, 44–45) argues against the identification of the modern state with freedom, as the state achieves its goals through projects of reform, progress and development that may be coercive or violent.

7. See also Strathern (2004) for an insightful discussion of the relationship between individual rights and social responsibility.

8. Although Richard Price (2013) suggests that the Maroon population has been radically undercounted and may now comprise 23 percent of the population of Suriname.

9. As Nikolas Rose (1999) argues, freedom is also a pervasive discourse of modernity that goes hand in hand with the state's capacity to organize and regulate the behaviour of its population.

10. This applies to human remains that have been identified as Native American but for which no lineal descendants or culturally affiliated Indian tribe has been identified.

REFERENCES

Anaya, S. James. 2004. *Indigenous Peoples in International Law*. 2nd ed. Oxford: Oxford University Press.

Anderson, Benedict. 1991. *Imagined Communities: Reflections on the Origin and Spread of Nationalism*. London: Verso.

Barsh, Russell Lawrence. 1994. 'Indigenous Peoples in the 1990s. From Object to Subject of International Law'. *Harvard Human Rights Journal* 7: 33–86.

Bessire, Lucas. 2014. *Behold the Black Caiman: A Chronicle of Ayoreo Life*. Chicago: University of Chicago Press.

Bowen, John R. 2000. 'Should We Have a Universal Concept of "Indigenous Peoples' Rights"? Ethnicity and Essentialism in the Twenty-First Century'. *Anthropology Today* 16(4): 12–16.

Brown, Michael F. 1998. 'Can Culture Be Copyrighted'? *Current Anthropology* 39(2): 193–222.

———. 2003. *Who Owns Native Culture?* Cambridge, MA: Harvard University Press.

Bulkan, Christopher Arif. 2008. 'The Land Rights of Guyana's Indigenous Peoples'. PhD dissertation, York University, Toronto.

Carsten, Janet. 2003. *After Kinship.* Cambridge: Cambridge University Press.

Chakrabarty, Dipesh. 2000. *Provincializing Europe.* Princeton: Princeton University Press.

Clifford, James. 1988. 'Identity in Mashpee'. In *The Predicament of Culture: Twentieth-Century Ethnography, Literature and Art,* edited by James Clifford, 277–346. Cambridge, MA: Harvard University Press.

Colchester, Marcus. 2002. 'Response to Ian McIntosh, *Defining Oneself, and Being Defined as, Indigenous'. Anthropology Today* 18(3): 24.

Colwell-Chanthaphonh, Chip, and T.J. Ferguson, eds. 2008. *Collaboration in Archaeological Practice: Engaging Descendant Communities.* Lanham: AltaMira Press.

Coombe, Rosemary. 1998. *The Cultural Life of Intellectual Properties.* Durham: Duke University Press.

Dominguez, Virginia. 1986. *White by Definition: Social Classification in Creole Louisiana.* New Brunswick: Rutgers University Press.

Fayard, Kelly. 2011. '"We've Always Known Who We Are": Belonging in the Poarch Band of Creek Indians'. Doctoral dissertation, University of Michigan, Ann Arbor.

Feeley-Harnik, Gillian. 1991. *A Green Estate: Restoring Independence in Madagascar.* Washington, DC: Smithsonian Institution Scholarly Press.

Fine-Dare, Kathleen S. 2002. *Grave Injustice: The American Indian Repatriation Movement and NAGPRA.* Lincoln: University of Nebraska Press.

Gilbert, Jérémie. 2006. *Indigenous Peoples' Land Rights under International Law: From Victims to Actors.* Ardsley: Transnational Publishers.

Goodale, Mark. 2009. *Surrendering to Utopia: An Anthropology of Human Rights.* Stanford: Stanford University Press.

Goodland, Robert, ed. 2009. *Suriname's Bakhuis Bauxite Mine: An Independent Review of SRK's Impact Assessment.* Paramaribo: Bureau VIDS.

Greely, H.T. 1998. 'Legal, Ethical, and Social Issues in Human Genome Research'. *Annual Review of Anthropology* 27: 473–502.

Harmon, Amy. 2010. 'Indian Tribe Wins Fight to Limit Research of Its DNA'. *New York Times* electronic document, April 21. http://www.nytimes.com/2010/04/22/us/22dna.html, accessed 22 April.

Henare, Amiria, Martin Holbraad, and Sari Wastell, eds. 2006. *Thinking through Things: Theorising Artefacts in Ethnographic Perspective.* New York: Routledge.

Hirsch, Eric, and Marilyn Strathern, eds. 2004. *Transactions and Creations: Property Debates and the Stimulus of Melanesia.* New York: Berghahn.

Kambel, Ellen-Rose. 2002. 'Resource Conflicts, Gender, and Indigenous Rights in Suriname: Local, National and Global Perspectives'. Doctoral dissertation, University of Leiden, Leiden.

Kirsch, Stuart. 2001. 'Lost Worlds: Environmental Disaster, "Culture Loss" and the Law'. *Current Anthropology* 42(2): 167–98.

——. 2004. 'Property Limits: Debates on the Body, Nature, and Culture'. In *Transactions and Creations: Property Debates and the Stimulus of Melanesia,* edited by Eric Hirsch and Marilyn Strathern, 21–39. New York: Berghahn.

——. 2011. 'Science, Property, and Kinship in Repatriation Debates'. *Museum Anthropology* 34(2): 91–96.

——. 2012. 'Juridification of Indigenous Politics'. In *Law against the State: Ethnographic Forays into Law's Transformations,* edited by Julia Eckert, Brian Donahoe, Zerrin Özlem Biner and Christian Strümpell, 23–43. Cambridge: Cambridge University Press.

——. 2015. Affidavit, Kaliña and Lokono Peoples v. The Republic of Suriname. Case 12.639 of the Inter-American Court of Human Rights. 27 January. 32 pages + appendices.

Kuper, Adam. 2003. 'The Return of the Native'. *Current Anthropology* 44(3): 389–402.

Lessig, Lawrence. 2001. *The Future of Ideas: The Fate of the Commons in a Connected World.* New York: Random House.

Li, Tania Murray. 2000. 'Articulating Indigenous Identity in Indonesia: Resource Politics and the Tribal Slot'. *Comparative Studies of Society and History* 42: 149–79.

Mackay, Fergus, ed. 2013–2014. 'Indigenous Peoples and United Nations Human Rights Bodies. A Compilation of UN Treat Body Jurisprudence, Reports of the Special Procedures of the Human Rights Council, and Advice of the Expert Mechanism on the Rights of Indigenous Peoples'. Volume VI. Moreton-in-Marsh: Forest Peoples Programme. http://www.forestpeoples.org/sites/fpp/files/publication/2015/06/cos-2013-14.pdf, accessed 1 July 2015.

Maclean, Neil. 1994. 'Freedom or Autonomy: A Modern Melanesian Dilemma'. *Man* 29: 667–88.

Macpherson, C.B. 1964. *The Political Theory of Possessive Individualism: Hobbes to Locke.* Oxford: Clarendon.

Maine, Henry Sumner. 1986 [1861]. *Ancient Law.* Tucson: University of Arizona Press.

Malinowski, Bronislaw. 1935. *Coral Gardens and Their Magic.* London: Routledge and Kegan Paul.

McIntosh, Ian. 2002. 'Defining Oneself and Being Defined As, Indigenous. Response to J. Bowen and M. Colchester'. *Anthropology Today* 18(3): 23–34.

McLaren, John, A.R. Buck, and Nancy E. Wright, eds. 2005. *Despotic Dominion: Property Rights in British Settler Societies.* Vancouver: University of British Columbia Press.

McLennan, John F. 1865. *Primitive Marriage.* Edinburgh: Adam and Charles Black.

Merlan, Francesca. 2009. *Caging the Rainbow: Places, Politics, and Aborigines in a North Australian Town.* Honolulu: University of Hawai'i Press.

Mihesuah, Devon A., ed. 2000. *Repatriation Reader: Who Owns American Indian Remains?* Lincoln: University of Nebraska Press.

Morgan, Lewis Henry. 1870. *Systems of Consanguinity and Affinity of the Human Family.* Washington, DC: Smithsonian Institution.

Muehlmann, Shaylih. 2013. *Where the River Ends: Contested Indigeneity in the Mexican Colorado Delta.* Durham: Duke University Press.

Niezen, Ronald. 2003. *The Origins of Indigenism: Human Rights and the Politics of Identity.* Berkeley: University of California Press.

Nowotny, Helga, Peter Scott, and Michael Gibbons. 2001. *Re-Thinking Science: Knowledge and the Public in an Age of Uncertainty.* Cambridge, UK: Polity.

Overing, Joanna. 1986. 'Men Control Women? The Catch 22 in the Analysis of Gender'. *International Journal of Moral and Social Studies* 1(2): 135–56.

Pálsson, Gísli. 2007. *Anthropology and the New Genetics.* Cambridge: Cambridge University Press.

Pocock, J.G.A. 1992. 'Tangata Whenua and Enlightenment Anthropology'. *New Zealand Journal of History* 26(1): 28–56.

Povinelli, Elizabeth. 2002. *The Cunning of Recognition: Indigenous Alterities and the Making of Australian Multiculturalism.* Durham: Duke University Press.

Pratt, Mary Louise. 1992. *Imperial Eyes: Travel Writing and Transculturation.* London: Routledge.

Price, Richard. 2011. *Rainforest Warriors: Human Rights on Trial.* Philadelphia: University of Pennsylvania Press.

——. 2013. 'The Maroon Population Explosion: Suriname and Guyane'. *New West Indian Guide* 87: 323–27.

Rabinow, Paul. 1996. *Essays on the Anthropology of Reason.* Princeton: University of Princeton Press.

Radin, Margaret Jane. 1993. *Reinterpreting Property.* Chicago: University of Chicago Press.

Ramos, Alcida Rita. 1998. *Indigenism: Ethnic Politics in Brazil.* Madison: University of Wisconsin Press.

Richards, Janet. 2010. 'Spatial and Verbal Rhetorics of Power: Constructing Late Old Kingdom History'. *Journal of Egyptian History* 3(2): 339–66.

Riding In, James. 2000. 'Repatriation: A Pawnee's Perspective'. In *Repatriation Reader: Who Owns American Remains?,* edited by Devon A. Mihesuah, 106–22. Lincoln: University of Nebraska Press.

Rose, Carol M. 1994. *Property and Persuasion: Essays on the History, Theory, and Rhetoric of Ownership.* Boulder: Westview Press.

Rose, Mark. 1993. *Authors and Owners: The Invention of Copyright.* Cambridge, MA: Harvard University Press.

Rose, Nikolas. 1999. *The Powers of Freedom: Reframing Political Thought.* Cambridge, UK: Cambridge University Press.

Rosengren, Dan. 2002. 'On "Indigenous" Identities: Reflections on a Debate'. *Anthropology Today* 18(3): 25.

Sahlins, Marshall. 1999. 'What is Anthropological Enlightenment? Some Lessons of the Twentieth Century'. *Annual Review of Anthropology* 28: i–xxiii.

Sakharov, Andrei. 1968. 'Reflections on Progress, Peaceful Coexistence, and Intellectual Freedom'. *New York Times,* July 22, A14–A16.

Saramaka People v. Suriname. 2007. 'Preliminary Objections, Merits, Reparations and Costs. Judgment of 28 November 2007'. Series C No. 172, at para. 194–96. Electronic document. http://www.corteidh.or.cr/dos/casos/articulos/seriec_172_ing.pdf, accessed 15 July 2010.

———. 2008. 'Interpretation of the Judgement on Preliminary Objections, Merits, Reparations and Costs. Judgment of 12 August 2008'. Series C No. 185. Electronic document.   http://www.corteidh.or.cr/docs/casos/articulos/seriec_185_ing. pdf, accessed 15 July 2010.

Sax, Joseph L. 2001. *Playing Darts with a Rembrandt: Public and Private Rights in Cultural Treasures.* Ann Arbor: University of Michigan Press.

Schneider, David Murray. 1980. *American Kinship: A Cultural Account.* Chicago: University of Chicago Press.

Sen, Amartya. 1999. *Development as Freedom.* New York: Random House.

Shah, Alpa. 2010. *In the Shadows of the State: Indigenous Politics, Environmentalism, and Insurgency in Jharkhand, India.* Durham: Duke University Press.

Shelton, Diana L. 2008. 'Saramaka Judgment'. *Yearbook of International Environmental Law 2007.* Vol. 18, edited by Ole Kristian Fauchald and David Hunter, 168–72. Oxford: Oxford University Press.

Simmel, Georg. 1978. *The Philosophy of Money.* Translated by Tom Bottomore and David Frisby. London: Routledge and Kegan Paul.

Simpson, Audra. 2014. *Mohawk Interruptus: Political Life across the Borders of Settler States.* Durham: Duke University Press.

Sinopoli, Carla. 2010. 'NAGPRA Spurs Potential Collaboration between U-M Museum and Native Tribes'. *Consider* 24(9): 2.

Smith, Andrea. 2005. *Conquest: Sexual Violence and American Indian Genocide.* Cambridge, MA: South End.

Speed, Shannon. 2008. *Rights in Rebellion: Indigenous Struggle & Human Rights in Chiapas.* Stanford: Stanford University Press.

Stillman, Amy Ku'uleialoha. 2009. 'Access and Control: A Key to Reclaiming the Right to Construct Hawaiian History'. In *Music and Cultural Rights,* edited by Andrew N. Weintraub and Bell Yung, 86–109. Champaign: University of Illinois Press.

Strathern, Marilyn. 1992a. *After Nature: English Kinship in the Late Twentieth Century.* Cambridge, UK: Cambridge University Press.

———. 1992b. *Reproducing the Future: Anthropology, Kinship and the New Reproductive Technologies.* New York: Routledge.

———. 1996. 'Cutting the Network'. *Journal of the Royal Anthropological Institute* 2(3): 517–35.

———. 1998. 'Comment on Michael F. Brown, Can Culture Be Copyrighted?' *Current Anthropology* 39(2): 216–17.

———. 1999. *Property, Substance and Effect: Anthropological Essays on Persons and Things.* London: Athlone.

———. 2004. 'Global and Local Contexts'. In *Rationales of Ownership,* edited by Lawrence Kalinoe and James Leach, 107–27. Wantage: Sean Kingston Publishing.

———. 2005. *Kinship, Law and the Unexpected: Relatives Are Always a Surprise.* Cambridge, UK: Cambridge University Press.

Thomas, David Hurst. 2000. *Skull Wars: Kennewick Man, Archaeology, and the Battle for Native American Identity.* New York: Basic Books.

Trope, Jack F., and Walter R. Echo-Hawk. 2000. 'Native American Graves Protection and Repatriation Act: Background and Legislative History'. In *Repatriation Reader: Who Owns American Remains?,* edited by Devon A. Mihesuah, 123–66. Lincoln: University of Nebraska Press.

US Government. 2010. 'Native American Graves Protection and Repatriation Act Regulations: Disposition of Culturally Unidentifiable Human Remains'. *Federal Register* 75(49): 12377–405. http://www.regulations.gov/search/Regs/home.html #documentDetail?R=0900006480abd3e5, accessed 15 June 2012.

Weiner, Annette. 1976. *Women of Value, Men of Renown: New Perspectives in Trobriand Exchange.* Austin: University of Texas Press.

Weiner, James F. 2006. 'Eliciting Customary Law'. *Asia Pacific Journal of Anthropology* 7(1): 15–25.

Ziman, John. 2000. *Real Science: What It Is, and What It Means.* Cambridge, UK: Cambridge University Press.

Stuart Kirsch is Professor of Anthropology at the University of Michigan. He is the author of *Reverse Anthropology* (Stanford University Press, 2006) and more recently of *Mining Capitalism* (University of California Press, 2014). Kirsch has consulted widely on indigenous rights and environmental problems in the Pacific and the Amazon. These projects are the subject of his next book, *Anthropology beyond the Text*, which examines the politics of engaged research.

Chapter Five

Pacifist Devices

The Human-Technology Interface in the Field of Conflict Resolution

Yael Navaro

TECHNOLOGY FOR PEACE

In 1996, at a time when the border between north and south Cyprus was shut and crossing was not allowed to communities on either side of the green line, the Cyprus Neuroscience and Technology Institute based in the south and directed by Dr Yiannis Laouris started an initiative under the rubric *technology for peace*. The rationale was to forge links, via technology, between communities who were banned from meeting and interacting with one another due to political blockades to movement. Laouris and his colleagues thought that modern technology could transcend the barriers to access across the border and create a space for communication between Greek and Turkish Cypriots.

This 'space' which was imagined by the makers of the Tech4Peace project was virtual. The reference was to cyberspace. The website of the project favourably presented the uses of information and communication technologies in the service of peace, stating, 'The Internet can overcome the challenge posed by physical separation, whether due to geographic, political or other reasons, by effectively moving discourse into cyberspace'.[1] Here, the internet was being conceived as an instrument for recreating contact between two communities which had been banned from communicating for more than twenty years. The rationale for the project was described as follows:

The specific vision which underpins the project 'Technology for Peace' is to enhance in Cyprus one of the most basic human rights, the right of communication, by applying modern technology in the service of peace with emphasis on the usage of the internet and internet-based applications. A promising and creative way to enhance intercommunal communication where there exist substantial hindrances to direct contact between peoples is through the use of the Internet.[2]

The project coordinators promised to employ the internet as a device with pacifist objectives. Technology enabled new kinds of communication and relationality, making political barriers to movement and contact redundant. Here, the internet was conceptualized as a tool for postconflict reconciliation, for the remaking of social relations in the aftermath of war.

In a blog under the rubric *technology initiatives for peace,* a commentator spelled out the rationale for the Tech4Peace project:

We would substitute the technology of peace for that of war. If our responsibility is to separate creative potential from the capacity to destroy, then let us get at it. Technology is an engine of change, but an engine is run by human hands. If not, it is automated. The automation is nevertheless programmed by a human mind with human sensibilities.[3]

This blogger was proposing what I will call a 'humanist ethic' as a rationale for the technology for peace initiative. Accordingly, if technology has been predominantly used for military purposes up until the present, a project like Tech4Peace could enlist new technology, like the internet, for contrary purposes.

Rather than having technology run its own 'automated' route, as, by implication, the military sciences do, Tech4Peace would maintain a human agency upon the use of technology and therefore ensure its users, products and outcomes against mechanization. The blogger specifies what he implies by his use of the term 'human', 'human hands', and 'the human mind': he associates such agency with what he calls a 'human sensibility'. We could interpret the 'human' in this humanist ethic as having been conflated with the notion of the humane and, therefore, there is a moralizing undertone to the way in which the human-technology interface is imagined by the receivers of this new technology in a postconflict situation. A human sensibility would, in this reading, be oriented towards nonviolent ends. Another blogger provides a more exact contrast with weapons research:

The process of studying and developing technologies for non-violent action provides a contrast to weapons R & D [research and development]. Most

military R & D is carried out by government or corporate laboratories, with
scientists and engineers taking a leading role. Testing is done in labs and by
the military itself, in exercises and on the battlefield. Thus, the whole process
of military R & D is dominated by specialists, including scientists, engineers,
and military personnel. In contrast to this military model, non-violent defense
depends fundamentally on popular participation ... As a general rule, technologies supportive of non-violent action are those that allow or foster participation, such as telephones or faxes for communication or do-it-yourself
building materials.[4]

The point and the priority in a technology for peace initiative is, according
to this commentator, to 'reorient technology from military priorities to the
goal of supporting nonviolent action', in other words, to hijack technology and appropriate it for 'pacifist' purposes.[5] Here, there is a proposal to
change the purpose and goal of technology. The imagined shifter of the gear
is once again conceptualized (or put into discourse) as human.

The initiative I outlined and the framework for it provided by blog-
gers could lead us to think that the peace sciences and peace activism
have assumed a new face and portfolio through the assumption of technology. This could certainly be studied as a new development, at least
in the self-portraits of peace practitioners. Until this shifting of gears, the
peace sciences would associate technology with mechanization and automation and (therefore, by implication) with military science and practice
against which they were argued to have been created as a practice, a
rationale and an ethic. Before the assumption of technology, peace scholars and practitioners could be situated as unproblematically humanist in
their outlook.

Here, I employ the term 'humanism' to refer both to the liberal humanist project in philosophy (see, e.g. Hayles 1999; Pickering 2001) and to the
blurring of the distinction between the 'human' and the (morally) 'humane'
in the notion of *humanitarianism* (see, e.g. Malkki 1994; Douzinas 2007).
Based on my evidence, I would argue that a humanist outlook amongst
contemporary peace practitioners is precisely based on a conflation of the
difference between the notions of the human and the humane. Effectively,
these practitioners would argue that their initiatives are humanistic, meaning that they are oriented towards the preservation of human life as against
its destruction.

My question in this paper, however, is different: I am interested in
exploring what has happened to social relations in a site identified as 'prone
to conflict' (such as Cyprus) in the aftermath of the assumption of new technologies by practitioners intending to reforge contact between the divided

communities. Marilyn Strathern has pioneered the study of the reimagining of kinship relations through the assumption of new reproductive technologies (1992). Following this work, I ask, how are social relations in postconflict situations reconfigured through the introduction of technical devices built for the purposes of reconciliation? At one level, reflecting on my ethnographic material, it could appear as though the assumption of technology would have led local peace practitioners and their user groups to move from a humanist to a posthuman (or cyborg) phase. But the evidence proves more complicated.

In what follows, my ethnographic route leads me to observe how the human-technology interface has moved Cypriots to assign agency to technology in their projected horizons for reconciliation in an unprecedented manner. We could determine that this is partly due to the fantasies (see Navaro-Yashin 2002) developed by the initiators of technology for peace as to the potentialities, promises and intrinsic values of technology. In other words, I would argue that the relation with technology is not merely practical or instrumental.

Technology is also assigned certain mystical, magical and phantasmatic qualities, as well as a potency for resolving conflict, in this instance, precisely due to being nonhuman. In other words, certain modernist projections have been reflected onto technology from a space, like Cyprus, which has been oriented towards an accelerated modernizing project. Technology, then, is not solely a tool or instrument, but also a 'phantasm' (see Ivy 1995) that promises to transcend the fragility, subjective inclinations, vulnerability, bias, partiality and limitations of a merely human approach.

And yet, I would argue, based on the material to be presented in this paper, that Cyprus has not simply turned posthuman through the introduction of new technologies. First, we could reflect, following Strathern, that 'there was never any pre-cyberculture' (1994), and like Latour, that the human-nonhuman interface always existed even before so-called modernity (1993). But in my own material from Cyprus, I have observed an ambiguity: a humanistic cloud hovers over the human-technology interface, which has been forged through the assumption of new technology in the arena of peace practice. In other words, humanism and the posthuman coexist in the practices of peace activists who employ technology.

More specifically, though engaging with each other through a nonhuman medium, peace activists have maintained a liberal humanist outlook (or ideology) for their practices. This is an attempt to don technology with a humanist cloak, a wish to humanize technology. Here, in no way would I take any notion of the human (or the machine) for granted. Instead, the point of this exercise is to ethnographically situate what might be understood by the human and the technological in a postconflict situation where they are interlinked and intermeshed. What specifically do Cypriot peace practitioners imply by the human? I do not study this merely by reference to Cypriots' discourses about the human.[6] Instead, here following Strathern (1988), I am interested in anthropologically exploring the manner in which the human might be a category (if at all) in Cypriot personhood in a specific conjuncture: that of the human-technology interface in the field of conflict resolution.

A DEVICE FOR PEACE

The tool for reconciliation introduced through Tech4Peace has a specific content, a genealogy and history. Its creators at the Cyprus Neuroscience and Technology Institute trace it back to systems theory and cybernetics. Yiannis Laouris, one of the inventors of this particular technology geared for peace, has a background in neurophysiology and systems engineering and experience in applying cybernetic models in the behavioural sciences.[7] After years of training and research in Germany and the United States, Laouris returned to Cyprus, in his account, 'with a vision to re-direct and expand my research in the interface of human and artificial intelligence. I desire to design research projects that are socially relevant and responsible'.[8]

On his curriculum vitae, Laouris lists several artefacts which he was instrumental in developing in the field of computer systems design. Most of these products (or computer programs) are in the area of software development for educational purposes. One of them is the *IT for peace* initiative which he has codirected along with a team of Greek and Turkish Cypriots whose scientific credentials are emphasized.

Laouris's work coincides with that of Dr Alexander N. Christakis, a well-known Greek American systems scientist. Christakis is known for developing what he has called the structured dialogic design process (SDDP), a technology-based methodology for mediating the relations between parties who experience dissonance or conflict with one another. Christakis first devised this technique through inspiration from his training in the systems sciences and applied it in his consultancy work for businesses and corporations which were experiencing some form of internal dispute.

Before being applied to the Cyprus problem, SDDP was employed in the field of natural resource management, healthcare, pharmaceutical drug development, the tribal affairs of Native American communities, environmental protection and the management of forestry, among other things. In an interview I held with him via Skype, Christakis described the difference between a 'workshop' and what he called a 'collaboration'. 'A "workshop"', he said, 'can be a gathering of people with common interests', such as biologists, anthropologists or other academics meeting to present their research results.

> However, if you are going to bring people with different points of view with some dissonance or conflict between them, they will not be able to communicate without help. We say that we are going to engage them in a 'collaborative dialogue'. They will be able to come out of the 'collaboration' with a common understanding.

Christakis also emphasized that the collaboration approach 'requires resources' (i.e. funding). He also stressed that this technique advocates using a 'consensus method' in conflict resolution.[9] In a coauthored article, Laouris and Christakis describe SDDP as follows:

> The Structured Dialogic Design Process (SDDP) is a deeply reasoned, rigorously validated methodology for dialogic design, which integrates knowledge from mixed participants in strategic design settings. It is especially effective in resolving multiple conflicts of purpose and values and in generating consensus on organisational and interorganisational strategy. (2007, 132)

In other words, this program is meant to facilitate the amelioration of conflict between parties to a divide, be this an intraorganizational dispute within a corporation or something like 'the Cyprus problem'. The authors are explicit about the theoretical genealogy of SDDP. They write, 'SDDP is scientifically grounded on six laws of cybernetics' (Laouris and Christakis 2007, 132). The references go back to the Turkish systems thinker Hasan Ozbekhan, who, according to the authors, first envisioned 'the need for such a scientific methodology to facilitate democratic dialogue' (ibid.).

Tracing the route of this tool which contains the knowledge which went into its making, the authors refer to the previous incarnation of SDDP in the form of interactive management (IM), which was developed by Christakis, along with Warfield, in the 1970s. SDDP represents an advancement in the area of IM with the development of 'software specifically designed for the purpose [of dialogue enhancement]'. Laouris and Christakis provide a history for IM and SDDP, particularly referring to these devices' comparatist credentials: they have been applied before in the context of dispute resolution in 'businesses, governments, NGOs, and international organisations' (2007, 132). Their application in the arena of political conflict is, by implication, therefore deemed more valid and valuable because or due to these techniques' prior uses in other institutional and disciplinary settings.

Particularly promoting the use of interactive communication technologies in the area of development and peace practice, Laouris and Christakis write the history of the regeneration of the bicommunal peace movement in Cyprus by reference to technology. In this narrative, technology does not simply appear as a human invention for which Laouris and Christakis take credit. It could, by way of reflection on the agentive role ascribed to it by these practitioners, be analyzed as a nonhuman actant in the Latourian (1993) sense which had its own specific role in generating and enabling contact between communities across the divide, as well as, significantly, in boosting the development of a distinct bicommunal peace movement in Cyprus with several branches, offshoots and initiatives. According to the historical narrative presented by Laouris and Christakis, in 1994 and 1995, IM was introduced to Cypriot peace activists through an American Fulbright scholar named Benjamin Broome, who was a forerunner of the 'cogniscope' methodology for dialogue design.

Broome facilitated bicommunal 'colaboratories' between Turkish Cypriots and Greek Cypriots, where the participants, through moderation, created a collective vision statement for the resolution of the Cyprus problem.[10] In the following couple of years, some of the Cypriot participants, who had been trained in IM, applied SDDP methods 'to create more than 25 bicommunal groups', among them groups of women, educators, youth, citizens and students (Laouris and Christakis 2007, 134). In 1998, when the checkpoints at the border between north and south Cyprus were still shut and access was banned, the Tech4Peace initiative was launched. 'Participants from the two sides of Cyprus were engaged in negotiation exercises using virtual communication tools, without ever meeting physically' (ibid.). This led to the creation of a peace portal, 'which hosts today more than 5,000 pages and enjoys more than 40,000 monthly hits' (ibid.).

As a result of these cumulative interactions, which were centred on the use of interactive technology for the creation of dialogue across the two Cypriot communities, Laouris and Christakis argue that a robust 'peace movement' was formed. The results even trickled upwards towards the assumption by the United Nations of plans for the resuscitation of the Cyprus problem. Some of the peace activists trained in IM and SDDP conflict resolution methodologies acted as consultants in the drafting of the Kofi Annan peace plan led by the United Nations for the resolution of the Cyprus problem (Laouris and Christakis 2007, 135). Laouris and Christakis locate agency in the technology all the way to the making of internationally binding legal jurisdictions for peace. The failure of the Annan plan from passing a referendum which was put to the two Cypriot communities in 2004 is again interpreted as a failure in the technology. As a solution,

Laouris and Christakis propose ways to ameliorate the shortcomings of the technology by, for example, rendering SDDP more speedy and efficient. With better technology, one could have better conflict resolution!

But what kind of device is SDDP? What does it do? How does it work? As an initial opening for any such collaboration, virtual interaction is established between participants in a 'colaboratory' via broadband internet technologies. In Cyprus, this has meant establishing contact between a core group of Turkish and Greek Cypriots who knew one another from bicommunal gatherings in the UN-held buffer zone prior to bans on such interactions. A 'triggering question' having to do with the Cyprus problem is sent via email to all these participants, along with a 'factor electronic response worksheet' (Laouris and Christakis 2007, 136). One such question could be, for example: 'What factors contribute to the increasing gap between the two communities in Cyprus?' (ibid., 141).

All those linked up are asked to forward their responses to this question electronically to the knowledge management team (KMT) by a set deadline. The KMT meets to enter all the submitted factors on cogniscope software. A pdf version of the 'factors table' is subsequently sent via email to all the participants on which feedback is requested. Following this virtual interchange, a face-to-face meeting between all the participants is organized and participants are encouraged to introduce more ideas on the basis of the factors table. During a coffee break, a core group develops a 'clusters table' out of the common attributes between all the ideas proposed by the participants. The participants are then asked to vote on the clusters identified on the basis of their relative importance. All these votes are registered through the use of cogniscope software as a result of which a vision map is produced (Laouris and Christakis 2007, 136).

In the application of SDDP in conflict resolution initiatives in Cyprus, the responses of participants are first split in two: the Greek Cypriot and Turkish Cypriot 'problematiques', as they are called, assuming some sort of already existing intracommunal consensus and intercommunal difference. The responses of participants in each of these two groups are pulled out of context by way of being divorced from the specific positionalities of the people who entered them into the computer program. Once they are flagged, these responses are blended and clustered into categories or groups. The KMT then presents these clusters for voting to all the participants, after which the issues are listed by order of importance. Through the process of SDDP, the issues raised by the participants undergo several steps of removal from their source of articulation. These issues take a different form once they are listed, computer processed and categorized into groups by order of relatively assigned relevance.

The resulting proposal for the solution of the Cyprus problem is a framework which could not have been developed were it not for the human-technology interface – or the computer program's specialist way of blending the materials presented to it is an intrinsic part of this technique. Nothing like this could have been produced if participants only depended on face-to-face interactions without technology. In the process of employing SDDP, several factors which would have entered a face-to-face conversation are eliminated. Amongst these could be an emotional outburst on the part of a participant in a group, a traumatic memory articulated by a war refugee, the heartbreak of participants in response to the words of one another, the built-up anger of members of one community against another, the complicated power dynamics between several participants from one or another community, the silences of certain participants who dare not speak, the tensions between them, et cetera.

But this elimination of such complications precisely because this methodology leans on mediation by technology is presented as the strength of SDDP. SDDP, from the point of view of its inventors' rationale, succeeds in ridding conflict resolution of the fragilities, ideologies, vulnerabilities, power relations, subjectivity and emotionality of participants. It could be concluded that SDDP's emphasis on the agentive and central role of technology in conflict mediation relies on the undermining of attributes particularly associated with the human. In another interpretation, we could argue that these propensities, which cannot figure in a collaboration organized with SDDP techniques, are ones which are discursively attributed to femininity.[11] The ideal dialogue scenario then, where technology takes centre stage, is achieved only by way of avoiding certain expressions, issues and properties which could not have been escaped were the interaction between participants conducted merely intersubjectively.

Now, how are we to conceptualize a device? I take a cue from the recent work of Michel Callon et al. on 'market devices' (2007). The authors emphasize the role of tools and instruments in the performance of economics in an arena where the tactility of practice has been ignored in favour of abstract numeration.[12] They write:

> We believe that the notion of 'market device' – a simple way of referring to the material and discursive assemblages that intervene in the construction of markets – can be useful . . . After all, can a market exist without market devices? From analytical techniques to pricing models, from purchase settings to merchandising tools, from trading protocols to aggregate indicators, the topic of market devices includes a wide array of objects. (Callon et al. 2007, 2)

Only, Callon et al. note a precaution. They would not like their proposed notion of 'the device' to imply any split agency between subjects and objects.

Instead, routing their argument through Deleuze and Guattari's notion of 'agencement', they argue, 'The subject is not external to the device. In other words, subjectivity is enacted in a device' (Callon et al. 2007, 2).

Were we to follow this argument, we could be left to search the manners in which subjectivities are enacted through techniques and technologies and vice versa. However, I would like to be led by my material on conflict resolution technologies in Cyprus to observe what exactly happens in the assumption and use of certain devices. I would argue that we cannot simply and categorically observe that the human-technology interface is an *agencement* in the Deleuzian sense, an enmeshment between subject and object in their jointly enacted agency, making this binarism irrelevant.

Instead, and here I speak as an ethnographer in tune with my specific empirical material, I would argue that the human-technology interface can be instrumentally enacted as a distinction between the human and the machine in order to achieve certain goals. For the strategic purpose of achieving some sort of consensus between parties to a collaboration, more agency is granted to technology in order to eliminate the messy emotionalities or vulnerabilities which an embodied subjective interaction would involve. In other words, the managed social relations which I have observed rely upon the creation of an ideal dialogue scenario which leans on the machine as the symbolic model for a more rational interchange between parties to a conflict. Therefore, I would differ from Callon et al. (2007), who have asserted that subjectivities are always 'enacted in a device', or experienced through devices. In the case I am trying to interpret, the device of SDDP, which I have rhetorically called a 'pacifist device', effectively works only by way of pushing aside or avoiding certain aspects of embodied subjectivity.

As a device, SDDP is indeed a human-technology cyborg. And yet, for its efficacy this device relies upon technology's symbolic model and technical prowess against the subjectively human. This is considered the success of this device!

Reflecting on this technological tool for conflict resolution, we can trace a paradox in the Cypriot context for the human-technology interface. On the one hand, the technology for a peace initiative takes on an explicitly humanist outlook. It does this in a special way, which must be ethnographically specified and analyzed. The objective is to employ technology for purposes other than war, to orient technology towards more humane ends. We could interpret that the objective of the creators of Tech4Peace is to humanize (or anthropomorphize) technology, to make technology more humane by directing it to nonviolent ends.

In this specific humanist outlook, violence is eliminated from the perception of the human and associated with mechanized war. Against this association of war with the machine, we can observe a naïve (I dare say) notion of a peacefully inclined human being. The project of the inventors of Tech4Peace is to design a computer program modelled on this idealized notion of a pacifist and dialogue-oriented human being. The cogniscope technique developed under this project is the perfect example for that: a technological device modelled on an idealized notion of peaceful interaction between human beings.

But paradoxically this utopian scenario cannot be created without the use of technology. In other words, the human beings participating in this project cannot enact their humanity as idealized by the inventors of the technique but for the interventions of technology. The technology, in other words, will assist the human beings in being properly human (or humane)! This technology has been modelled on a discourse about the ideal pacifist human being. The technology, then, is more human than the actual human being. In one reading, one can only attain (or achieve) one's humanity virtually. The dependence on technology for interaction eliminates the accidents, inconsistencies and surprises of the flesh and bone.

Virtually mediated interaction between human beings cancels out embodiment. Or, we could realize that those aspects of the human (such as the emotions, affectivities, traumas, power relations, subjectivity, memories, fantasies, ideologies) which are associated with embodiment are eliminated in favour of some idealized notion of a peacefully and dialogically inclined human being.[13] We could go further and understand that the human imagined (and imposed) through SDDP technologies is nongendered or modelled on a male participant devoid of any female properties or attributes.

Is this particular occasion of human-computer interaction humanist or posthuman then? By way of being ethnographically very specific, I would argue that in the case I am studying, the specific interaction between human beings via technology in a conflict resolution scenario is both humanist and posthuman at the same time. There is, as I have illustrated, an emphasis on the human. In other words, peace activism has not yet found a non- or posthumanist vocabulary for itself. Pacifism remains resolutely humanist in its philosophy and ideology. This means that special and positive particularities (like the humane) are attributed to human beings or are at least favoured amongst human potentialities. In this vein, if technology is to be employed in a project for peace, the technology must be not just geared by humans but oriented towards humane ends, as well.

This is a technology devised with a humanist rhetoric. But on the other hand, in the Tech4Peace project there is also a key emphasis on the technology. The humanism of this particular pacifist project cannot be enacted just by humans on their own. Human beings cannot be properly human without technology.

Only when linked up online via technology can human beings be extracted out of their bodies to be rendered ideally human for conflict resolution purposes. The technology, modelled on this idealized notion of humanity (the dialogic intersubjective mise-en-scène), is to teach and assist human beings in being human in this particular and desired way. Therefore, we could suggest that contemporary peace activism in Cyprus as well as being humanist in its rhetoric is posthuman too, for its humanism is necessarily dependent on posthuman (or cyborgstyle) interactions (and, we could argue, vice versa). The distinction (or opposition) between humanism and the posthuman proposed by Andrew Pickering (2001), then, becomes obsolete. The ethnographic case described here survives and employs both humanist and posthuman tactics for strategic purposes, in this case for an honourable one, like peace!

LIBERAL HUMANISM AND CYBERNETICS

Tracing the genealogy of SDDP brings us straight to the origins of the cyborg. It is via the work of Alexander Christakis (and his collaboration with the systems thinker Hasan Ozbekhan at the Club of Rome) that SDDP techniques were introduced to Cyprus. Christakis is explicit about the origins of SDDP, locating it in systems theory and cybernetics. Following the route of this knowledge practice back through its path can assist us in understanding how humanism and the posthuman may be intertwined (rather than being opposed to one another, or mutually exclusive, as philosophies).

The science of cybernetics, according to Peter Galison, was born out of a device originating in military science. In the 1940s, the MIT mathematician and physicist Norbert Wiener's research was focused on systems of preempting strikes by enemy airplanes, in this case German ones. He developed a computational technique which would anticipate an attack by an alien war plane (Galison 1994, 228). This technique was presented as a device called the 'antiaircraft (AA) predictor', which was 'designed to characterize an enemy pilot's zigzagging flight, anticipate its future position, and launch an antiaircraft shell to down his plane' (ibid., 229). But according to Galison, Wiener's ambitions did not stop there. Out of this antiballistic device, he imagined an entire scientific domain which transcended the conditions of possibility of World War II:

Wiener came to see the predictor as a prototype not only of the mind of an inaccessible Axis proponent but of the Allied antiaircraft gunner as well, and then even more widely to include the vast array of human proprioceptive and electro-physiological feedback systems. The model then expanded to become a new science known after the war as 'cybernetics,' a science that would embrace intentionality, learning, and much else within the human mind. Finally, the AA predictor, along with its associated engineering notions of feedback systems and black boxes, became, for Wiener, the model for a cybernetic understanding of the universe itself. (Galison 1994, 229)

Cybernetics would develop into a study of feedback loops in information mechanisms, whether these loops were routed between machines, human beings or both. It employed methodologies emerging from communication technology as well as nonlinear processes (Galison 1994, 232). And cyberneticists specialized in generating computational systems to create equilibrium in mechanisms that experienced some kind of turbulence or dissonance.

But equally interesting is the manner in which the AA predictor, first devised by Wiener, came to inspire the imagination for the cyborg. Galison argues, 'As the AA predictor came to fruition, Wiener came to see it as the articulated prototype for a new understanding of the human-machine relation, one that made soldier, calculator, and firepower into a single integrated system' (1994, 235). The scientific-technical content of this device is what inspired this imagination about the trans- or posthuman. Wiener carried his research into mathematical and calculational methods in servomechanisms ('feedback devices such as thermostats or self-guided torpedoes') into his imagination of the AA predictor (ibid.). This preemptive antimissile calculator would be able to predict the intentionalities and direction of an airplane-pilot unit.

The AA predictor emerged as a reimagination of the relation between the human being and the machine. Wiener articulated 'the psychological and philosophical implications of the predictor' (Galison 1994, 245). He argued that out of this could be developed a general theory of behaviour, which would be 'equally applicable to living organisms and machines' (ibid.). Galison argues, 'Beyond any particular features of humans and machines lay Wiener's deep-seated commitment to a behaviourist vision of both' (ibid., 246). In Wiener's imagination an enemy warplane was man and machine at one and the same time, cancelling the notion of a human-machine distinction. Likewise did he consider his AA predictor a device which glossed over any difference between human and mechanical intentionality (ibid., 251).

From this device was born the notion of the cyborg. Cybernetics, the scientific field on which the notion of the cyborg is based, grew to become radically interdisciplinary, studying the way in which communication takes place in both animate and inanimate beings through the exchange of orders and commands (Galison 1994, 255). The development of this field motivated the scientific imagination in ways which would transcend the bounds of philosophical humanism by making it possible to consider intentionality as shared between human and machine or as comparable between humans and nonhuman entities.

Andrew Pickering is one philosopher of science who has used his research into cybernetics to devise a posthuman philosophy. This philosophy is firmly based on the notion of the cyborg, which Pickering, too, traces back to cybernetics. 'The word "cyborg"', Pickering writes, is 'an abbreviation for "cybernetic organism" denoting a part-human, part-machine actor in which the two parts are constitutively coupled to one another' (1995, 3). He argues that a whole range of cyborg objects and sciences owe their origin to World War II (ibid., 5). Whilst historically contextualising the emergence of the cyborg, Pickering develops from it a posthumanist philosophy (or theory). He writes, 'We need a posthumanist social theory: one that recognizes from the start that the contours of material and human agency reciprocally constitute one another' (2001, 164). In a passage reminiscent of Latour and actor-network theory, Pickering writes:

> Posthumanism directs our attention to encounters between human and nonhuman agency, and we might therefore be encouraged to write a history of agency (or a sociology of agency, or a philosophy – these are no longer very different endeavours), which would center on great, enduring, and conspicuously visible sites of encounter of human and nonhuman agency, such as the factory (standing for the whole field of organized production) and the battlefield (standing for organized destruction) (and even the home in its historic transition from production to consumption). (2001, 165)

In promoting posthumanism as a theoretical trajectory, Pickering is inspired by cybernetics. He writes that he is amazed by 'the considerable congruence that exists between the cybernetic world-view and the posthuman' (Pickering 2001, 171).

Similarly studying the historical origins of the cyborg by way of researching cybernetics, Katherine Hayles provides a more nuanced analysis. In the work and mindset of Norbert Wiener, Hayles studies not simply a transcendence of humanism but, rather, a conflictual interrelation between liberal humanism and the posthuman outlook provided through the cyborg. Hayles observes that humanism and the posthuman paradoxically coin-

habit the practices and worldview of Norbert Wiener and of cybernetics as
a scientific discipline. She writes:

> The revolutionary implications of the [cybernetic] paradigm notwithstanding,
> Wiener did not intend to dismantle the liberal humanist subject. He was less
> interested in seeing humans as machines than he was in fashioning human
> and machine alike in the image of an autonomous, self-directed individual.
> In aligning cybernetics with liberal humanism, he was following a strain of
> thought that, since the Enlightenment, had argued that human beings could
> be trusted with freedom because they and the social structures they devised
> operated as self-regulating mechanisms. For Wiener, cybernetics was a means
> to extend liberal humanism, not subvert it. The point was less to show that man
> was a machine than to demonstrate that a machine could function like a man.
> (1999, 7)

In this subtle reading of Wiener's complicated standing vis-à-vis the
notion of the human, in no way does Hayles intend to resurrect the subject of liberal humanism (Hayles 1999, 5) – nor do I, in trying to decipher
the complex positionality of Cypriot peace practitioners in relation to the
notion of the human. Hayles argues that one cannot observe a radical break
with liberal humanism with the inspiration about the human-machine interface provided by cybernetics. Instead, she posits that 'the human and posthuman coexist in shifting configurations that vary with historically specific
contexts' (ibid., 6). In this paper, I am attempting to study and decipher the
specific configuration of the human and posthuman in a particular historical conjuncture amongst Cypriot peace practitioners. Such configurations
cannot be universalized. Nor are they transhistorical. In the case of SDDP
as used in Cyprus, the genealogical roots which lead us back to cybernetics
are relevant, as they assist us in locating the paradoxical coexistence of a
humanist and a transhuman outlook within the guise of a device.

Pertinent for the purposes of our inquiry into the genealogical origins
of SDDP, in Wiener's work Hayles observes what she calls a 'contradiction':

> The tension between Wiener's humanistic values and the cybernetic viewpoint
> is everywhere apparent in his writing. On the one hand, he used cybernetics to
> create more effective killing machines (as Peter Galison has noted), applying
> cybernetics to self-correcting radar tuning, automated antiaircraft fire, torpe-
> does, and guided missiles. Yet he also struggled to envision the cybernetic
> machine in the image of the humanistic self. Placed alongside his human
> brother (sisters rarely enter this picture), the cybernetic machine was to be
> designed so that it did not threaten the autonomous, self-regulating subject of
> liberal humanism. On the contrary, it was to extend that self into the realm of
> the machine. (Hayles 1999, 86)

It is here that Hayles's careful analysis of the humanistic underpinning of the posthuman project can assist us in understanding the similar but particular cohabitation of the humanistic and the cyborg in the context of Cypriot peace activism.

CONCLUSIONS

'Knowledge that goes into the making of something travels with the product itself', writes Marilyn Strathern in *Commons and Borderlands*. 'This is how we commonly think of technology: know-how embedded in the artefact. When it is a product manufactured for the market, the price one pays includes the price of knowledge, whatever went into the research and development' (2004, 18). In this paper, I have begun to trace the knowledge route, in Strathern's sense, of one such 'product': a technological tool devised for the amelioration of conflict and the management of social relations between different parties to a dispute. Going back to the beginnings of cybernetics, I have explored the theoretical and practical history of a technological product which today appears in the guise of a technique for conflict resolution. If we follow Strathern, this genealogy matters for a product which travels interdisciplinary, institutional and temporal and spatial distances.

'So let's go back a stage', writes Strathern, 'to the actual site of the creation of the product, to the point at which everyone is working together, and the outcome is still in the future' (2004, 20). In this ethnographic and historical tracing, Alexander Christakis's SDDP appeared as 'the future' of Norbert Weiner's AA predictor. If, as Strathern notes, the knowledge contained in a tool travels along with it wherever it goes, then it makes sense to explore the paradoxes which reigned at the time of the germination of this tool. Subsequently, I have found a parallel between the paradoxical position of Wiener vis-à-vis the cyborg and that of contemporary cyberneticists like Christakis: a cohabitation of liberal humanism and the posthuman or a double commitment to a humanist philosophy and a transcendence of the human subject through the assumption of technology.

If the cyborg has been represented idealistically by certain feminist thinkers (like Donna Harraway 1991), as a hybrid form which unilaterally transcends the uniform visions of humanism, such positive or negative features cannot be attributed to a device if one follows its ethnographic and historical features, what we could call its specificities, contingencies, peculiarities or particularities. A cyborg is not the same in its cyborgness wherever it goes. In the features it has assumed in the conflict resolution industry, here under the guise of SDDP in Cyprus, the cyborg retains some of the original paradoxes which went into its making: that tension between humanism and the posthuman.

But to go beyond asking questions about the ethnographic specificities of the human-technology interface, in this paper I have begun to research, in conflict resolution, what we could call, following Strathern, 'one kind of culture on the make' (2000, 1). In audit cultures, Strathern noted the emergence of new regimes of accountability across institutions and geographies, something which she identified as a 'distinct cultural artefact' (ibid., 2). It is precisely in this guise, as a cultural artefact, that conflict resolution has entered places like Cyprus which have been identified as sites of and for conflict. Locally, Cypriots (both Greek and Turkish) know and recognize conflict resolution precisely as a new culture which arrived in Cyprus with its baggage of associated practices, forms of training, jargon and bureaucracy, as well as tools of trade. What this 'culture' does, as I have observed, is bring a new idea (and a type) of relationality into a foreign space: an idealized one, which is projected into the future of a conflict-ridden scenario.

Relationality now is no longer to be naturally (or simply) practiced but to be appropriately learned and acquired, if possible through training provided all across the board in conflict scenarios by conflict resolution practitioners and experts. A tool like SDDP stands in for the ideal form in which relationality in a future-projected 'peace' is to be practiced. This relationality is to be acquired as a technique. It can be learned as a tool of the trade, as certificate-carrying conflict resolution trainees will attest. SDDP, like other conflict resolution techniques, structures and manages what the practitioners call 'dialogue' and 'communication'. But this notion of a dialogue, we could observe, is no neutral notion. Were we to trace the genealogy of this concept, we would find its roots in liberal European political philosophy, for instance in the work of the likes of Jurgen Habermas and his notion of 'communicative rationality' (1984).

For Habermas, an ideal communication scenario is only to be achieved through reasoned deliberation between different parties to an argument. Many have taken the ideas of Habermas as emblems for the notion of *democracy* (see, e.g. Benhabib 1996). Habermas was explicit in associating his idealized 'communicative rationality' with a Western 'modernity' and most specifically with the bourgeois public sphere of nineteenth-century Europe (1989). Many have critiqued Habermas and Habermasians for their Eurocentrism and for their unanalyzed privileging of a male and bourgeois participant in dialogue (see, e.g. Butler and Scott 1992). But such philosophical ideas about dialogue and communication have taken practical routes via policy in the guise of development practice and democratization in Eastern Europe and the Third World.[14] It is through such a route that SDDP has popped up in Cyprus, under the name and emblem of 'conflict resolution'. SDDP stands in for what its practitioners would like to present as an ideal model for relationality and communication between different parties.

Such a model, at present, can only be achieved, according to the crafters of this tool, by intervention and teaching, through the introduction of a specific technique. As I have tried to argue, this technique is no neutral technique. It arrives with the baggage of cultural associations: Western notions of idealized communication, something which is quite ideologized today in the guise of democracy. So what appears rather honourable and benign, a tool for peace or dialogue, when traced back through its routes, looks rather more complicated.

Of course, when turned into a practice, a tool of knowledge, including a body of theory or a philosophy, may acquire certain properties which were not necessarily intended by its originators. That, too, is a paradox contained in the specificities and peculiarities of a knowledge practice, if we follow it through the routes it takes. What I have observed in my recent work on conflict resolution practices in Cyprus (as comparatively linked regionally and interdisciplinarily elsewhere) is that knowledge is rendered valid and valuable in such enterprises only insofar as it is considered useful. Of course, there is an instrumentalist, a functionalist, a goal- or use-oriented approach to knowledge in this practice-geared industry.

And like the notion of *dialogue,* whose partiality I began to trace, the notion of *usefulness* is no neutral notion either. This is something which has again been studied by Strathern in her Isaiah Berlin Lecture titled 'Useful Knowledge' (2006). In response to an economically geared knowledge industry (including the academy) which would value knowledge mainly insofar as it has a use ('relevance' or 'importance' are other terms for this), Strathern has made an argument for the value of 'useless knowledge' (ibid., 73–75). In the application of cybernetics and systems theory in the field of conflict resolution, we find quite the opposite: a body of knowledge geared specifically towards use.

Knowing that use is no neutral matter, as I asserted at the start of this paper, the crafters of the technology for peace initiative are reflexive about the uses towards which they orientate the technologies which they create. And they are especially explicit about the use towards which they would not want to gear this technology: war. It is one specific, military, kind of use of technology against which the Tech4Peace initiative bases its morals and rationale. As in my coining of the term 'pacifist devices' to name this technology, SDDP, like other conflict resolution techniques, is meant for nonviolent ends as projected and desired by its community of crafters, experts, trainees and practitioners. But my genealogy of the past routes of this technology brought me to other venues, other purposes: in this case, Norbert Weiner's AA predictor, a specifically military device which has been found to be at the origin not only of cybernetics as a scientific practice but also of the cyborg as a philosophical imaginary.

So the AA predictor and SDDP are relatives: if the ancestor was a device put to military ends, its offspring has been employed in the service of peace. We must ask: does it matter what the origin of a technology in its kinship and its past was? Does it matter that a so-called pacifist device today had origins in military R & D? My answer would be yes as well as no. And this is no moralizing answer, only an observation, an analysis. We could first respond and say, yes, perhaps. How could it not matter if the roots of the cybernetic imagination can be traced back to weapons research? Both Galison and Pickering ask and engage with this question.

But Ian Hacking would advise us against such a track of thinking. He writes, 'From time immemorial weapons have been a product of human knowledge. The relationship became reciprocal. A great deal of the new knowledge being created at this moment is a product of weaponry' (1999, 166). Hacking takes the origins of many forms of knowledge in weapons research for granted. He argues that this is a given. He would not like a moralizing critique of military science to shadow his analysis into scientific knowledge practices. He therefore writes, 'Despite the notable counterexamples, and despite the exciting peaceful spinoffs, much of our new knowledge has been made in the pursuit of new weapons. This conclusion raises vast issues both for morality and for policy. I deliberately avoid them' (ibid., 169). Likewise, I would argue that the fact that cybernetics has military origins cannot be an analysis of this scientific practice or its variegated uses, only a moral judgement. Instead I have taken a route which would ethnographically study the specific transmogrifications of a device through the distances it travels, the peculiar, if paradoxical, forms it assumes as it goes far. The pacifist device is honest in its pacifism. But that is not my analysis. What is interesting is the way in which a particular knowledge practice employs the notions of the human and the machine for particular ends.

In SDDP, the technology has been presented as a model for what an idealized communicative scenario should look like between parties to a dispute. The technology stands in for an idealized mise-en-scène of peaceful human relationality. But the notion of *technology* (or *the machine*) here employed is one which specifically employs the terms and language of humanism. This technology is to be geared to humane ends, its practitioners will say – a specifically humanistic machine, a humanistically oriented technology: that is what its practitioners will argue is to be found in the pacifist device, a humanist project which employs the cyborg, a paradox in the making.

NOTES

1. Since the original publication of this essay in 2008/9, the website of Tech4Peace has been deactivated. The citations that thus became inaccessible have since been sourced elsewhere. The citation was previously found at File:///Volumes/KINGSTON/technology%20&%20peace/tech4peace.webarchive, and a digital remnant can now be sourced on Wikipedia: https://en.wikipedia.org/wiki/Technology_for_peace
2. Ibid.
3. This citation has similarly had to be resourced; it was originally found at file:///Volumes/KINGSTON/technology%20&%20peace/Technology%201...%20TIP:%20Towards%20a%20Technology%20of%20Peace%20:.webarchive and was accessed for republication on http://tipfaq.blogspot.com/2005_06_01_archive.html.
4. The original citation was taken from file:///Volumes/KINGSTON/technology%20&%20peace/Technology%20IN...ogy,%20violence%20and%20peace,%20by%20Brian%20Martin.webarchive. It has since been found on http://www.bmartin.cc/pubs/99encyclopedia.html.
5. Ibid.
6. For an example of a study on the discourses of humanitarianism, see Maalki (1994).
7. See http://www.nets-uni.net/yiannis-laouris.
8. Ibid.
9. Alexander Christakis, interview by Yael Navaro via Skype, 8 April, 2009.
10. See Broome's own work on conflict resolution (2002). Also see Laouris (2004).
11. For a study of gender and peace activism in Cyprus, see Cockburn (2004).
12. Also see Andrew Barry (2001, 7–9).
13. Katherine Hayles (1999, 5–7) has argued that cybernetics, like liberal humanism, works against the grain of embodiment.
14. For a study of the introduction of ideas of 'democracy' and associated practices in Eastern Europe, see Coles (2007).

REFERENCES

Barry, Andrew. 2001. *Political Machines: Governing a Technological Society.* London and New York: Athlone Press.
Benhabib, Seyla, ed. 1996. *Democracy and Difference: Contesting the Boundaries of the Political.* Princeton: Princeton University Press.
Broome, Benjamin. 2002. 'Participatory Planning and Design in a Protracted Conflict Situation: Applications with Citizen Peace-Building Groups in Cyprus'. *Systems Research and Behavioral Science* 19: 313–21.

Butler, Judith, and Joan Wallach Scott, eds. 1992. *Feminists Theorize the Political.* New
    York: Routledge.

Callon, Michel, Yuval Millo, and Fabian Muniesa, eds. 2007. *Market Devices.*
    Oxford: Blackwell.

Cockburn, Cynthia. 2004. *The Line: Women, Partition, and the Gender Order in Cyprus.*
    London: Zed.

Coles, Kimberley. 2007. *Democratic Designs: International Intervention and Electoral
    Practices in PostWar Bosnia-Herzegovina.* Ann Arbor: University of Michigan Press.

Douzinas, Costas. 2007. 'The Many Faces of Humanitarianism'. *Parrhesia* 2: 1–28.

Galison, Peter. 1994. 'The Ontology of the Enemy: Norbert Wiener and the
    Cybernetic Vision'. *Critical Inquiry* 21: 228–66.

Habermas, Jurgen. 1984. *The Theory of Communicative Action: Volume One. Reason and
    the Rationalization of Society.* Boston: Beacon Press.

——. 1989. *The Structural Transformation of the Public Sphere: An Inquiry into a Category of
    Bourgeois Society.* Cambridge: Polity.

Hacking, Ian. 1999. *The Social Construction of What?* Cambridge, MA and London:
    Harvard University Press.

Harraway, Donna. 1991. *Simians, Cyborgs, and Women: The Reinvention of Nature.* New
    York: Routledge.

Hayles, Katherine N. 1999. *How We Became Posthuman: Virtual Bodies in Cybernetics,
    Literature, and Informatics.* Chicago and London: University of Chicago Press.

Ivy, Marilyn. 1995. *Discourses of the Vanishing: Modernity, Phantasm, Japan.* Chicago and
    London: University of Chicago Press.

Laouris, Yiannis. 2004. 'Information Technology in the Service of Peacebuilding:
    The Case of Cyprus'. *World Futures* 6: 67–79.

Laouris, Yiannis, and Alexander Christakis. 2007. 'Harnessing Collective Wisdom
    at a Fraction of the Time Using Structured Dialogic Design Process in a Virtual
    Communication Context'. *International Journal of Applied Systemic Studies* 1(2):
    131–53.

Latour, Bruno. 1993. *We Have Never Been Modern.* London: Pearson.

Malkki, Liisa. 1994. 'Citizens of Humanity: Internationalism and the Imagined
    Community of Nations'. *Diaspora: A Journal of Transnational Studies* 3(1): 41–68.

Navaro-Yashin, Yael. 2002. *Faces of the State: Secularism and Public Life in Turkey.*
    Princeton: Princeton University Press.

Pickering, Andrew. 1995. 'Cyborg History and the World War II Regime'. *Perspectives
    on Science* 3(1): 1–48.

——. 2001. 'Practice and Posthumanism: Social Theory and a History of Agency'.
    In *The Practice Turn in Contemporary Theory,* edited by Theodore R. Schatzki,
    Karin Knorr-Cetina and Eike von Savigny, 163–74. London and New
    York: Routledge.

Strathern, Marilyn. 1988. *The Gender of the Gift. Problems with Women and Problems with
    Society in Melanesia.* Berkeley: University of California Press.

——. 1992. *Reproducing the Future: Essays on Anthropology, Kinship and the New Reproductive
    Technologies.* Manchester: Manchester University Press.

——. 1994. 'Response to Escobar'. *Current Anthropology* 35(3): 225–26.

——. ed. 2000. *Audit Cultures: Anthropological Studies in Accountability, Ethics and the Academy.* London and New York: Routledge.

——. 2004. *Commons and Borderlands: Working Papers on Interdisciplinarity, Accountability and the Flow of Knowledge.* Oxford: Sean Kingston Publishing.

——. 2006. 'Useful Knowledge' (the Isaiah Berlin Lecture). *Proceedings of the British Academy* 139: 73–109.

Yael Navaro is Reader in Social Anthropology at the University of Cambridge. She is the author of *Faces of the State: Secularism and Public Life in Turkey* (Princeton University Press, 2002) and *The Make-Believe Space: Affective Geography in a Postwar Polity* (Duke University Press, 2012). For the past few years, she has been conducting research in south Turkey as principal investigator on a European Research Council Consolidator grant under the title 'Living with Remnants: Politics, Materiality and Subjectivity in the Aftermath of Past Atrocities in Turkey'.

Chapter Six

Audit Loops and Audit Implosion

Casper Bruun Jensen and Brit Ross Winthereik

Implosion is a process in which objects are destroyed by collapsing on themselves. The opposite of explosion, implosion concentrates matter and energy. An example of implosion is a submarine being crushed from the outside by the hydrostatic pressure of the surrounding water.[1]

In the imploded time-space anomalies of late twentieth-century transnational capitalism and technoscience, subjects and objects, as well as the natural and the artificial, are transported through science-fictional wormholes to emerge as something quite other.

Haraway 1997

THE NATIONAL AUDIT OFFICE

The mandate of Denmark's National Audit Office is to audit the state accounts. More specifically, it is to verify that funds are used according to parliamentary decisions. Organizationally, the office refers to the Public Accounts Committee, yet it conducts its tasks independently to ensure impartiality and objectivity. In general terms, the prevalence of audits testifies to the strength of the *audit explosion* thesis (Power 1994). However, although the National Audit Office appears to be the epitome of external control, its modes of operation also embody the organizational and epistemological frictions that we propose to characterize as *audit implosion*.

The office has undergone substantial organizational changes since 1986.[2] It has halved the number of office workers it employs and increased the number of employees with academic backgrounds, mostly in social science. The more than 250 employees still working in the office come from a wide range of backgrounds 'reflecting the many tasks that the institution is performing'.[3] These tasks include forms of auditing that go considerably beyond traditional evaluations of accounts and budgets (which of course remain central). 'Auditing in many ways'[4] is the term used to describe these activities on the office's homepage.

Carrying out these diverse tasks involves addressing questions such as what should be audited and where, as well as questions about the use of methods and the interpretation of data. The variety of critical decisions that need to be made before and during an audit provided us with an initial sense that, although the office is committed to an ideal of procedural objectivity, this ideal coexists with a far more mixed and diffuse sense of obligation to assist organizations and help them learn. Yet, this ambition can create tensions, since too much 'assistance', may be seen by sceptical outsiders as demonstrating a lack of objective impartiality.

Accordingly, the auditors with whom we have talked are in a situation at once epistemologically interesting and practically challenging. They deal reflexively with questions about validity, objectivity and methods that are reminiscent of issues that continue to haunt social science more broadly. However, since the office operates with a political mandate that relies largely on a positivist and quantitative understanding of what performance audit is and what it can and should do, they navigate difficult terrain.

AUDIT EXPLOSION

According to Michael Power's famous diagnosis, Euro-American society had become an audit society around 1994. The term audit was used with 'growing frequency' (Power 1994, 6), and audits were conducted in ever more contexts: 'In addition to financial audits', Power wrote, 'there are now environmental audits, value for money audits, management audits, forensic audits, data audits, intellectual property audits, medical audits, teaching audits, technology audits, stress audits, democracy audits and many others besides' (ibid). Indeed, Power suggested, an audit *explosion* could be witnessed in the mid-1990s. As an organizational and societal tool, audit is intimately bound up with issues relating to control, accountability and transparency. Audit is not only or even primarily about performance measurement; instead it concerns evaluating the governing qualities of systems. It is about the 'policing of policing' (ibid., 11).

Power's analysis emphasized that this metagovernance relied on quantification to an unprecedented degree. His critical observation was that the excessive interest in quantifying practice risked undermining trust, dialogue and autonomy, replacing these values with measurement, expertise and discipline. Power's analysis was picked up by scholars in various fields, including organizational theory (e.g., Munro and Mouritsen 1996) and social anthropology (e.g., Gefou-Medianou 2000; Pels 2000; Strathern 2000c). Anthropological commentators, in particular, have argued that although the audit explosion undoubtedly has engendered organizational change processes, another pertinent issue concerns the implications of auditing understood as cultural form.

Seen as cultural form, auditing becomes amenable to ethnographic scrutiny. As Marilyn Strathern suggests, such scrutiny would facilitate the delineation of 'some of the scale and pervasiveness of the way in which the twinned precepts of economic efficiency and good practice are being pursued' (Strathern 2000c, 2). Offering an entry point for redescribing audit relations, such an approach would entail a simultaneous investigation of the conventions of audit modes of operation and aspiration and a diagnostic exploration of how audit may be morphing into new social, cultural and organizational shapes. Exploring the ubiquitous practices of monitoring that unfold in the Danish National Auditing Office's department of performance auditing, the present chapter is guided by these lines of inquiry.

From early on Michael Power himself posed the question What is 'beyond audit' (1994, 32). In line with his general critical argument, he suggested, 'We seem to have lost an ability to be publicly skeptical about the fashion for audit and quality assurance; they appear as "natural" solutions to the problems we face' (ibid., 32). Yet, Power also identified managerial fashion as a crucial vector of change. Thus, 'just as other fashions have come and gone as the basis for management thinking, the audit explosion is also likely to be a passing phase. The seeds of a change may be there' (ibid., 32).

Yet perhaps the question of what these seeds are, and what they might grow into, has not been addressed sufficiently. Indeed, it might be viewed as somewhat surprising that Power's general diagnosis remains standing more than twenty years after he first suggested the possibility of further transformation of the audit paradigm. Here we suggest that one of these developments is audit implosion. If audit explosion pointed to the extraordinary proliferation of audit initiatives across very numerous Western practices, audit implosion characterizes a situation in which auditing, as a particular form of control ('policing of policing') that is based on a specific ideal of 'objective' knowledge, threatens to fragment or, indeed, collapse under its own weight.

In the context of performance audits carried out by the National Audit Office, we have observed efforts similar to those described by Power, which aim to redesign the audit process 'in the direction of a business service' (Power 2000, 2). In particular, audits are increasingly seen to fulfil a dual role of controlling audited organizations and creating opportunities for them to learn. Here we aim to capture some transformative dimensions of these efforts. We add specificity to the notion of audit implosion by characterizing some ways in which performance auditing operates through loops of control and learning.

PROCEDURES FOR MAKING KNOWLEDGE

Our initial encounters with the auditors generated a sense of surprise. We expected to meet a group of 'dusty accountants' concerned mainly with keeping the audited organizations at arm's length in order to ensure the objectivity of their reports. These expectations were not met. Instead we found ourselves talking to staff whose concern was how to carry out performance audits in a way that would inspire learning organizations to internalize robust accounting practices.

It was not difficult to get in contact with auditors. One reason might be that, as a Danish public institution, the office has a legal obligation to respond to inquiries like ours. But auditors also exhibited a general willingness to discuss their tasks. Thus, we managed to set up initial interviews with relative ease. Nevertheless, the openness extended only so far. Our requests to observe auditors' daily work, join internal meetings and participate in discussions with 'clients' were politely turned down, and joining auditors on a 'field trip' turned out to be impossible. Accordingly, our analysis is based on four open-ended interviews lasting between one and two hours, on documents we were given by the auditors and on a study of the guidelines, brochures, reports and other documentation that are publicly available on the web. Using this material, we drafted a first version of the present chapter.

However, this turned out to be the end neither of our empirical studies nor of our analytical endeavour. For after we sent our informants copies of the draft, we were summoned to a meeting with the head of office and one of our 'key informants'. During this meeting we discussed not only empirical details but also analytical content and the 'aesthetics' of our argumentation. The meeting, and several ensuing rounds of email discussions and revisions, produced additional data.

As auditors saw it, this process helped to correct our mistakes, prevent flawed generalizations and clarify points of procedure. As we saw it, these interactions exemplified and mimicked the hybrid relation between controller and counsellor that we aimed to characterize in the first place.

Specifically, the exchanges seemed to replicate the ways in which audit reports are themselves finalized in collaboration with audited organizations. This is a sort of participatory validation process in which drafts of reports are sent back and forth between auditors and audited organizations, which are encouraged to offer points of clarification and give critical feedback to be taken into account in subsequent revisions of the reports.

One outcome of this process is that most quotations from auditors' correspondence had to be removed out of concern that 'colourful' expressions could be traced back to individuals. Because some of our interviewees were no longer employed at the office, we were told that it would be hard to ask for their permission to be quoted. As we saw it, this was a somewhat protective stance that exemplifies the importance the office attaches to formal procedure rather than individual 'opinion'. As our contact persons saw it, the issue was one of research ethics.

The aforementioned dialogue has thus not only informed but literally 'track changed' this chapter. Recursively, the argument that we present has itself been subject to a version of the audit practice it describes. This is analytically relevant because it indexes how maintaining a sense of control in situations where authority of the audit office is perceived as potentially at risk is still very important. In our particular case, the challenge of authority was handled 'backwards' with reference to all the formal procedures and guidelines that are in place to ensure that the office's products can be trusted (even in the context of an open and collaborative attitude).

This process had stylistic repercussions as well. Thus, one important effect of the removal of quotations and the toning down of any potentially controversial statement is the somewhat bland presentation of what follows. We urge readers to consider this blandness as indexing a kind of textual internalization of what the ethnography allows us to argue about performance auditing: the importance of retaining a neutrally, descriptive or 'epistemologically objective' tone of voice, even in, or especially in, a context in which auditing is increasingly influenced by new forms of partnership and attendant reflexive ways of making knowledge about organizations.

To some extent, then, the formal, procedural style we have just pointed to, and which this chapter replicates to an extent, stands in contrast to what we learned from our interviews about auditing as a highly reflexive and contingent endeavour. The more general point is that 'procedural' or 'formal' auditing and the participatory and reflexive endeavours we describe as *audit loops* coexist and coevolve. As our self-exemplifying case suggests, such coevolution may create both epistemological and procedural friction. Our interactions with the office regarding both the form and the content of the present chapter highlight what we demonstrate in more detail below: that auditing works recursively through a series of loops of control and learning.

APPROACHING IMPLOSION

In the introduction to *Audit Society,* Michael Power began envisaging a shift in auditing practice that he designated 'audit implosion': 'In the context of external financial auditing . . . it may be more appropriate to speak here of an "audit implosion" whereby organizations have become more "reflexive" and where company directors have been forced to require responsibility for internal control systems and risk management' (Power 1997, xviii). The shift identified in this quotation is one in which audit ceases to be an externally imposed measure and increasingly becomes a matter of ongoing reflexive self-monitoring. In later work, Power continued to emphasize this transformation, arguing, 'The growth of interest in internal control systems in the last ten years has accompanied an audit *implosion* meaning that auditing and inspection are now part of what organizations do to themselves' (2007, 162).

Power related this change in particular to financial auditing practices. In a working paper titled 'The Audit Implosion' (Power 2000), he proposed to view the implosion of audit as involving 'an ongoing contraction in the significance of the external audit as a force in corporate governance, as compared to internal mechanisms and agencies of control' (ibid., 2).

Power, however, is not the only social science scholar to make analytical use of the metaphor of implosion. As we saw in the introductory quote, for the feminist historian of science Donna Haraway (1997), implosion, too, is a tool with which to understand contemporary sociotechnical and organizational forms of 'collapse'. Whereas Power's focus on implosion is rather concrete, having to do precisely with the internalization of auditing, Haraway makes it clear that implosion has far broader implications for cultural diagnosis. In particular, she considers implosion to have emergent and unforeseeable effects on broader patterns of science, technology and enterprise. This is why she uses the metaphor of 'wormholes' from which objects and practices are likely to 'emerge as something quite other' (ibid., 4). Her analytical interest in unforeseen effects ties in with the anthropological attention to audit cultures, which, in Strathern's formulation, take particular interest in how 'audit and ethics are structuring social expectations in such a way as to create new principles of social organization' (2000b, 281).

Of course, Power's identification of audit implosion understood as a 'reflexive' internalization of audit practices exemplifies one 'new principle of social organization'. However, inspired by Haraway's argument that implosion heightens attentiveness to 'heterogenous and continual construction through historically located practice' (1997, 68), we suggest that the wormholes of auditing have a number of additional ramifications.

Audit implosion, in the Harawayian sense, has to do with things other than the internalization of auditing in organizations that have begun to institutionalize 'second-order self-descriptions' (Strathern 2000d, 313). As we continue to discuss, this transformation centres on the emergence of increasingly complex auditing loops, a notion we use to index mutually shaping interactions between auditors and auditees that cross organizational barriers in multiple directions, both 'downstream' and 'upstream'.

In this situation, implosion characterizes a situation where both the *epistemology* and the *form* of audit are put under pressure, as external and internal modes of monitoring begin to work in tandem through such loops. In a broadly diagnostic, but also unavoidably speculative, vein, we end this chapter by considering audit loops as a response to a contemporary situation of knowledge production that Marilyn Strathern has referred to as 'postplural'.

AUDITING PERFORMANCE

The National Audit Office is divided into five departments.[5] One deals with administration, support and international collaboration; two are in charge of financial accounting and two conduct performance audits. The fact that the organization has a department dedicated to performance audits as a type of audit that is distinct from financial accounting is itself worth noting. The differences show in the organizational set-up but also in the different strategies defined for the departments. The strategy for the financial accounting departments aims to ensure the quality of the material based on which Parliament approves the state budget, to verify that the accounts of companies follow good accounting practice and to set standards for good public accounting practice. These are rather unsurprising objectives.

However, the strategy for the department for performance audits looks quite different. Its goals are to prepare high-quality reports on the effectiveness of the administration to the Public Accounts Committee and to Parliament, to strengthen the development of effective administration by conducting cross-cutting and internationally based inquiries and to inquire into areas where administration runs the risk of not functioning effectively for citizens and businesses. The latter two points, in particular, are indicative of the explosive expansion of audit into new areas.

Generally, the department for performance audits conducts two forms of audit. One is carried out at the request of the Public Accounts Committee and is mandatory. However, the department also initiates its own investigations. One of the recurrent tasks of the department is to carry out annual 'risk analyses' of the ministries. On top of this, the department also conducts 'strategic analyses'. Inquiries begin with a prestudy, a three-month period of intense preliminary investigations to determine whether it is worth the effort to plan and conduct a full audit.

A number of other reasons suggest why prestudies make excellent organizational sense. The first relates to the fact that ministerial areas might be said to be rather broad and diffuse. If the aim of auditing were exclusively to inspect the annual budgets, as is the case for financial audits, perhaps this problem would be less pressing. But how is an entity like the Ministry of Foreign Affairs to be monitored and evaluated with a view to identifying areas with a risk of inefficient administration? Many simultaneous uncertainties are at play here, relating both to the question of where to look (the central office or the embassy in Vietnam; the internal monitoring unit or the communication department?) and what to look for (questions about meeting structure, collaborative process, strategic visions, incentives or something quite different?).

The broad diversity in themes that can hold auditing interest is manifested in some of the final reports that came out in 2008. Titles such as 'Development Aid to Bhutan and Bangladesh', 'Management of Government IT Projects', 'The Effects of the Efforts Made to Integrate Newly Arrived Immigrants', 'The Restoration of the Railway Infrastructure' and 'The Danish Defence's EH-101 Helicopters', although by no means comprehensive, are indicative of the breadth and width of audit topics.[6] If the examples cited above suggest that the National Audit Office is operating in an environment characterized by audit explosion, its consequences are manifest in the perplexity auditors confront. If everything (or at least many things) can be audited, and if the auditing outcome (administrative effectiveness or risk) is hard to measure and quantify, what then should be looked for and how should it be done? Paying closer attention to how auditors in the department deal with these challenges will allow us to begin specifying some implications of audit implosion.

UNCERTAINTIES OF AUDITING

As noted, performance audits can be instigated at the behest of either the Public Accounts Committee or the auditor general (based on input and suggestions from the employees in the department for performance auditing). However, the department also spends considerable energy defining its own strategic focus areas, which guide later choices of audit themes and specific topics. At the time of prestudies many decisions have thus already been made. One does not conduct a prestudy of the Ministry of the Environment *at large* but in relation to a circumscribed set of strategic areas.

Among other things, strategic importance relates to what is referred to as 'being at risk'. There is a double specification at work: topics must be important for citizens or politicians, *and* they must involve processes and decisions that are perceived as risky (that is, there must be concern that the organization may not follow legal rules and requirements). This broad requirement, however, is not selective enough to *determine* focus areas. Each spring, a strategic process is initiated in the department in order to designate themes of special importance for the subsequent auditing period. Among other things, this process entails inviting various high-profile researchers to offer input to the strategy process. These researchers do not directly propose audits. Instead, they make suggestions and provide inspiration for the choices the office makes. Examples of strategic focus areas might include effective administration or (during the recent financial crisis) economizing.

The specification of these themes narrows the potential scope of audit considerably. Still, because of their generality, the relation of these themes to the specific set of concrete questions addressed by any particular performance audit remains underspecified. This prodded us to look further into the grounds for choosing specific audit topics and questions rather than others. However, we were told that, aside from the circumscribing strategic decisions just mentioned, there are no general grounds for such choices. In explaining how specific inquiries are chosen, an interviewee had recourse to astrological metaphor, explaining that auditors look for 'signs in the sun and moon'. We were quite surprised by this choice of imagery. Asking where one might look for such signs, we were told that interesting suggestions might be found in the media but also internally in the organization. For example, good ideas might be developed in conversation with colleagues from the regular accounting departments who also spend significant amounts of time interacting with audited organizations.

Thus, the 'signs in the sun and moon' came from a variety of sources, which also convey a sense of the uncertain political climate in which the national audit operates. Deciphering these signs entails paying attention to a heterogeneous set of potential factors, something that is necessary even when one is working within the strategic framework. Somewhat naively, we had expected auditing decisions to be guided by wholly formal, objective criteria. However, it became obvious that such criteria were not in themselves specific enough to determine particular, practical choices about what to audit and how.

According to the formal description of the process, performance audits follow a rigidly standardized schedule. First comes the prestudy, which is initiated by written contact to the selected organization or agency. An initial meeting follows, which clarifies the reason for the audit, the topics of investigation, and expectations as to what materials must be made available and which specifies contact persons. The next document that is produced outlines the overall and particular auditing goals, accounting criteria and accounting actions; it also explains the procedure by which the audit will be conducted. The design is spelled out in detail in the accounting tree, which specifies accounting criteria (at two levels), accounting actions and what documentation is required. The accounting tree and the audit plan are then presented to management in a collaborative process that generates further input and comments on them.

The second phase is data collection and analysis. Then, an accounting note is produced to summarize the documentation and to offer preliminary evaluations and comments. This note is submitted to the organization that is to be audited, which has a chance to comment on and qualify the evaluation. Based on this response another document is produced and circulated. It is eventually followed by the final report, which is submitted to the Public Accounting Committee at a specified time and date. Subsequently it is made public. As should be clear, this is a very regimented set-up. At the time of our interviews, the prestudy was presumed to take one to three months, and the data collection and analysis phase *plus* the series of notes and reports that follow between six and nine months.[7]

This formal mode of operation perfectly exemplifies what the historian of science and administration Theodore M. Porter refers to as an epistemology of 'mechanical objectivity' (Porter 1995, 4), that is, objectivity obtained by following the rules. Rule following, as Porter explains, provides a 'check on subjectivity: they should make it impossible for personal biases or preferences to affect the outcome of an investigation' (ibid., 4). However, Porter qualifies this ideal in two important ways. First, 'following rules may or may not be a good strategy for seeking truth' (ibid., 4). Second, 'mechanical objectivity can never be purely mechanical' (ibid., 5). Indeed, it is because mechanical rule following cannot remain mechanical, and because it may not always be a 'good strategy,' that auditors are required to [comment: or "need to be"] constantly vigilant, supplementing their formal rule books with 'signs in the sun and moon' such as input from colleagues, the news media, and researchers. As we shall see, performance audit in action also depends in important ways on qualitative, interpretive processes.

GOING TO THE FIELD IN SEARCH OF RELEVANT CONTEXT

According to auditors, two general types of information are available: written information and information gathered by auditors during audit visits. To explore how these forms of information work together to produce audit knowledge, we consider a recent audit of the Ministry of Foreign Affairs that focused on development aid activities in an African country.

To operationalize and narrow the scope of this audit, a number of subgoals were defined in the accounting tree. They included answering whether the development goals were being met, whether guidelines for monitoring and evaluation followed best practice and whether knowledge about aid effects and results were being used systematically. Each of these questions had several subquestions, and for each subquestion relevant documentation was identified. It included items such as: 'performance assessment framework', 'status reports', 'reviews', 'analyses from other donors', 'programme completion reports', 'review aide memoires', 'guidelines for monitoring', 'evaluation policies', 'administrative manual', 'correspondence and contracts concerning evaluation' and much more.

As this lengthy list suggests, it is a basic condition of the performance audit that one works with very large amounts of documentation. In contrast to the experiences social scientists may occasionally have: that information relevant to their research can be hard to come by, since auditors can in principle get access to almost anything, they must deal with the question of how to delimit their material. This problem of what to look for is exacerbated by the fact that many of the audited areas, including the development aid sector, are huge 'paper mills', and thus the body of potentially relevant documentation is always enormous. The tension embedded in the auditing process is that this material must be analyzed in such a way as to answer the predefined questions and it must fit into an accounting note no longer than thirty pages.

The question of *condensation* is thus omnipresent. Furthermore, *interpretation* is always necessary since auditors have to estimate the quality of arguments used in these reports and the interests behind them. To explain why one has to be on guard for ulterior motives cropping up in reports, an auditor conjured the example of a fictive report, which argued that 'everything went wrong but it was not the fault of the ministry, it was all because of an external partner'. Because it is always possible for reports to invoke uncontrollable, external factors to account for problems, auditors can never take them at face value.

This type of situation illustrates that audited organizations are themselves not neatly bounded but rather operate through interactions with many other partners. Because there are usually multiple stakeholders and because any project's outcome is caused by interactions between them, there is rarely a single causal explanation for any particular problem. This is one reason performance audits raise issues of interpretation. To contain the problems of interpretive flexibility posed by such 'multicausal' complexity, performance audits invariably require making empirical and analytical 'cuts' that allow auditors to delimit the scope and relevance of information. This includes making choices about what are the right data, and it involves assessments of its reliability.

If something 'looks peculiar' in the available material and data itself do not explain why that is so, then auditors are faced with an interpretive gap. Sometimes this gap can be bridged by triangulation with other documents, but the oddness may remain. It is, among other things, to strengthen interpretive capacity that auditors go beyond written documentation. To do so they go on audit visits, where, to be sure, they acquire even more documents, but during which they also interview a variety of people, participate in meetings and attempt to put together a coherent perspective on the mass of data. Audit visits thus help to ensure the quality of documentary evidence as well as of auditors' own interpretations and analyses. To some extent this is a matter of developing a 'gut feeling' for what is going on in the field.

To illustrate: during an audit visit to an African country, auditors realized that it would be possible to participate in the annual general budget support review meeting; accordingly, they scheduled their visit around this meeting. This was seen to be very useful, since it enabled auditors to get a sense of the 'backstage' of project collaboration – that which isn't visible at the surface level of documentation. For example, a report might 'openly' acknowledge that certain issues are difficult to discuss at meetings, but it will rarely spell out in much detail precisely how or why these issues cannot be discussed openly.

Such statements therefore obscure as much as they make visible. By attending meetings, however, auditors can get a sense of context. What kinds of things are discussed, and how difficult is it actually to discuss them? Participation in concrete activities thus provides auditors with interpretive anchors that they can use to evaluate the statements found in reports. For similar reasons, auditors also usually conduct interviews with a variety of stakeholders, for example, evaluators, consultants, embassy employees and local collaborators. Although the extensive formal documentation analyzed by auditors provides the basis for the final report, it matters a great deal to be able to look people 'deeply in the eyes'.

Field experiences enable auditors to develop shared understandings of how to interpret the statements and actions of different stakeholders. At best they facilitate a 'quantum leap' in understanding the situation. Further, even while auditors are focusing on the particular questions specified in the accounting tree, they may pick up on other things, collateral issues, which suggest that something strange may be going on in the organization. In turn, this may lead to supplementary queries, interviews or conversations that allow the auditors to put their overarching auditing questions in a broader context. Thus, the 'quantum leap' takes the form of a changing context for interpreting what the issues and risks at hand are.

These descriptions of auditors' 'field work' demonstrate the extent to which qualitative, participatory methods have been invited into the auditing process. It was obvious to us that these methods to an extent resembled those used in our own research practice. But how did they form an evidence base for the performance audits? Queried about the resemblance between qualitative audit knowledge and the interpretive analytics of social science, the auditors readily acknowledged the similarity. The process they described was based on judgement and estimation.

Their pragmatic stance was that they had to 'start out with what is there' and, getting that, decide whether it was good enough. The auditors also explained how, upon returning from the field, they faced the challenge of fitting their amorphous data, observations, intuitions and interpretations into a report that must be bulletproof before it is made available for public scrutiny. One important way of ensuring validity is to be in close dialogue with the organization being audited and to use that organization's critical comments to pinpoint weaknesses in the auditors' own arguments.

Yet in spite of the similarities, the methods, analytics and outcomes of social scientific methods and auditing methods also differ in crucial ways. We have already noted that, at least in principle, auditors have 'access to everything'. Consequently, the auditors' problem is not usually how to get their hands on data but rather how to 'define when enough is enough'. Additionally, whereas anthropologists and sociologists have recourse to theories and concepts that help them shape their questions and concerns, auditors relate their choices to 'how the real-world works'.

And because the facts of the case are presupposed, in the end, to speak for themselves, this analysis must be made entirely on the basis of guidelines and procedures, without relying on any guidance from concepts or theories. Only in this way can auditors ensure the 'mechanical objectivity' of the audit process and, thus, the legitimacy of auditing.

ENSURING LEGITIMACY

The mandate of the National Audit Office expresses a dual aim: to ensure that good accounting practices are followed and to strengthen the development of effective administration. Accomplishing these two aims requires that auditing be trustworthy. Institutionally, the National Audit Office is kept institutionally separate from legislators, since it belongs to the judiciary. Despite this formal separation, there have been stories in the media in which auditors' judgements have been challenged and auditors have been presented as biased. In one sense, participatory methods such as fieldwork help to ensure the legitimacy of the final product because the auditors *have been there and seen what is going on*. At the same time, though, basing judgements and recommendations on the experiences of audit visits poses a threat to auditors' legitimacy.

During an interview, one auditor emphasized that audit visits are invested with considerable importance. Aside from the interpretive anchoring, on which we remarked above, he explained, audit visits can have a legitimizing function. This auditor said that certain reports had been written in which the audit visit had made no difference whatsoever because all relevant documentation was at home. The sole reason for travelling, in such cases, was to guard against the accusation by the organization under scrutiny that the report had been mere 'desk work'. In order to demonstrate accountability to the organization that is being investigated, apparently, auditors must show their faces. The broader issue here is that, to be seen as trustworthy, auditors must, to an extent, be perceived as on the same team as those they audit, even if one central purpose of getting closer to organizational realities is to inspect whether something fishy is going on within them.

But establishing trustworthiness by 'stepping into practice' (Jensen 2007) only works in relation to audited organizations. In order to ensure the legitimacy of audits to politicians and to the public, reference to having experienced real-world complexity is insufficient; it might even turn out to be detrimental. For to these audiences, the important legitimating issue is rather the reverse; to be able to demonstrate that the audit remains 'outside practice'. Retaining distance, in these interpretive contexts, provides a guarantee of the objectivity of the evaluation.

For such reasons, auditors repeatedly emphasized that care must be taken in preparing the final notes and reports so that there is absolutely 'no room for error'. Even though huge sets of information are gathered in preparation for writing the final report, most of the information never makes it onto paper. If one is only 90 per cent certain about the material it cannot be used. Spontaneously comparing audit to research, one interviewee said the main difference was that auditors have 'no leeway for making mistakes'. And because they have no leeway, they are required to always make conservative judgements.

In conjunction with the demand that each question and subquestion defined by the accounting tree be rigorously addressed, and with the fact that reports are relatively brief, the conservative requirement to avoid error at all cost is central to the usage of information. The most immediate consequence is that formal quantitative documentation always forms the backbone of the evaluations offered in reports. Whereas it might be possible to construct a strong 'accounting proof' based on qualitative material, it would be 'bloody difficult', since it would require a large-scale audit comprising surveys and interviews, with, potentially, hundreds of people. And even in such a case the issue of self-censorship among interviewees would need to be methodically addressed. This is a kind of audit, we were told, that one would only consider under very special circumstances.

This raises the question of how efforts to plan and go on audit visits, participate in meetings, do interviews, interpret qualitative data and so on then *matter* in relation to external accountability. It also raises the question of whether knowledge made through such processes is an interesting but ultimately inconsequential 'subjective supplement' to the quantitative information or whether it has a more substantial role to play. To understand how qualitative knowledge matters, one needs to pay attention to how the *interpretive* endeavour is rendered implicit and condensed in the final reports. In these reports, we were told, interpretations are conveyed: 'in the choice of words and the space given to particular topics'.[8]

Thus, the data collected on the basis of qualitative data has to be both absent and present. It has to be absent for the report to function as a legitimately objective evaluation in the eyes of Parliament and the general public. But it also has to be obliquely present for the qualitative knowledge gained from participatory methods to have a chance to guide the attention of those who have a chance to induce organizational change.

LEARNING FROM AUDITING

The ambition of strengthening organizational control measures was central to the New Public Management initiatives of the previous decades (Bloomfield 1995; Du Gay and Salaman 1992). Gradually, however, that ambition has been complemented with an interest in enabling organizations and agencies under scrutiny to *learn* from audits. The self-disciplining and internalization of audit goals that Power describes as a result of the audit explosion can thus also be identified in the way the auditors speak of what they hope to be long-term outcomes of their work.

When a final report is publicized the ministry or agency under scrutiny is obliged to address each point of criticism. If problems with information technology have been indicated, for example, the ministry might respond that information technology consultants have been contacted or that new contracts are being negotiated. Few problems can be resolved within a few months, the auditors recognize, but organizations have to demonstrate that they take the criticism seriously by responding with a plan for how to address the issues. After a few years a follow-up investigation will be conducted. Still, determining whether reasonable progress has been made often remains a matter of judgement.

But how can auditors know whether an organization has institutionalized ways of thinking and best practices appropriate to the 'accountable organization'. How can they detect whether learning has occurred? At stake is an experience that the office shares with ministries involved in ongoing evaluations, such as the Ministry of Foreign Affairs, which must account for the effects of development aid. An auditor illustrated the dilemma by emphasizing that while measuring output may be easy, measuring outcome is often very difficult. For example, he said, the number of wells dug in the course of a development project (an output) can be counted, but how the wells have contributed to improved health in a region (an outcome) is much harder to show.

Nevertheless, performance audits must deal with output and outcome simultaneously. That is, they have to both evaluate outputs and induce organizations to internalize a specific 'conduct of conduct' (e.g. Dean 1999; Larner and Walters 2004; Rose 1999) that leads to better outcomes over time. As noted, this tension is managed in practice by requesting the audited ministry or agency to write a note that outlines its plans for responding to the identified issues. Even so, this formal feedback tells little about whether and how much the ministry has actually learned from the audit. It is not easy to decipher, from such responses, whether an audit has led to a process of internal reflection, leading to an organizational change process, or whether it is intended to 'satisfice' (Simon 1957) – that is, to merely *signal* that demands and suggestions are taken seriously, while in reality the organization is doing little to address the underlying issues.

In addition, auditors are aware that their inquiries are imbued with a sense of threat that may run counter to their aim of helping organizations learn. Ministries, for example, may be fearful of an audit because they worry about negative publicity. Thus, auditors engage in consciousness raising in the form of attempts to convey to ministries that they ought not be afraid. One auditor suggested that organizations are generally too worried. Worry usually is unnecessary and even counterproductive, he felt, since 'we are not gangsters out to kill people'.

Occasionally, however, there might be good reason to be frightened by an audit, for sometimes organizational members really have not been doing a good job. Still, this auditor also pointed to how the feeling of threat works against organizational learning. His ideal was to have an audit culture in which organizations would *welcome* a 'brutally honest report' and use it to move ahead. The difficulty in establishing such a culture, in his view, was bound up with the fact that audited organizations are enmeshed in a political system in which reputation and legitimacy tends to be seen as more important than organizational improvement.

The same auditor went on to argue that, from the perspective of the National Audit Office, goal achievement in a narrow sense is not always the most interesting issue. If one wants to know how some organization is doing, he argued, there are many more relevant questions to ask than whether it has achieved a particular goal. At least as important, in his view, is assisting organizations preventively by helping them identify issues that may become urgent later. Such assistance ties auditors and organizations together in a continuous feedback loop, simultaneously shaping the knowledge and concerns of both parties.

Assisting organizations, however, is difficult also because organizational actors may have internally different strategies that may themselves be in friction, or may even be mutually exclusive. For example, successful short-term financial management may impede efficient long-term sustainability of project goals. An auditor used the example of measuring the efficiency of the educational system. Schools usually do not wish to do everything as cheaply as possible, because their main aim is to teach children to be skilled at reading, mathematics and so on. Of course the ability of the educational system to provide those competencies to children can be measured. But that takes time and costs money, and meanwhile the schools must continue to operate. The sensible thing to do in this situation is to realize that objective measurement is a long-term goal, and the system will have to run for a while before there is anything useful to measure anyway.

Interestingly, this type of argumentation goes against the explosion of audit. It suggests that it is senseless to channel a constant stream of resources into audits requiring efforts by people who ought to spend their time differently. Thus, learning from auditing is, in part, also learning about how to circumscribe and make reasonable use of auditing itself. Audit, at least as seen by some auditors, should apparently not explode *too much*.

AUDIT LOOPS

The situations we have described in previous sections are indicative of a gradual change perceived by auditors themselves. This is a change towards what we might call proactive auditing, that is, auditing that will not only control organizations but also enable their enhancement. One consequence of the requirement that audit should ideally 'add value' is that the National Audit Office becomes increasingly implicated with what it evaluates. Here we are entering the audit wormhole. Through processes of proactive auditing, the office and audited organizations become tied together in feedback loops of information sharing, of recommendations, suggestions and responses. Ambiguity in the relation between the external and the internal may follow.

In a down-to-earth estimation, we were told, 'It is a balancing act'. Holding the balance is crucial, however, since politicians or the media may jump at an opportunity to argue that the office is less than objective.[9] 'As soon as you touch these things', one interviewee noted, 'you are in the political sphere'. Since auditors, simply by doing their job, run the risk of being drawn into the political sphere, it is crucial for them to avoid being seen as taking sides. The auditors we spoke with thus insisted on objectivity, neutrality and formal transparency even as they aimed to provide learning opportunities.

This is also why it is crucial to the audit office that performance audit be seen by the public, including by members of Parliament, as a straightforward evaluative process. Data flow from the organizations and agencies that are being investigated by the audit office. Suggestions and criticisms flow from the office and back. Responses and clarifications are written. Recommendations are received and put to use. In contrast to this linear, procedural self-description, we suggest that the framing of auditing, the production of audit knowledge, the recommendations and demands such knowledge gives rise to and the subsequent responses are recursively implicated. Through loops of ongoing interactions, these phases become 'folded together', and the question of what constitutes the inside and the outside of auditing is rendered ambiguous.

The situation can be explicated with reference to the previously mentioned notion of mechanical, rule-following objectivity. As Porter notes, this form of objectivity is 'especially prominent where inside and outside are not sharply differentiated' (1995, 229). This lack of sharp differentiation precisely characterizes the loop-like interactions through which performance audit knowledge is made and validated. This is the kind of situation, Porter argues, that 'encourages the greatest extremes of standardization and objectivity, a preoccupation with explicit, public forms of knowledge' (ibid., 229).

Such a preoccupation is also a prevalent feature of performance auditing. It is manifest, not least, in the way the indisputability of final reports are seen as depending exclusively on 'objective' data, even though the quality of such reports is acknowledged to rely to a significant extent on qualitative knowledge and observations 'in the field'. Because of these coevolving but also competing and, to an extent, contradictory tendencies, auditors encounter challenges when engaging in loops to support organizational learning.

As noted, these are loops through which information continuously flows back and forth between auditors and auditees, transforming the knowledge of both parties in the process. Such audit loops, we argue, are *constitutive* of performance audit because they are absolutely necessary for the production of relevant audit knowledge. At the same time, these loops have contradictory implications. They are both generative and troublesome. They form the basis for both control and learning while also threatening both aspirations. And they involve interaction and mutuality in a way that cannot be accounted for according to the epistemology of mechanical objectivity that both informs public and internal understandings of auditing and sustains the organizational legitimacy of the National Audit Office.

Although we have illustrated audit loops with material from performance audit at the National Audit Office, they are by no means confined to this setting. Indeed, audit loops swirl in and out of innumerable organizations (see Jensen and Winthereik 2013). For instance, internal auditing offices of large organizations collaborate with the National Audit Office as well as with other external consulting bodies concerning questions such as how to implement and improve their own infrastructures of accountability. Thus, audit loops connect the National Audit Office with its clients, just as they connect the internal auditing bodies of these clients with those they monitor. But loops of information and knowledge making also extend in the opposite direction, as we discovered when we queried whether the office is itself audited.

It was in the context of addressing this question that we were told how auditors have 'no leeway for making mistakes', since any mistake risks tarnishing the reputation of the organization as a whole. One could certainly argue that having in principle no leeway for making mistakes does not protect an organization against actually making them. Yet it is to minimize this possibility that the office enters into further audit loops in order to ensure *its* accountability.

Thus, since 2000 the office has requested external reviewers to evaluate the quality of all its reports. In 2006, the office collaborated with the supreme audit institutions of several other countries, in a process in which colleagues from these institutions conducted a peer review of the office and offered criticisms and recommendations. The detailed report and the organizational plans for addressing the identified shortcomings followed much the same format as the one usually used by the office for its performance audits. These documents are also publically available online.[10]

Accordingly, we might say that even if no one forces the office to 'take its own medicine', it willingly does so anyway. It engages in exercises that help it perform as the kind of learning organization that it hopes to induce other organizations to become.

AUDITING AND POSTPLURALITY

> 'Forster foresaw connectedness in the form of an intermediary (a participant-
> observer) making repeated excursions between separate realms, domains or
> entities, and drawing comparisons by coming to terms with the *regularities of
> life* practiced by each as he interprets them'. This is the merographic amalgam
> of pluralism. A postplural world has 'lost' this mathematics insofar as it can
> no longer enumerate such different domains
> (Strathern 1992, 215n41, quoting Rapport; emphasis in original).

In preceding sections, we used activities relating to the conduct of performance auditing to illustrative purpose. In particular, we have aimed to elucidate some conventions and cultural forms of auditing and explored some ways in which they may be changing. Inspired by Marilyn Strathern and Donna Haraway, we see such 'seeds of change' as relating to a process of cultural transformation in which auditing is imploding on top of, or alongside, its explosions.

In the quotation above, Strathern refers to a 'merographic amalgam of pluralism'. Pluralism is here understood epistemologically, as indicating that many perspectives might always be taken in any given case. The notion of merography (a word whose root, *mero,* means 'fraction') points to the – often implicit – pluralist idea that each perspective taken on a case adds to a general body of knowledge. In epistemological pluralism, knowledge is thus gained in a dual process. On the one hand, one gets to 'know more' by examining more cases. On the other hand, one may 'know more' by adopting new perspectives on existing cases.

In a formulation that resonates with the view from performance auditing that we have tried to establish, Strathern notes that 'if the assumption is that much of what is invisible is what is simply *not yet made* visible, then there will always be more to learn about the organization, further realities to uncover' (2000d, 312). The proliferation of performance audit and its ambition to delve into evermore aspects of the regularities of organizational life seem, indeed, to point in this direction.

Strathern's central observation in the introductory quote, however, is that 'a postplural world has "lost" this mathematics'. The postplural designates a world in which epistemological pluralism is fragmenting and, in a sense, collapsing under its own weight. On the one hand, this is a consequence of the *empirical observation* that one will never be able to exhaust the cases that can be investigated. On the other hand, it is a consequence of the *analytical realization* that the proliferation of perspectives, embedded in methods, approaches and questions do not *add up*, because they continues to *open up* to an indefinite horizon of inquiry that can have no endpoint. We might say that the postplural indicates a situation in which the idea that 'the more you know, the more you know that you don't know' – and, indeed, cannot know – is taken to its logical end. This line of thinking provides us with some tentative signposts of where auditing might be headed. The proliferation of audit loops provides us with a sense of direction.

As we have argued, auditors operate simultaneously on a terrain of control and a terrain of learning. This duality is operationalized in an infrastructure of auditing that takes the form of a series of interactive loops, weaving in and out of organizations, through which audit knowledge is made. Here we make the further suggestion that this looping infrastructure makes the question of perspective central to this navigational feat. This is contrary to how auditors see it; for, as we have seen, their epistemological authority and their organizational legitimacy are premised precisely on having *no perspective, just procedure.*

Nevertheless, perspectives are embedded in audit processes in multiple ways. There are views (for example, from research) that lead to strategies, there are signs that lead to specification of particular audit themes and areas and there are choices that lead to even more specific audit questions. Finally, there are concrete decisions about what will count as the relevant data sets (of formal documentation) and about how to interpret the relation of this documentation to the mass of informal, qualitative knowledge gathered from audit visits. Additionally we have noted how the need to access deeper and, in some ways, more relevant knowledge about organizations has required the more or less ad hoc adoption of participatory social science methods, shorn, however, of explicit conceptual guidance. Rather than mechanically determined by procedure, auditing is thus also contingent and perspectival in multiple ways.

In particular, perspectives proliferate because the making of audit knowledge engages auditors in complex loops of interaction with those they evaluate and those who, in turn, evaluate them. One consequence of this situation is that audit organizations become subject to tensions comparable to those present in the organizations they monitor. These loops, we have suggested, are nudging auditing into a kind of Harawayian 'wormhole' from which it may emerge as a 'quite other' form of knowledge-making practice.

Specifically, audit loops are indicative of a situation in which there are multiple auditing aims, which do not necessarily add up to a larger whole and in which partners proliferate alongside the questions that may be asked of organizations. This is the sense in which, even as auditing may have exploded, as Power argued, it is also imploding. This argument doesn't involve any predictions about the disappearance of audit as either a form of control or knowledge making. As Haraway reminds us, although 'implosion of dimensions implies loss of clear and distinct identities', it doesn't entail any 'loss of mass and energy' (1997, 69). And, obviously, auditing as a set of everyday activities shows no sign of vanishing.

What does seem to be imploding is auditing as a cultural form of evaluation based on formal detachment and rigid procedural rule following and as an epistemology relying on 'mechanical objectivity'. The ideal of detachment is imploding in a situation where auditing by necessity implicates organizations and auditors in a looping infrastructure.[11] And the ideal of mechanical objectivity is challenged in a situation where a multiplicity of perspectival choices and decisions underpin audit knowledge – in which knowledge is constructed through (redescribing) relations rather than through an 'objective gaze'.

Even so, formal detachment and mechanical objectivity remain central to auditors' own conceptualization of their work and roles. Thus, an epistemology very akin to Porter's mechanical objectivity is upheld as the official ideal, though it does not characterize the practice of auditing very precisely. In this sense formal and participatory auditing processes coexist, coevolve and alternate at different moments in time. We see these simultaneously complementary and frictional aspects of auditing as generated by practical efforts to contain and manage the paradoxes of postplural knowledge making in a world still assumed to be plural.

CONCLUSION

In this chapter we have picked up on the notion of the audit explosion by considering aspects of a particular audit culture. Specifically, we have tentatively proposed that certain 'seeds of change' are present in practices and conventions of the performance audit. We have thus moved from audit explosion via audit loops towards audit implosion. What is the purchase of this diagnosis? In conclusion we take up this question by contrasting our analysis with some anthropological studies critical of audit (e.g. Pels 2000; Shore and Wright 1997).

Conventional anthropological approaches tend to view contemporary audit as an especially predominant and efficacious structure of control. In the characterization of Peter Pels, for example, 'The stated goal of making the inner workings of organizations more visible goes together with a positioning of the audit process itself as an increasingly private and invisible expert activity'. Audit, Pels continues, 'actively constructs the environments in which it operates, making them more "auditable" at the same time that it renders itself thereby invulnerable to its own failure' (Pels 2000, 142).

In this description, audit becomes performative in a double sense. It *constructs the environment in which it operates* in order to make it more auditable. Since the organizational environment is in each case specified by monitoring procedures, the audit system *closes on itself,* and thus it is blinded to its own failures and limitations. But then the failures of audit simply call for more auditing. The very activity (and ideal) of audit is *rendered invisible* in this process, and this is why audit is *made invulnerable* to failure. In this context, sociologist of science Leigh Star's question (addressed to designers of computer systems) – *quis formabit formatores,* 'Who will formalize the formalizers'? (Star 1995, 101) – becomes pertinent as 'Who will audit the auditors'? (cf. Ciborra and Failla 2000, 124).

But is audit made invulnerable to failure? Contrary to other studies of organizational accountability, such as Steven Brown and Gordon Lightfoot's (2002), which found that transparency requirements do not enter into the managers' 'control room' where the really important decisions are made, the National Audit Office strives to make its own practices available to further scrutiny through additional audit loops that will make the office as auditable and transparent as it requires other organizations to be. Contrary to the idea that the office provides the final link in a chain of accountability, the infrastructure extends both 'forwards' and 'backwards' from the office. Since the infrastructure consists of loops, rather than a chain, it is not possible to reach a final instance of auditing at all.

If detachment is seen as a prerequisite for mechanical objectivity, this might be perceived as indicative of a situation in which auditing, rather than an encompassing form of objectivized control, becomes contextualized and relativized. But in a postplural condition, the stark oppositions between objectivity and relativity, between detachment and attachment, lose much of their purchase. Clearly, there can be no auditing closure in a situation in which audit knowledge depends on a looping infrastructure. Each new level of auditing simply creates more monitorable contexts and issues.

Our analysis has brought audit loops into view as a conceptual tool for describing certain gradual transformations of state bureaucracy, tendencies illustrated, in the context of audit, with the gradual supplementation of quantitative control with qualitative participation. This draws out one important implication of Strathern's observation: 'The concept of audit ... has broken loose from its moorings in finance and accounting; its own expanded presence gives it the power of a descriptor seemingly applicable to all kinds of reckonings, evaluations and measurements' (Strathern 2000c, 2).

In this situation, the 'power of the description' of audit becomes challengeable simultaneously from within and without. This is one consequence of implosion, one, we venture is likely to engender further transformations of the conventions, demands and expectations of auditing.

NOTES

This essay is a modified version of 'Wormholes: Loops of Auditing and Learning' in *Monitoring Movements in Development Aid: Recursive Partnerships and Infrastructures* (Jensen and Winthereik 2013), reprinted with permission from the MIT Press.

1. Available at http://en.wikipedia.org/wiki/Implosion_(mechanical_process).
2. Some of the details of formal organization and process mentioned here are from Justesen (2008).
3. See http://www.rigsrevisionen.dk/about.
4. Translated from the Danish front page of the homepage: http://www.rigsrevisionen.dk/.
5. The following is based on interviews with staff members from Department D in 2009 and 2010 and on an interview with staff members from Department A in March 2009.
6. Available at http://www.rigsrevisionen.dk/composite-1303.htm?pagechildren tab=1108.
7. Since then the process has been made more flexible, and the timeline is now decided for each individual case.
8. To be able to refer to meetings, the reports will occasionally use the formulation 'the ministry has revealed . . .' Such formulations allow for the identification of 'subjective' perspectives.
9. For example a recent case concerns a report that criticized the then liberal government for paying very expensive fees to private hospitals. Politicians interpreted the report as a critique of the ideological choices that led to determining the level of the fees. It was thus considered 'political'.

10. Available at http://www.rigsrevisionen.dk/media(267,1030)/Peer_review.pdf.
11. Meanwhile, the rigidity of procedure is never more stringent than when applied retrospectively – as suggested by the audit loop through which the veracity of this chapter was established.

REFERENCES

Bloomfield, Brian P. 1995. 'Power, Machines and Social Relations: Delegating to Information Technology in the National Health Service'. *Organization* 2(3–4): 489–518.

Brown, Steven D., and Gordon Lightfoot. 2002. 'Presence, Absence and Accountability: E-mail and the Mediation of Organisational Memory'. In *Virtual Society? Technology, Cyberbole, Reality,* edited by Steve Woolgar, 209–22. Oxford: Oxford University Press.

Ciborra, Claudio, and Angelo Failla. 2000. 'Infrastructure as a Process: The Case of CRM in IBM'. In *From Control to Drift: The Dynamics of Corporate Information Infrastructures,* edited by Claudio Ciborra, 105–25. Oxford: Oxford University Press.

Dean, Mitchell. 1999. *Governmentality: Power and Rule in Modern Society.* London: Sage.

Du Gay, Paul, and Graham Salaman. 1992. 'The Cult(ure) of the Customer'. *Journal of Management Studies* 29(5): 615–33.

Gefou-Medianou, Dimitra. 2000. 'Disciples, Discipline and Reflection: Anthropological Encounters and Trajectories'. In *Audit Cultures: Anthropological Studies in Accountability, Ethics and the Academy,* edited by Marilyn Strathern, 256–79. London and New York: Routledge.

Haraway, Donna. 1997. *Modest_Witness@Second_Millennium.FemaleMan_Meets_ OncoMouse – Feminism and technoscience.* New York: Routledge.

Jensen, Casper Bruun. 2007. 'Sorting Attachments: Usefulness of STS in Health Care Policy and Practice'. *Science as Culture* 16(3): 237–51.

Jensen, Casper Bruun, and Brit Ross Winthereik. 2012. 'Recursive Partnerships in Global Development Aid'. In *Differentiating Development: Beyond an Anthropology of Critique,* edited by Soumhya Venkatesan and Thomas Yarrow. Oxford and New York: Berghahn.

———. 2013. *Monitoring Movements in Development Aid: Recursive Partnerships and Infrastructures.* Cambridge, MA and London: MIT Press.

Justesen, Lise. 2008. 'Kunsten at skrive revisionsrapporter. En beretning om for-valtningsrevisionens beretninger'. PhD Thesis. Copenhagen Business School, Frederiksberg.

Larner, Wendy, and William Walters, eds. 2004. *Global Governmentality: Governing International Spaces.* New York and London: Routledge.

Munro, Rolland, and Jan Mouritsen, eds. 1996. *Accountability: Power, Ethos and the Technologies of Managing.* London: International Thomson Business Press.

Pels, Peter. 2000. 'The Trickster's Dilemma: Ethics and the Technologies of the Anthropological Self'. In *Audit Cultures: Anthropological Studies in Accountability, Ethics and the Academy,* edited by Marilyn Strathern, 135–73. London and New York: Routledge.

Porter, Theodore M. 1995. *Trust in Numbers: The Pursuit of Objectivity in Science and Public Life.* Princeton: Princeton University Press.

Power, Michael. 1994. *The Audit Explosion.* London: Demos. http://www.demos.co.uk/files/theauditexplosion.pdf.

———. 1997. *The Audit Society: Rituals of Verification.* Oxford: Oxford University Press.

———. 2000. *The Audit Implosion: Regulating Risk from the Inside.* London: ICAEW.

———. 2007. *Organizing Uncertainty: Designing a World of Risk Management.* Oxford: Oxford University Press.

Rose, Nikolas. 1999. *Powers of Freedom: Reframing Political Thought.* Cambridge: Cambridge University Press.

Shore, Cris, and Susan Wright, eds. 1997. *Anthropology of Policy: Critical Perspectives on Governance and Power.* London: Routledge.

Simon, Herbert A. 1957. *Models of Man: Social and Rational.* New York: Wiley.

Star, Susan Leigh. 1995. 'The Politics of Formal Representation: Wizards, Gurus and Organizational Complexity'. In *Ecologies of Knowledge: Work and Politics in Science and Technology,* edited by Susan Leigh Star, 88–119. Albany: State University of New York Press.

Marilyn Strathern. 1992. *After Nature: English Kinship in the Late Twentieth Century.* Cambridge: Cambridge University Press.

———. 2000a. 'Afterword: Accountability . . . and Ethnography'. In *Audit Cultures: Anthropological Studies in Accountability, Ethics and the Academy,* edited by Marilyn Strathern, 279–305. London and New York: Routledge.

———. ed. 2000b. *Audit Cultures: Anthropological Studies in Accountability, Ethics and the Academy.* London and New York: Routledge.

———. 2000c. 'Introduction: New Accountabilities'. In *Audit Cultures: Anthropological Studies in Accountability, Ethics and the Academy,* edited by Marilyn Strathern, 1–19. London and New York: Routledge.

———. 2000d. 'The Tyranny of Transparency'. *British Educational Research Journal* 26(3): 309–21.

Casper Bruun Jensen is Senior Researcher at Osaka University and Honorary Lecturer at Leicester University. He is the author of *Ontologies for Developing Things* (Sense, 2010) and *Monitoring Movements in Development Aid* with Brit Ross Winthereik (MIT, 2013) and the editor of *Deleuzian Intersections: Science, Technology, Anthropology* with Kjetil Rödje (Berghahn, 2009) and *Infrastructures and Social Complexity* with Penelope Harvey and Atsuro Morita (Routledge, 2016). His present work focuses on delta ontologies and environmental infrastructures in South-East Asia.

Brit Ross Winthereik is Associate Professor at the IT University of Copenhagen in the Technologies in Practice faculty group and the author of *Monitoring Movements in Development Aid* with Casper Bruun Jensen (MIT, 2013). She is lead investigator of *Marine Renewable Energy as Alien: Social Studies of an Emerging Industry* with Laura Watts and head of the ETHOS Lab – an experimental space for ethnography of/through the digital. She has published on ethnographic methods, accountability, information infrastructures, ontology and critique. Presently, she focuses on innovation cultures within renewable energy.

Chapter Seven

Slow Motions [Extended Remix]

Comments on a Few Texts by Marilyn Strathern

Eduardo Viveiros de Castro and Marcio Goldman
Selections and Translation by Ashley Lebner

With the work of Marilyn Strathern the world has become more complicated, or should we say describing the world has become more complicated?
We (EVC and MG) are still learning how to know Strathern's anthropology.
She has an extensive oeuvre in progress that we have not read exhaustively;
and, more importantly, she has created a new language for the discipline,
whose conventions must be absorbed little by little to adequately appreciate all the power of invention contained therein. It is a difficult language,
not only because its writing is stylistically demanding (including for native
speakers) but also because it is the instrument and the site of a complex analytical movement, the controlled interference of two diverging ethnographic
fluxes – the Melanesian and the Euro-American – which are allowed to
interact with and counteraffect two discourses that are themselves distinct:
the theoretical discourse of anthropology and the political discourse of feminism (and/or vice versa).

These fluxes and these discourses have different thematic attractors,
which we will highlight, due to the texts that we have chosen for commentary, the theme of knowledge, the theme of property and the theme of
kinship. The recursive application of each one of these three themes on the
other two produces a marvellously intricate descriptive weave. The master
concept that will serve as a frame for all of these gestures of connection
and separation, this polyrhythmic alternation (or perspectival exchange)
between the ethnographic flux and the analytical cut, is the conceptual

multiplicity known as the 'relation'. Strathernian anthropology is the most sophisticated theory of the relation that our discipline has produced since Lévi-Strauss's structuralism.

In the interview she gave to *Mana* (this volume[1]), Strathern said that she belongs 'to the other camp, that which chose to deliberately exaggerate the differences, simply because this obliges us to think'. Her work emphatically involves a 'stop to think', a slow deliberate gesture of standing back, a kind of infinite slowness of analytical thought that at the same time projects itself forwards at a vertiginous speed: a heady heedfulness, as it were. Slowness and velocity are metathemes in Strathern's work, as are almost all of the issues she explores.

The idea of slowness – the approach to the question of movement from the point at which its difference in relation to immobility is minimal – seems strategic to us. We need to stop to think, in order to not stop thinking. Strathern has written caustic and luminous pages on the pseudochanges that have overtaken the university world: the ideology of productivity and high intellectual turnover of managerial efficiency, of value for money, in short, the audit culture, the 'enterprising-up' of academia, the hell we have come to know only too well.

In the case of anthropological research in particular, time is a fundamental variable, or perhaps I should say constant. Slowness is absolutely indispensable to the process of knowledge. One needs to let things mature. There is a certain time in the field (most of the time, actually) in which it seems that nothing is done, nothing happens, within as well as without; there is a moment in writing in which it seems we are bogged down for good, nothing moves, thought is blocked. But that is just where things start; in the deadening times ideas are born. Where nothing happens – that is where everything begins to change.

Thus, let us recursively apply the rule: we are not in a rush, we are not trying to understand the texts of Marilyn Strathern hastily, because they are slow, hesitant texts, folded within themselves, texts that heave and halt and keep coming back to where they started. This slowness is, naturally, partial and partially deceptive. Suddenly, the analysis jumps – more to the side, you understand, in a direction that the reader was not expecting. The texts move as if in a flash to unforeseen positions. The extreme slowness is shot through with sudden scintillations, surprising effects of action at a distance.

NO PARTS, NO WHOLES

('Parts and Wholes', 1992)

'Parts and Wholes' is a key article in the work of Marilyn Strathern. It was presented in a colloquium organized by Daniel de Coppet, an eminent Melanesianist who was the major advocate of the work of Louis Dumont in France. We owe de Coppet the maintenance of a vigilant orthodoxy relative to the nature of *fundamentum inconcussum* to be attributed to the ideas of totality and hierarchy within anthropological theory. The success of this vigilance in the French academic context was, shall we say, moderate and, moreover, somewhat redundant, since the local theoretical sensitivity has always been strongly preadapted to a Dumontian outlook.

Strathern, from her position of 'standing back' from the concept of society as totality, also intends to bypass the concept of individual, while Dumontians start from a critique of the concept of the individual in order to reconstruct an even more totalizing notion of society. These are, in fact, two totally antipodal movements, even though Strathern seeks a possible passage between them (or merely appears to seek; nothing is simple here). What is in play for her is the issue of how to move from a pluralist vision of society to a notion of sociality as multiplicity. Note that she does not use the word multiplicity at any point in 'Parts and Wholes'.

We take it she is aiming at something extremely close to the Deleuzian concept of multiplicity, though. She does use the word 'plurality' on various occasions to say that the plural world is the characteristic world of modernity and that the problem, for various reasons, is how to leave it, or how to theoretically articulate the anthropological fact that we have already left it –from plurality to multiplicity, therefore, because the postplural world is everything but a unitary and unified world. It is not a question to leave (or have left) a plural world to rejoin the One, wherever and whenever it exists/ed.

In that essay, Strathern retraces some crucial moments of the history of British social anthropology of the past fifty years. She operates on the reciprocal effects of the ethnoanthropological Euro-American discourse and the discourses (or descriptions) upon which the former elaborates – for example, the Melanesian – pointing to the vacuousness of whatever pretension to produce an analytical discourse that is not immanently ethnographic. There is a radicalization of the idea that ethnography is theory and vice versa.

Strathern says that it is necessary to rethink a certain 'arithmetic' of the micro and macro, of the part and the whole, of the one and the plural. The introduction to the notion of the 'fractal', in this context, is a means to reengage and rethink the problem of the metonymy, the trope that will mark all of poststructuralist anthropology. One should not imagine the whole as greater than the sum of its parts, nor is it equal to the sum of its parts: the whole is a version of the part and the part is a version of the whole. The passage from the whole to the part and from the part to the whole is ontologically smooth: the whole is as relative as its parts. With this, the distinction is destabilized. Instead of wholes and parts we have something like multiplicity and singularity.

If there is neither part nor whole, neither is there inside and outside, as these are movements of the exteriorization and interiorization of relations rather than zones or domains. And, finally, there is neither individual nor society. There is an interconvertibility (version, conversion) without residue between the concept of person and the concept of relation. Persons are relations in the 'corpuscular' phase or mode, and relations are persons in the 'wavelike' mode. And by the bye, there is nothing algebraic in imagining persons composed of relations; on the contrary, it means effectively defining a geometry – rather than an algebra – but a non-Euclidean geometry (Archimedean, perhaps) in which the force fields are prior to the forms that emerge in them, and the objects are not defined by their perimeters of circumscription but, rather, by their centres of expansion or radiation.

There is thus a kind of principle of complementarity of the Melanesian person. It appears either 'in person' (the figure of the person against the continuous ground of relations) or 'in relation' (the movement of the relation against the particulate ground of persons). It is here that Strathern introduces the notion of an exchange of perspectives or of perspectivism, a terribly important notion for Tânia Stolze Lima and me, which we used to describe what is happening in Amazonian cosmopraxis. However, we employed the notion of perspective in a homonymic rather than synonymic sense to Strathern's usage (but the tightening of the connection is currently in progress).

The exchange of perspectives that Strathern finds in Melanesia brings a whole new perspective (literally) to the concept of exchange: the determination of the concept of exchange by the concept of perspective. As Wagner (1967) showed for the case of the Daribi, matrimonial exchange produces its own terms, the givers and the receivers. There do not exist groups who exchange, there are exchanges that group and all grouping is a perspective. Strathern contrasts the exchange of perspectives of Melanesia with modernist perspectivism, or cultural relativism: the idea that there are infinitely numerous points of view on the world. In that view, perspectives cannot be exchanged (the impossibility that characterizes cultural relativism). A perspective can only perceive another perspective by transforming it into a part of itself – by hierarchizing the perspectives, as it were. This is exactly what anthropology does in the classical, presymmetrical mode, when it conceives the culture of the native as a part, a subset of the nature-culture twosome that characterizes the West.

Strathern proposes to redescribe the West from the concept of perspective that she develops in the Melanesian context. She makes an interesting observation with respect to the postmodern idea of fragmentation, of the collapse of totalities. The notion of the fragment supposes a whole that is lost forever and, therefore, a whole still more powerful than the old Durkheimian totality – a bit like the dead father in *Totem and Taboo,* who is much more terrible than the living father. The whole appears there, then, as the agent of repression within anthropology's discourse. That is why the multiplicity that Strathern attributes to the Melanesian mode of social existence is not a fragmentation; it is not a proliferation of pieces, but a state that we could call an incessant ontological alternation or an intrinsic movement of scaling. Why is she so interested in scale? Because the individual is society in miniature and society is the individual expanded. Both are relational mixes.

The figure of the Melanesian person is instructive, because through it we can conceptualize the difference between Melanesians and us. It is not about substituting the Euro-American concept by the Melanesian concept as the best candidate for impersonating the Universal: the Melanesian person is not a better proposition than the former, it is no more faithful to the true essence of the Human than the Western individual. The notion of the Melanesian person only emerges in the context of an attempt to conceptualize the difference between Melanesians and Euro-Americans. Classic British social anthropology is a subparticular discourse, a rather minor episode in the discourse of Euro-American societies on other societies.

Yet Strathern is not suggesting we substitute these discourses (the minor and the major) by a superdiscourse that would be less particular, something like the word of God, a point of view of nowhere (or everywhere) that would transcend and encompass both Euro-American discursivity and the Melanesian. What she proposes is, far more modestly, a new manner of relating these two discourses without retroprojecting something like a greater common denominator of all cultures: human nature.

There are, thus, two different relationalisms in Strathern: the relational notion of the (Melanesian) person and the relational conception of (anthropological) knowledge. The recursive relation between them is just what makes her anthropology interesting, because it is deliberately unstable (or 'metastable', as a reader of Gilbert Simondon would say). **EVC**

Refusing dualisms

In Strathern's texts, the anthropology of the West and the anthropology of Melanesia intercept one another; they mix, they critique and they mutually transform one another. It is important to first emphasize the importance of feminist discourse. In the case of *The Gender of the Gift,* this is very clear. In the interview she gave to *Mana* (this volume), she says that the importance of feminist work for her came from the fact that they did not take anthropological paradigms for granted. Now, if from the point of view of Melanesia it is obvious that neither anthropology nor the West as a whole is necessarily visible, it can also happen that even from the point of view of a Western, more or less anthropological practice (like feminism) they are not either, because these practices, which obviously are 'Western', reveal other potentialities of this 'West,' – different, for example, from those that anthropology developed and explored.

These practices can be part of the analysis in various ways: as a substantive contribution, as a catalyst, as a marker of differences. In other words, they can allow us to tune our ears, or to rearrange our material, in a way that we were not accustomed to arranging them in. Strathern emphasizes in 'Parts and Wholes' a critique that is assiduous in feminist thought: that of the dichotomy between public and private, political and domestic, which is absolutely constitutive of anthropology, especially in British social anthropology. We know that one of the aims of feminist discourse is precisely to abolish these dichotomies, these distinctions. And this is for obvious reasons women being condemned to the domestic and the domestic being considered inferior to the public.

If we take this seriously, if we stack this against the predominant anthropological discourse, what happens? Not taking the anthropological paradigm as given means that we do not have to believe that dichotomies like public and private, domestic and political have to structure our discourse anymore. And whatever experience is enabled by feminist output could be remade with other discourses of resistance, like those connected to race or ethnicity. And we know that anthropologists have strange reactions when they are confronted with these discourses.

Another way that *The Gender of the Gift* departs from ethnographies on Melanesia is through the opposition between commodity and gift. For Strathern, it is neither about accepting nor refusing nor even transcending this dichotomy. It is about, more modestly perhaps, beginning by admitting that in Melanesia this dichotomy might not be pertinent. And this is different than saying that in Melanesia the gift reigns, while here the commodity reigns. This dichotomy is, nevertheless, a good point of departure but not of

arrival, as the aim is to problematize this very dichotomy. What is not opera-
tive in the Melanesian universe might be the dichotomy itself! In *The Gender
of the Gift* Strathern stretches this argument almost to its limit, assuming that
when we define our relation to Melanesians as an opposition between commodity and gift, it is necessary to recognize that this opposition is ours; it is
internal to our economy and to our thinking.

What emerges clearly in 'Parts and Wholes' is that the relation between
part and whole is closely connected to the opposition between individual
and society. The question is: do we have to choose between one or the
other of these dichotomies? As Eduardo said just now, in fact they want to
oblige us to choose! But who says that we are obliged to? The central argument is that there is no way to choose between the poles of either of these
dichotomies.

On the first page of 'Parts and Wholes', Strathern says something
that deserves attention. 'The society that we think up for the 'Are 'Are,
Melanesians from the Solomon Islands, is a transformation of the society
we think up for ourselves (1992, 90). The crucial word is *transformation*. Not
projection, not inversion, but *transformation* – forgery perhaps, as Eduardo
suggests. It is that which we are not that allows us to identify ourselves
more easily – and the notion of transformation in an almost Lévi-Straussian
sense. It allows us to think of two 'societies' or 'peoples' as reciprocal transformations of one another. There is no ontological judgement about reality
here, about the ultimate nature of the real. Eduardo referred to 'versions',
which is also a Lévi-Straussian way of formulating the problem. Societies
are myths in a certain sense; all are versions of each other, and there is no
original myth. **MG**

It is clear in the text of Lévi-Strauss that myths are in fact versions of
each other and that there is no original myth. But there is a myth of reference. In what sense? We have to begin somewhere. 'M1' is the first by
chance. To a certain point Western society is the M1 of anthropology, not
because it is a transcendent possibility but because it has methodological
privilege: we have to start with it. **EVC**

Someone can ask whether if, to guarantee transformation and, as such,
to make anthropology work there needs to be a common nature. Strathern
does not ask herself this question. She takes a step to the side and asks
another question: do we have the descriptive capacity to speak of these
societies as transformations of one another? It's a hell of a lot of work, but
it is the work that proves that it is possible. We stand before a process of
infinite expansion, and we expand other dimensions to keep presenting
themselves. **MG**

THE LANGUAGE OF DESCRIPTION

('The Ethnographic Effect I' and 'The Ethnographic Effect II')[2]
The analytical texts of Strathern are continuous with the subjects they treat. That is why they present that already-mentioned stylistic complexity: their organization is deliberately motivated by what they are speaking about – hence the sensation that the Strathernian text is a strange text because, in truth, it looks like its own object. This is an object, needless to say, that is constructed by the text or, rather, in the text and as a text – but it is a text that does not construct itself as castles in the air are constructed. 'Ethnographies are the analytical constructions of scholars; the peoples they study are not' (Strathern 1988, xii).

At the end of 'The Ethnographic Effect I', Strathern concludes that 'the ethnographic method ... begins to look extremely promising' (Strathern 1999a, 25–26). Slightly before, she states that her work 'is neither a matter of piling on theoretical antecedents nor a matter of going where no one has been before'. We should go precisely where we have always been, that is, again to the immediate here-and-nows from which we have created our knowledge of the world. This implies working with the retrospective vision of the possibility of unforeseen results and with the consciousness that the simple being-in-the-present permits the investigator to recuperate materials that previous investigators did not know they were collecting. That is why ethnography is 'extremely promising'.

At the end of the preface of *Property, Substance and Effect* there is a passage that I ask permission to cite *in extenso*, as it constitutes an especially scintillating moment of Marilyn Strathern's theoretical project:

> These essays are ... retrospective. That personalises a professional conviction that social anthropology does not always do enough with its past. It has contributed uniquely to human knowledge by its studies of human knowledge. In doing so, it draws attention to one consistent characteristic of social life, namely the complex kinds of reflection upon themselves that people afford one another through their relations with one another ...
>
> I wish to note where I stand in the division of labour between myself and my colleagues [NB that is a reflexive application of the phrase that came before]. These essays document, among other things, a continuing struggle with the language of description. Description presupposes analysis, and analysis presupposes theory, and they all presuppose imagination. The issue is how we may best describe knowing the effect which descriptions have on one another, that one description is always interpreted in the company of others and nothing is in that sense by itself. Social anthropologists make the question explicit: they work openly through other people's descriptions. (Strathern 1999e, xi–xii)

A struggle with language: 'language can work against the user of it' (ibid., 18). The struggle is visible, and this visibility is part of the author's 'aesthetic' – to coin a term. The language of Strathern always gives a strong overall impression of ambiguity, but this does not seem to us to be a defect; it is, rather, an effect. As computer software programmers are fond of saying: 'it's not a bug, it's a feature'; in the present case, this, for once, is true! Marilyn Strathern's incessant struggle with language reproduces itself in the reader, who is engaged in a constant struggle with the language of Marilyn Strathern. Please note that I am not complaining.

Let us consider the above example. It is not completely clear for me, in this long passage, whether we are facing the general demand that, when one describes something, the analytical consciousness must never lose sight of the effects that the descriptions produce on one another (so as to factor in and/or out such effects), or whether it addresses a more specific objective, namely to describe the effects that descriptions produce on one another. These are two slightly different things. How can we describe in the best possible way the fact that we know that the effects that descriptions have on one another have implications? Or how can we describe something in the best possible way, knowing the effects that descriptions have on one another? That ambiguity is intrinsic to the text of Strathern, and only a native speaker could, perhaps, resolve the enigma (if there is one!).

The author concludes, tersely:

> Those descriptions invariably include people referring to fellow people as thinking and feeling beings, and attribute what they say and do to how they think and feel, but that is not the same as studying how people think and feel and this is not intended to be such a study. As on other occasions, the present work remains agnostic as to the emotions, states of mind or mental processes of the people mentioned here. (Strathern 1999e, xii)

That observation allows us to evaluate the distance that separates the intellectual project of Marilyn Strathern from what almost all of our colleagues are intending to do – or think that they are doing. But is it really a great distance, or is it only a slight displacement of perspective – a change that changes everything? A battle with the language of description: with the very language of description, mind you, not with the language of others, the language of those who are being described (whose language, in other words, is being described). In short, she is not aiming to interpret the language of others with the help of the theoreticotheological devices currently used to interpret the 'emotions, states of mind or mental processes of the people' (Strathern 1999e, xii).

It is important to note that Strathern does not make much of terms like 'interpretation' or 'explanation'. She favours another technical word: 'description'. Interpretations and explications are modes of description. All description is always interpreted, and this always occurs in contrast with other descriptions. There is no description that is not relative to the descriptive context, that is, to the set (virtual and actual) of other descriptions. In sum, I understand that for Marilyn Strathern all description includes explanations and interpretations, explanations and interpretations made by those – anthropologists or natives – describing the actions of other persons (human or otherwise), describing, that is, the 'mental states' of other persons. But precisely, this does not mean defining anthropology as the study of the mental states of persons, either directly or through their simulation in the mind of the analyst.

There is a well-known distinction in philosophy between first-person descriptions and third-person descriptions. Strathern seems to be looking for something between these two modes of description. The first-person description is a phenomenological dream: 'I must be capable of subjectively experimenting the way in which the native thinks and feels the world'. On the other side is the positivist project: 'I will produce an objective, impersonal account of the way in which the native thinks and feels the world'. This would be a pure third-person description of a physical system, or a would-be physical system (the mind of the native) that goes through states we call thoughts, feelings, emotions, reasonings – in sum, energetic states that are detectable by certain objective indices (the blood pressure of the speaker, an MRI of her cortex, etc.). Marilyn Strathern does not at all propose a third-person perspective. But neither does she assume the first-person perspective; she is agnostic, exactly what the phenomenologist is not (he spent all of his agnosticism at the moment of the phenomenological reduction).

Strathern proposes something different, a relational description. The first and third persons are weak relational positions; by employing the third person we are of course radically different than what we describe, but in employing the first person, we are also, perhaps even more, different, because we are describing ourselves and no one can do that in our place. Maybe Marilyn Strathern has invented a kind of nondialogic second person, as it does not deal with dialogue; she invented a complex variation of free indirect speech. We do not find in her texts many direct citations of the phrases of natives; there is, in general, little cited discourse.

But, at the same time, her free indirect descriptive speech does not follow the classical model of narrating as if the author has privileged access to the mental states and silent inferences of the native (who remains, nevertheless, a native, that is, whose 'first-impersonation' by the analyst does not prevent the latter from crucially modulating the description with ever so slight an amount of epistemic irony). With Strathern's texts, something very different happens; finding its exact 'enunciation point' (as when one says 'melting point' or 'boiling point') is a challenging task, that is because this point is variable, varying most when the author passes from Melanesia to Euro-America.

In short, what Marilyn Strathern is proposing is a perspectivist theory of description that takes as its privileged object the exchange of perspectives, which is of the same order as the relation between her discourse and that which she analyzes. Hence the vertiginous or labyrinthine effect of her writing. The exchange of perspectives is for her the prototype of all anthropological analysis, the ethnographic moment, a kind of recurring hallucination, a primal conceptual scene as it were. Strathern's 'description' – the exchange between the language of the subject who describes and that of the subject who is being described – is a structural transformation of the exchange of perspectives.

This is necessarily effectuated by the social relation as a 'double duplex': both analytical tool and object of analysis, both a conceptual entity and an affective movement. There is, then, a kind of recursive imbrication that is the mark of an analytical device far more powerful and consequential than, say, a whimsical preference for the baroque *concetto*.[3] Everything happens as if there was no other possibility for anthropology as a discipline – either we do that, or we will not get much further (at best) than a noble engagement in the struggle for human rights. I am not saying that fighting for human rights is without value but simply that one does not need to be an anthropologist to do it. It is enough to have a minimum of 'human' decency. From there on in, everything gets much more complicated. **EVC**

* * * * *

In defence of exchange

The Marxist critique of Mauss was influential. It maintained that what is important is not exchange, but production, as exchange does not explain how things were produced to then be exchanged. This is a critique that was directed at *The Gender of the Gift* by Lisette Josephides, a Marxist anthropologist. For Josephides, Melanesian women, who have their productive work on pigs eclipsed, are like proletarians, as men extract a kind of surplus value from their work, which is the prestige obtained in the circulation of the pigs.

In sum, the pigs are what allow for exchange, and women make them. But Strathern shows that, in the first place, the pigs are not only made by women; they are made by women and men. In the second place, she questions this bizarre idea that people are the owners of what they make and that there is a natural property relation between a person and their property. Strathern rebuts the Marxist critique of exchange with another critique of exchange, this time the contractualist and individualist Hobbesian model of exchange. In this model, exchange is merely one variant of the social contract that avoids chaos, the war of all against all. It is in this sense that Sahlins interprets the 'Essay on the Gift' as an 'anti-Leviathan', as a social contract no longer based on the abdication of individual liberties in the name of a sovereign but on exchange.

Strathern writes *The Gender of the Gift* at a moment in the history of anthropology when the notion of exchange was unpopular. But *The Gender of the Gift* is a theory of exchange, a theory of Melanesian exchange, an articulation between the theory of exchange and the theory of gender, an explanation of production by exchange. She transforms production in a moment of exchange, instead of taking, as in classical models, exchange as a moment that connects production with consumption. Strathern defines the relation between husband and wife, which is a relation of production in the classical sense of the term that evokes the idea of the division of labour, as a relation of exchange and, more specifically as an unmediated relation of exchange.

According to Strathern there are two types of exchange in Melanesia. The first is mediated exchange, that is, made by means of objects, the incarnations of relations and typically enacted within a universe of persons of the same sex. The exchange of women between men is a mediated exchange, because it occurs between two terms of the same sex. What she calls unmediated exchange, typically enacted among people of the opposite sex, includes sex itself, work, conjugal life, and so on. Remember that for Engels, the relation between man and woman is the most fundamental relation of production. In this sense, Strathern commits a kind of theoretical sacrilege, as she affirms that production is a type of exchange. She responds to the critique of exchange via the notion of production and puts production at the moment of exchange.

As Alfred Gell proposed, Strathern creates a model 'M', for Marilyn and for Melanesia. But this model is much more than Melanesian. It is not a particular model of Melanesia, but it is not a general theory either. It is a perspective on society produced by Melanesian ethnography, a perspective through which the issue of the exchange of perspectives becomes the fundamental one. My impression is that the Strathernian contribution to the theory of exchange has not been sufficiently absorbed by the theoretical discourse of anthropology. Many people stopped with Pierre Bourdieu's theory, with the critique that he made of the gift or with the idea that exchange is only the name of exploitation or that, in sum, it is a secondary activity in the ontological sense of the term.

What happens if we forward the idea of the exchange of perspectives proposed by Strathern? Note that she makes the important argument that what is exchanged in Melanesia are not conch shells, but perspectives. Conch shells, and objects in general, embody relations and what is being exchanged as perspectives in relation to these relations. The gifts that move from one side to the other are not things, not values, they are positions, relations. In the exchange of women, for example, what is produced is the capacity to see that woman, whether from the point of view of the brother or the point of view of the husband, and in a certain sense this is what creates the woman as such. There only exists woman because there exists a difference between sister and wife, and not the other way around. A Jivaro myth recounts that in the past there were no women in the world, only men, and then two cross-cousins had sexual relations and the one who was on the bottom became the first woman.

The myth is genius, as how could there be cross-cousins if, for them to exist, you need a brother and a sister, that is, siblings of the opposite sex? What this myth says is the following: there aren't cross-cousins because there are women, there are women because there are cross-cousins. In other words, there are women because there is exchange between cross-cousins, between brothers-in-law. Brothers-in-law exist before women. In other words, the difference between brother and brother-in-law or between sister and wife comes before the difference between man and woman.

The difference of a woman is created from the difference between men. The opposite could also be said. In sum, the term follows the relation: it was not the existence of women that created matrimonial exchange; it was matrimonial exchange that created women – in the literal sense of myth, in the magical sense of myth, in the logical sense of theory. The history contained in the Jivaro myth returns us directly to Strathern's theory in *The Gender of the Gift*: we can only speak of gender where there is the relation between same sex and cross-sex, relations of the same sex and intersex relation. Gender is not a relation between sex A and sex B but a relation between two relations.

There is still a question that pursues me: what is the status of the concept of exchange after the work of Strathern, after the idea of the exchange of perspectives? Also, what is the status of the notion of perspective, a notion that was also castigated in the poststructuralist era as being derived from a visualist, Eurocentric, masculinist perspective? Poststructuralism considered vision to be a model of Western, sexist, colonialist knowledge.

Vision penetrates, vision denudes. The object is feminized, the subject is masculinized. A whole critique of Western visualism was developed, which made the idea of perspective seem like a conceptual vice. In Strathern's texts, exchange and perspective come back together. There is a double and deliberate anachronism in her discourse in the idea of the exchange of perspectives. This is a question that I would prefer to leave open. **EVC**

The three perspectivisms

At the end of 'The Ethnographic Effect II' Strathern juxtaposes three perspectivisms: the exchange of perspectives in Melanesia, the Western notion of perspective, which has two versions – the renaissance and the postmodern – and Amazonian perspectivism. On the notion of Western perspectivism, there is, on the one hand, the point of view of God and, on the other, pluralism, the idea that there are multiple perspectives, in other words, relativism. She uses the term perspective to describe these different cases, but the meanings attributed to them are very diverse. Each one of them is a theory of social relations, a theory of social life, of sociality. In principle, she does not hierarchalize them. She does not say that the Melanesian or Amazonian theory is the most true. It is very difficult for an anthropologist to resist this temptation. My impression is that she struggles all the time against this tendency. **MG**

* * * * *

When Tânia Stolze Lima and I wrote about Amazonian perspectivism, we had not paid the slightest attention to this other meaning of perspectivism as elaborated by Marilyn Strathern. I had already read 'Parts and Wholes' (Strathern 1992) before writing my article 'Cosmological Deixis and Amerindian Perspectivism' (Viveiros de Castro 1998), but Strathernian perspectivism escaped me completely. It was only after having developed an Amazonian notion of perspectivism that I was able to make Melanesian perspectivism visible within my own conceptual aesthetic. I presume the same applies to Stolze Lima. Strathern pairs Amazonian perspectivism – with all of its shamanic significance, involving differentiated visions of each species – with the Melanesian theme of the exchange of perspectives and its strong gendered codification, which is a more 'sociological' perspectivism.

The exchange of Melanesian perspectives is not an exchange of seen worlds; it is an exchange of relations between 'giver' and 'receiver'. It is not a problem of 'vision' in the literal, sometimes anatomic sense one may encounter in Amazonian and similar worlds (different species have 'different eyes', etc.). Perhaps the gift, the object, the conch or the pig have eyes, but this is not the most important. I note that Strathern does not directly mention (if memory serves) that one can find, in Melanesia, cosmological complexes that are somewhat evocative of those found in Amazonia (the Kaluli's or the Korowai's, for example). But that is because it does not matter much, for Strathern, to know whether in Melanesia, in Malaysia or in Siberia there exist perspectivist ideas that are similar to the Amazonian. It is much more important, for her, to indicate different possibilities of interpretation of perspectivism – and much more interesting, for Amazonianists, that she does that.

In the triangulation done by Strathern, the Amazonian perspective and the Melanesian are on one side, and the modernist perspective on the other. In the case of Amazonia and Melanesia, one perspective assumes the perspective of another. In modern, pluralist perspectivism (the expression is mine), each individual exists with their vision of the world, always incomplete, and then there is the perspective of the whole, the society, which is incommensurable with the perspectives of individual parts. In that world, each perspective, by including another point of view as part of itself, has to exclude it as a perspective. In other words, there is a hierarchy. Marilyn Strathern emphasizes this contrast, as for her, fundamentally, modern perspectivism is a false perspectivism, or better, modern representational pluralism is a different regime from that which we could call the regime of perspectival multiplicity.

At the end of 'The Ethnographic Effect II' Strathern adds, 'I repeat the point that an exchange of perspectives is not to be confused with the European gaze. A mutual gaze in the contemporary Euro-American mode is two perspectives each from an individual standpoint on to the world' (1999b, 260). The exchange of perspectives to which Strathern refers should not therefore be confused with visualism, the European ocularcentrism. The mutual gaze in the contemporary Euro-American mode returns us to two points of individual views on the world.

It is a duplicated dualism, as we can see in the Euro-American model of filiation, in which a child can be seen from the point of view of the mother and the point of view of the father. In Euro-America, in sum, there are no exchanges of perspectives; there are simply accumulations of different and individualized perspectives on the world. In the Melanesian model, she continues, 'for which I have imagined a visual theory of sorts, any one perspective elicits another' (ibid.). The point of view of the father, as much as the point of view of the mother, are contained in the child, and the fundamental question is how these points of view alternate in the child. **EVC**

* * * * *

According to Strathern, to understand the modern or postmodern pluralist perspectivism, we have to look to renaissance perspectivism. What is
involved in renaissance perspectivism is the idea of encompassment, as
there is always a perspective capable of encompassing the others, and that is
the perspective of God. In the case of modern or postmodern perspectivism,
the only relationship between the plural perspectives is that one of them
encompasses the rest; it is one of them negating the others as perspectives.
Perhaps it is this that has permitted the definition of anthropology as the
study of the perspective of others. And the whole issue becomes this: is the
perspective of others a perspective, or not? **MG**

*   *   *   *   *

The focus on notions like exchange and perspective attend to a double
interest. In the first place, they are concerned with certain Melanesian/
Amazonian knowledge practices; in the second place, they relate to a
certain style of doing anthropology. 'Perspective' is a term that connects
(relates) the relation 'between' anthropological and Melanesian discourse
to what is happening 'inside' Melanesian discourse. By the same token, the
notion of exchange defines not only the exchange of perspectives between
Melanesians but also an exchange between the perspective of the anthropologist, modernist or Euro-American, and the perspective of the native.
Exchange and perspective are transepistemological notions inasmuch
as they establish a continuity between the object of description and the
description itself.

In sum, the process of anthropological description is, itself, a process of
the exchange of perspectives. This contrasts with the idea that an anthropological description is the encompassment of the point of view of the other.
Strathern wants to escape the alternative between 'pluralist' or 'liberal' relativism, on the one hand, and 'imperialist' or 'conservative' universalism, on
the other. It is not necessary to choose between these two alternatives, another
world is possible . . . We have there an epistemological alterglobalism.

In a certain sense, the reflections on the Amazonian and Melanesian
perspectivisms are already given in the ethnographic material. But, beyond
the specificities of both ethnographic areas, the idea of perspectivism connects the discourse of the 'observer' and the 'observed' in ways that are
definitely nontraditional. Classically, the encompassment of the native's
perspective by that of the anthropologist is one of the conditions of possibility of the discipline – perhaps *the* condition. In other words, it is imperative
that the anthropologist be able not to take the native too seriously; this way
the former can reconstruct the latter's 'point of view' without losing any
sleep over it.

The alternative to that epistemic colonialism is to transform the notion of perspective in a notion that in fact destabilizes anthropological discourse, obliging it to assume the perspective of the other as such. In Melanesia, writes Strathern, the subjects assume the perspectives of others above all because they are obliged to. The gift consists precisely in obliging the partner to the exchange, in producing an effect. Effect is, by the way, a keyword here, as effectiveness is found in opposition to reflexivity. Melanesian knowledge practices consist in producing effects on other people; they thus constitute a theory of social action. Something different is produced by the theory of Western knowledge: it is less linked to the idea of effectiveness than to the idea of representation. **EVC**

FROM MELANESIA TO US

('The New Modernities'; 'Cutting the Network')[4]
The Strathernian discussion of the ideas of the authors who have examined the modern world (e.g. Bruno Latour and James Clifford) brings to mind the distinction between sociology and anthropology originally proposed by Lévi-Strauss in 1954 in his article 'The Place of Anthropology in the Social Sciences and the Problems Raised in Teaching It' (republished in *Structural Anthropology* 1963). Lévi-Strauss affirms that while sociology tries to do the 'social science of the observer', anthropology seeks to elaborate a 'social science of the observed'. Sociology, even when it takes as its object a different society, is solidary with the point of view of the observer. Anthropology, in contrast, elaborates a social science of the observed,

> either by endeavouring to reproduce, in its description of strange and remote societies, the standpoint of the natives themselves, or by broadening its subject so as to cover the observer's society but at the same time trying to evolve a frame of reference based on ethnographical experience and independent both of the observer and of what he is observing. (Lévi-Strauss 1963, 363)

On the basis of the ethnographic experience, anthropology would thus be able to establish an absolute point of view, independent of both the observer's and his object's. Here one sees the theological dimension of Lévi-Straussian anthropology. If we discount this dimension, however, we can transport the anthropology/sociology distinction to Strathern's encounter with the ideas of Latour and Clifford. Speaking in very broad terms, we could say that Strathern sees in Latour's and Clifford's analyses the work of sociologists, in no pejorative sense. Both authors occasionally speak of other societies using general anthropological propositions and have a very good grasp of our discipline's 'language game'. Still, Strathern suspects that they remain riveted to issues and problems that are very specific to the society to which they belong. If we use the vocabulary of 'The Limits of Auto-Anthropology', we can argue that there is a continuity between what these authors say and the knowledge practices of the society to which they belong.

In this article, Strathern distinguishes 'auto-anthropology' and 'anthropology at home'. Perhaps we could make a further distinction, between 'anthropology at home' and an 'anthropology from home' (or a 'home-made anthropology'), which would approximate the definition of sociology that we have just cited: a knowledge practice in total epistemic continuity with the questions raised by the society of the observer.

In 'Cutting the Network', Strathern asks herself about what effect the a notion of symmetrical anthropology can have for a Melanesianist. Let us recall that Latour introduced this notion to speak about science and, later, politics, the two overarching practicotheoretical modes of our society. My own reading of the reasoning of Latour is more or less the following: if an anthropologist who studies Melanesia aims at a type of understanding of Melanesians that is predicated on taking utterly seriously what they say, this does not mean that such an aim must be pursued in the same way and with the same means as when we work with scientists, because the points of departure are asymmetrical, and the operation of symmetrization does not mean to suppose that everything 'is the same thing'.

Symmetrization means choosing the right procedures, which may be the very opposite of those employed in a 'Melanesian type', so that the process is symmetrical, producing a certain epistemic discontinuity vis-à-vis the interlocutors. Latour seems to have little interest in what the scientists say about what they are doing. From the point of view of Strathern, his ethnography appears slightly strange, since, for her, everything we deal with are knowledge practices after their fashion, and, therefore, what the persons themselves have to say is absolutely constitutive of the object being investigated. On the other hand, there is no doubt that the kind of ethnographic observation practised by Latour affords him a crucial distance from the rationalist tradition of French epistemology and, more importantly, allows for a description that suspends the supposed privileged access to the real that we usually attribute to scientists.

This is a problem that anthropologists who study Amazonia or Melanesia do not need to deal with, because we do not normally take for granted that 'the natives' are the happy possessors of a particularly privileged definition of the real. The effort of these exo-anthropologists consists, on the contrary, precisely in being able conceptually to construct natives' definitions or descriptions as something real.

In his small book on fetishism, Latour uses the description of African 'fetishist' practices to arrive at modern 'anti-fetishism' (Latour 1996). He is little interested in what the 'fetishists' have to say about 'fetishism', presenting them like people who make an object and afterwards put it at the centre of a cult as if they had forgotten that they had made it themselves. What makes them similar to scientists, though, is that they also make an object to afterwards affirm that it had always existed. This kind of approach always seemed to me to be typical of sociology. The African fetishists serve only as a point of support, as supplementary material that helps us respond to a question that was not asked by them. Strathern, on the other hand, would seem to be favouring the old ethnographic tradition of anthropology, which would fall back to that well-known line of argument: 'Well, it might be like this here in the modern world, but there in my field site it isn't so'.

Normally, this is an objection that leads to a kind of grumpy relativism or to a paradoxical generalized particularism. Strathern, however, goes much beyond that. She uses the inadequacy resulting from the application of the familiar discourses of the observer to expand the anthropological concepts, not to restrict them. Taking some notions put forth by Latour – network and hybrid, for example – the problem of Strathern is how to simulate what happens when these concepts cross Melanesian material or are crossed by them. All of this is a problem of direction and application: either we simply apply the concept of network to the Melanesians – this is the traditional procedure in anthropology – or we do what Strathern does, which is exactly the opposite: apply the Melanesians to the notion of the network, that is, we redescribe the concept of network with the help of Melanesian realities. Everything happens as (if she were to say) the following: 'If Melanesians had the will and the patience to read Latour, what would they be able to say about it?'

In 'The New Modernities', Strathern launches a very interesting critique of the notion of scale, which brings us, among other things, to the Latourian question of the length of networks. According to Latour, the 'premoderns' have very short networks; they excel in thinking about hybrids but come short when the problem is generating them. Moderns are very good at generating hybrids and terrible at thinking about them. The nonmodern world, the alternative indicated by Latour, will be an ideal combination between the premodern and the modern, bypassing the postmodern. Latour seems to have begun with a modern (or postmodern) question and, in that sense, he cannot arrive anywhere else. The premodern material in his texts appears more like a corrective, as an example of how the modern 'constitution' can be improved. The premoderns are interesting to us to the extent that they can think about hybrids, but they are not sufficiently interesting, because they cannot expand their networks.

Anthropologists are interesting because they are capable of describing, on the same plane, the human and the nonhuman, but they are not sufficiently interesting because they are only able to do these things away from home. Latour simultaneously praises and rebukes anthropology, says Strathern. Her own critique consists in the dislocation of his question. One should not think about what a network is in Melanesia, but what a network would be for a Melanesian. A network for a Melanesian can be absurdly long, since they involve hundreds of names, types of being and planes of existence. Strathern's argument is therefore quite different from Latour's, for whom, in the final analysis, networks, as Melanesians conceive them, cannot exist (as Evans-Pritchard said of Zande witches). The networks promoted by science or by globalization (networks as scientists conceive them), on the other hand, can certainly exist.

Thus, in general terms, the basic Strathernian procedure is to ask Melanesians what would networks, or hybrids, be. The Latourian hybrid musters entities like animal, machine and human. A certain methodological or discursive presupposition that these things are both relatively homogeneous and exterior to one another seems necessary so that they can cross and hybridize. But in Melanesia this is not necessary. The social relations are already hybrid in themselves. Human beings are hybrids and (literally) heterogeneous. **MG**

* * * * *

On the other hand, we tend to index relations between humans and nonhumans as heterogeneous. In Melanesia this would be problematic, as a yam can be more like me than my brother-in-law. While for Latour you and your brother-in-law are the same kind of thing, the yam is another thing, and then the hybrid 'person-yam' is created. In Melanesia – in Dobu, let us say – the yam and the human are already seen as two faces of the personhood of the clan. **EVC**

* * * * *

Also in 'The New Modernities', Marilyn Strathern talks about the 'new culturalisms', using, once again, Melanesian examples. For Clifford, these new culturalisms are the symptoms of the generalized hybridization and globalization that he likes so much. Strathern begins her commentary by suggesting that the planetary process of environmental degradation can be coded in the key of witchcraft. For us, the environmental crisis is the result of a relationship between humans, on one side, and nature, on the other. For Melanesians, this is not exactly what is happening. Witchcraft is a kind of relational theory, and the environment appears as an objectification of social relations. For the Melanesians, it is social relations themselves that are objectified in the destruction of the environment. We can see here that while appearing to hold an apparently similar discourse concerning the destruction of the environment, Melanesians have a completely different theory, which must be taken seriously.

Another important point, which appears in 'Cutting the Network', is the notion of property, which has a constitutive relationship with the notion of the hybrid. The new technologies and the patenting of life also serve as analysts of this situation. Marilyn Strathern concludes that, in a certain sense, there is only property in hybrids. Property is by definition a hybrid, as it supposes an articulation between persons and things and assumes that they are different.

Strathern gives an example of a man who brings a case to a North American court alleging that his blood was used unlawfully by a multi-national company. He ends by losing the case and is even accused by the judge, who says that he has commercial interests. The multinational defends itself, saying that the patent is not the blood of the individual but a scientific discovery, a hybrid, a mixture of nature and culture. The problem of property appears exactly at the moment that Strathern filters it through Melanesia, where the notion of property does not appear to function very well, seeing that it presupposes an exteriority between persons and things.

Again she makes her procedures explicit: 'In anthropologising some of these issues, however, I do not make appeals to other cultural realities just simply because I wish to dismiss the power of the Euro-American concepts of hybrid and network. The point is, rather, to extend them with social imagination' (Strathern 1996: 521). What happens if we apply these and those concepts to these and those peoples' imaginations – and vice versa? This is the most important question.

In 'Cutting the Network', Strathern employs a vocabulary that does not appear in her other texts, including terms like flux and cut; these are absolutely central in the anti-Oedipus of Deleuze and Guattari, even though Strathern makes no reference to these authors. In essence, she defines a network like a cut within a flux. The network is not something absolutely unlimited, in unlimited expansion, but also a blockage. It works by connecting-and-cutting, flowing-and-blocking. Strathern offers examples of the new technologies. For example, a group of forty people sign a scientific article on hepatitis C. But, of these forty, only six apply for a patent. Scientific activity, the discovery of this virus, is a flux that we could trace infinitely. The work of objectifying the hepatitis C virus demands the presence of many people. The issue becomes not the length of the networks but where one could make the cut or, in other words, who will be the owner of this patent. The cut is the property. And the network is also a special way of cutting.

In 'Cutting the Network', Strathern relativizes the distance between the social networks of classical social anthropology of British transnationalism and the networks of actor-network theory. She also relativizes the distance between the classical theories of kinship networks and the studies of modern kinship. For her, what characterizes Western kinship is exactly the fact that it incorporates that which, it can be said, is not kinship. With this operation, the studies of kinship assume the same characteristic as the studies conducted with actor-network theory. In the West, there is no way to speak about kinship without speaking about biology, without speaking about the imbrications of the biological and the social, which is an exemplary case of the Latourian network. **MG**

* * * * *

We began this course by drawing attention to the value of anthropological studies of science for anthropology in general, as the anthropology of science examines the problem of the great divide between science and nonscience, the West and the Rest. Strathern inverts the direction, showing the value of classical anthropology – studies of kinship, for example – for the anthropological studies of science. The interest in Western kinship is that kinship can become a tool for the analysis even of science. Instead of simply applying science to kinship, let us also see what happens when we apply kinship to science: we get another science; we expand anthropology. The study of Western kinship is the Strathernian anthropology of science. **EVC**

NOTES

What follows are selections that were made and translated by Ashley Lebner from edited transcriptions of three lectures given in Portuguese in April 2006 at the National Museum (Museu Nacional) of the Federal University of Rio de Janeiro. A shorter and differently ordered version of this text was published in Deiringer and Lebner (2008/9; selections and translation also by Lebner). Naturally, the oral quality of the lectures that we decided to maintain was achieved through various rewritings of the original transcription; and the dated character of our statements (April 2006) hide a number of surreptitious insertions made in January 2009. These lectures were part of the postgraduate course Introduction to a Post-Social Anthropology:

Networks, Multiplicities and Symmetrizations. It experimented with new directions in anthropology created by the collision of certain concepts (invention/convention, reversibility, reflexivity, actor network, symmetry, partial connection and multiplicity, among others) proposed by authors such as Roy Wagner, Bruno Latour, Gilles Deleuze, Félix Guattari and Marilyn Strathern. The course was based on the collective text 'Symmetry, Reversibility and Reflexivity: Great Divides and Small Multiplicities' (http://sites.google.com/a/abaetenet.net/nansi/Home/simetria-reversibilidade-e-reflexividade) of the Abaeté Network of Symmetrical Anthropology, which influenced a series of dissertations, theses and other works by participants (and the network). The expression 'postsocial anthropology' should be understood as synonymous with 'pre-x anthropology', where x is an unknown. We only speak of 'postsocial' because we are imagining something still to come and we do not know, nor can we, what it is. We would like to thank those who taped our classes, with or without our knowledge; Fábio Candotti, for the transcription of the material and Renato Sztutman, for the preliminary editing of the transcripts.

1. The interview was first published in Portuguese (Strathern 1999d).
2. Strathern 1999a, 1999b.
3. Italian for 'concept', *concetto* was the name given in the Baroque era to certain complex, convoluted poetic images with metaphysical or religious implications.
4. Strathern (1999c, 1996, 1987).

REFERENCES

Deiringer, Sabine, and Ashley Lebner, eds. (2008/9). "Special Issue of Cambridge Anthropoloy: Bureacratic Knowledge Practices, the William Wyse Professorship and the Work of Marilyn Strathern. *Cambridge Anthropology*. 28: 3.

Latour, Bruno. 1996. *Petite réflexion sur le culte moderne des dieux faitiches.* Paris: Les em-pêcheurs de penser en rond.

Lévi-Strauss, Claude. 1963. 'The Place of Anthropology in the Social Sciences and the Problems Raised in Teaching It'. In *Structural Anthropology,* 346–81. New York: Basic Books.

Strathern, M. 1987. 'The Limits of Auto-Ethnography'. In *Anthropology at Home,* edited by Anthony Jackson, 16–37. London: Tavistock.

——. 1988. *The Gender of the Gift.* Berkeley: University of California Press.

——. 1992. 'Parts and Wholes: Refiguring Relationships in a Postplural World'. In *Conceptualising Society,* edited by Adam Kuper, 75–106. London: Routledge.

——. 1996. 'Cutting the Network'. *Journal of the Royal Anthropological Institute* 2: 517–35.

——. 1999a. 'The Ethnographic Effect I'. In *Property, Substance and Effect. Anthropological Essays on Persons and Things,* 1–28. London: Athlone Press.

——. 1999b. 'The Ethnographic Effect II'. In *Property, Substance and Effect. Anthropological Essays on Persons and Things,* 229–61. London: Athlone Press.

——. 1999c. 'The New Modernities'. In *Property, Substance and Effect. Anthropological Essays on Persons and Things,* 117–37. London: Athlone Press.

——. 1999d. 'No limite de uma certa linguagem'. *Mana* 5: 157–75.

——. 1999e. *Property, Substance and Effect. Anthropological Essays on Persons and Things.* London: Athlone Press.

Viveiros de Castro, E. 1998. 'Cosmological Deixis and Amerindian Perspectivism'. *Journal of the Royal Anthropological Institute* 4: 469–88.

Viveiros de Castro, Eduardo, and Marcio Goldman. 2008/9. 'Slow Motions. Comments on a Few Texts by Marilyn Strathern'. Special Issue of *Cambridge Anthropology: Bureaucratic Knowledge Practices, the William Wyse Professorship and the Work of Marilyn Strathern,* edited by Sabine Deiringer and Ashley Lebner 28(3): 23–42.

Wagner, R. 1967. *The Curse of Souw: Principles of Daribi Clan Definition and Alliance.* Chicago: University of Chicago Press.

Eduardo Viveiros de Castro is Professor of Social Anthropology at the National Museum, Federal University of Rio de Janeiro. He was Simón Bolívar Professor of Latin American Studies, Cambridge University (1997–1998) and directeur de recherches at the Conseil national de recherche scientifique (1999–2001). His major publications are *From the Enemy's Point of View* (Chicago, 1992), *A inconstância da Alma selvagem* (São Paulo, 2002), *Cannibal Metaphysics* (Minneapolis, 2014) and *The Relative Native* (Chicago, 2015).

Marcio Goldman is Professor in the Postgraduate Program in Social Anthropology, National Museum, Federal University of Rio de Janeiro; researcher for the Brazilian National Council of Research and a funded scholar at the Rio de Janeiro Research Foundation. He is the author of *Reason and Difference: Affectivity, Rationality and Relativism in Lévy-Bruhl* (1994), *Some Anthropology* (1999) and *How Democracy Works: An Ethnographic Theory of Politics* (London, 2013). He is working now on a book about Afro-Brazilian religions and beginning an investigation into native theories of miscegenation.

Conclusion

Thinking through Proliferations of Geometries, Fractions and Parts

Sarah Green

It is strange how easy it is to misremember stories, particularly ones that are important. For years, I remembered that my fascination with mathematics came from reading *The Phantom Tollbooth* as a child (Juster 1962). That part of the story is true. What is less true is my memory that the book was entirely about a boy's journey through a magical world of numbers (the boy's name was Milo). In fact, only a part of the book is about the 'kingdom of numbers'; much of the rest is about the kingdom of words, and the book as a whole concerns an unfortunate split between two brothers, Mathemagician and King Azaz, who were the respective rulers of each world, having divided their father's Kingdom of Wisdom into two, as they were unable to agree on anything. Milo's task was to bring them together again, and thus to restore Rhyme and Reason (two rather sensible young women) to their rightful place of reigning in the reunited Kingdom of Wisdom. Rhyme and Reason do not displace the kings of numbers and words (Mathemagician and Azaz), but they reunite the parts.

I went back to the book recently because of my sense that my repeated encounters with Marilyn Strathern's work, including reading refractions of it through the papers in this volume, involved something distinctly geometrical. And the part I remembered most clearly from *The Phantom Tollbooth* concerned a Dodecahedron, whom Milo encounters on his way from Dictionopolis to Digitopolis. Dodecahedron has twelve faces (each sporting a different facial expression), and he wears a rather fetching beret. After explaining his name, Dodecahedron asks Milo, 'What are you called?' And after Milo responds with 'Milo', Dodecahedron asks, 'Is everyone with one face called a Milo?'

> 'Oh no', Milo replied; 'some are called Henry or George or Robert or John or lots of other things'.
> 'How terribly confusing', [Dodecahedron] cried. 'Everything here is called exactly what it is. The triangles are called triangles, the circles are called circles, and even the same numbers have the same name. Why, can you imagine what would happen if we named all the twos Henry or George or Robert or John or lots of other things? You'd have to say Robert plus John equals four, and if the four's name were Albert, things would be hopeless'.
> 'I never thought about it that way', Milo admitted.[1]

Hopeless indeed. How could there be any understanding of the entities that add up to four (the two twos), never mind understanding what their combination, four, might be – if the first two is called Henry and the second two is called George and, on this occasion, the four's name is Albert, yet on a different occasion, a four's name might be something else (e.g. Fred)? Milo spends quite a lot of his time in the book being befuddled by such questions and wondering whether it is him, or the strange entities that he encounters, that are not entirely making sense.

I was right to return to the book. It captures something of the combined sense of confusion and exhilaration I had when I first began reading Marilyn Strathern's work. What is more, *The Phantom Tollbooth* captured that sensibility in a manner that put its finger (face?) on what it was that generated the simultaneous befuddlement and excitement: there was something about the combination of the mathematical abstraction of geometry (and its precision) with the diversity of names (terms, concepts and their proliferation of significance) being presented in Strathern's work that was simultaneously mind-bogglingly confusing and enormously thought-provoking. I have lost count of the times when, just as I thought I had grasped *the* point, the text would proliferate other points, none of them more or less important than the previous one.

I often experienced reading her texts as semirecursive loops (a concept also drawn upon by Jensen and Winthereik in this volume), where an idea is introduced like a thread, drawn in one direction for a while and then woven into related ideas, before the text returns to a previous thread only to be cut or nipped somewhere and then finding the beginning of a new thread nearby that may or may not be tied directly with the first one, or a different one. This recursive looping, threading and cutting occurs not only within one text but between texts, and Strathern herself often draws attention to this interweaving and repetition, the not-quite-replications that appear (for example) at one moment in *Partial Connections* (Strathern 1991) and a year later, reworked, in *After Nature* (Strathern 1992).

In an updated edition of *Partial Connections,* Strathern is perhaps at her most explicit about this, saying that the Euro-American issues of complexity and scale that she addresses in that book are reproduced in a different guise in *After Nature* as a form of Euro-American discursiveness she calls 'merographic' (Strathern 2004, xxix). A merographic way of thinking, she explains, means the idea that 'any part of one thing may also be part of something else' (ibid.). I made sense of this by imagining an individual located at the intersection between several overlapping circles or spheres of a three-dimensional Venn diagram.

For example, within modern forms of English kinship, persons could be thought of as being, amongst other things, the combined outcome of both nature and culture/society ('born and bred'): there is a whole domain of phenomena that are imagined to be natural and another, and different, whole domain of phenomena that are imagined to be cultural and/or part of society; and at the intersection between them, where they overlap, is both some principles of modern English kinship and the individual English person. Moreover, there are infinite numbers of other domains, in addition to nature and culture/society, of which individuals could be a part: gender, class, nationality and so on. An individual is only ever a *part* of any one of these whole entities (e.g. nature) because they are simultaneously also a part of something else (i.e. they are neither wholly natural nor wholly cultural), and potentially, they could be a part of an infinite number of other things (or domains). This generates a sense of plurality, Strathern says: infinite possible combinations, in which each result is a unique individual.

This is all fine, until Strathern reconfigures the geometry of this in two ways. First, she points out that the only way to think about individuals like that (i.e. to think about them merographically) is to imagine a pre-existing entity (the individual) who is related in some way to all these different domains, which is the key Euro-American trope that both makes merographic thinking possible and is also its outcome. Consider instead, she suggests, the Melanesian situation, in which persons are imagined literally as being relations: 'When a Melanesian looks inside a person (a relation), he or she finds other persons (relations)' (Strathern 1992, 79).

In that situation, there are no pre-existing entities (no individuals): it is not possible for a person to belong partly to one whole entity and partly to another and to potentially belong to infinite numbers of others. Instead, persons enact their relations, which makes those particular relations actual, rather than potential; there is nothing more than, nor less than, their relations. And there are also no infinite possibilities: the relations carry all the substance of the person within them. Within this understanding of persons, there is also no possibility of *choosing* relations: entities that are brought into existence by having and enacting relations cannot thereby choose one relation over another – there is no entity to do the choosing; the relation has to exist before any action can take place.

The geometric logic of this is both simple and inexorable, and yet, because it dragged me away from the heart of what I had previously been capable of imagining about persons and their relations, the thought, when I first encountered it, caused me to feel like Milo: I had never thought about it that way before. This was despite the fact that I had been trained in the same British social anthropology that Strathern draws upon to build her arguments. It took a mental geometric relocation, a shift from thinking from the location of the individual to thinking from the location of the relation, and then an erasure of the dot that stands for the individual and replacing it with a fleshy container full of relations,[2] for me to 'get' the Melanesian point.

Second, Strathern states in *After Nature* that the Euro-American plural, individual, merographic, way of thinking, which Strathern introduced in this book and that I spent quite a long time trying to understand, was perhaps in the process of disappearing. *What?* The logic of that was inexorable as well. Drawing on a combination of political sensibilities at the time (what would today be called the development of neoliberal logic) and technological transformations (especially new reproductive and genetic technologies), Strathern suggests that a world imagined in a 'postplural' way could be replacing the world imagined in a merographic (plural) way. Thatcher's Britain, which appeared to be typified by Thatcher's claim that there was no society, only individuals who choose – meaning consumer choice, in the market – combined with technological changes, particularly new reproductive technologies, which implied the difference between nature and culture was no longer a clear difference, seemed to be taking all the boundaries of the domains away.

If in this part of Euro-America people began to imagine that there is no society and no nature that is different from culture, then the most important domains (nature, culture, society) of which individuals are made up cease to exist as distinct domains. The implications were dramatic: 'The "postplural individual" is no longer imagined merographically,' Strathern says (1992, 135), which carried the implication that what this combination of this new political economy and new technologies was causing people to *think* could be fundamentally changing Euro-American concepts of persons. In the end to the prologue to the book, and after noting that the main ideological trope of this new approach appeared to be equating freedom with the freedom to choose (meaning consumer choice, which of course runs fundamentally against Mauss's logic of the gift), Strathern famously says:

> Such free-ranging access, such apparent freedom of choice, in the end turns the sense of plurality into an artefact of access or choice itself. An approximation to the insight, then, of what it might be like to belong to a culture whose next imaginative leap is to think of itself as having nothing to construct. It would not, after all, be after anything. (Strathern 1992, 9)

I have written about this elsewhere, so I will not repeat the point (Green 2015); suffice it to say here that in a postplural world in which these distinctions are blurred and turned instead into choice, there is no way of differentiating the key domains of nature, culture and society. None of the differences make any difference anymore, even if the differences proliferate at an alarming rate these days: one could say there is nothing *but* difference (a Deleuzian point, of course), with no way to choose between the differences, even though choice is all there is, the only logical option.

It is intriguing that most of the authors in this collection draw upon the strands of Strathern's thought which concern this Euro-American combined conceptual and political shape-shifting more than almost any other aspect of her work.

Greenhouse's consideration of the way US legal arrangements transformed individuals into statistical identity categories, rather than identities, as such; Corsín Jiménez's study of the transformations effected by managerial rescalings and equations, and efforts to create paperless offices; Kirsch's study of how indigenous rights claims can creatively cross domains to generate certain effects; Navaro's study of how a software program called a structured dialogue design process (the mind boggles), aimed at conflict resolution in Cyprus, is entangled in the postplural (posthuman, even) technical logic of mediating social relations; Jensen and Winthereik's study of the effects of audit on the auditing process itself (a kind of looping back); and perhaps even Strathern's own afterword: on the one hand, that text loops all the way back to Fortes's comments on the past fascination anthropology had with roles and statuses. Yet Strathern does this in order to create a commentary on the recent separation of the role of the William Wyse Professor of social anthropology at Cambridge from the office of head of department there and how that appears to reflect a move towards a personalized position (a Milo, a Henry, or a George), not an office with obligations and relations attached which contains a current incumbent (a circle, a square, number two or William Wyse Professor).

The exception to this general focus on conceptual shape-shifting in this volume is the dialogue between Viveiros de Castro and Goldman, in which the focus is more on their mutual efforts to gain a perspective on Strathern's work on perspectives (what they refer to as an 'exchange of perspectives'). That dialogue loops into an engagement between Strathern and Viveiros de Castro that takes place elsewhere, concerning the difference Strathern has evoked between a 'perspectivist' and a 'perspectival' approach (Strathern 2011). Strathern's comments on that were published in the same journal as Viveiros de Castro's 2004 paper, 'Exchanging Perspectives' (Viveiros de Castro 2004). I also read this debate as another form of geometry, but this time, one that involved a particular kind of engagement with the 'geo' part of geometry: an engagement with the logic of location, as such.[3]

The similarity between the words (perspective and perspectival) came together with my own work on the strange geometry of the Balkans (Green 2005), and my former readings of political philosophy in relation to the question of perspectives (especially Foucault and Nietzsche) to once again cause a deep sense of both confusion and intrigue with this debate. Fortunately, there is some reiteration here, some loops and partial connections back to what has been thought before and which made me realize that all my work on understanding what merographic might be about had not gone to waste.

One key difference between perspectivism and perspectivalism is the question of *choice;* another is whether relations are based on similarity or difference. The *perspectivalist* (Euro-American) approach imagines a pre-existing individual who could have many different perspectives, which depends on the individual's location at any given moment – in a sense, her position in the Venn diagram of overlapping domains. In contrast, within a *perspectivist* approach (Melanesian/Amerindian), each 'perspective' is based on relations – which, as relations create the person, they also generate the perspective, the location (or world, in a sense) from which things are viewed. 'To be perspectivalist acts out Euro-American pluralism, ontologically grounded in one world and many viewpoints; whereas perspectivism implies an ontology of many worlds and one capacity to take a viewpoint' (Strathern 2011, 92).

The distinction between perspectivist and perspectival 'views' in Strathern's terms thus concerns the logic used to generate the geometry of relations; it is not literally about 'seeing' things. In the perspectivalist (Euro-American) logic, there is a 'view' on something: the assumption is that there is in reality one world, and there can be many different 'views' on it. This of course again requires the pre-existence of a self-contained individual who *chooses:*

This notion of choice is a prop to the notion that relations (actively) link terms, parties, and entities, so that links can be made (more or less) anywhere in this regime of plenitude . . . it is over and again the terms, not the relation, that are regarded as prior, which means that Euro-Americans . . . continue to live in the perspectivalist world of things with preexisting attributes. (Strathern 2011, 100)

In contrast, within perspectivist logic, which Strathern regards as typified within Melanesian/Amerindian thought, there are many parallel worlds created out of relations. The example of the relation of brother-in-law comes in more than once: brother-in-law is a relation generated by kinship rules, in which one man has a sister who is another man's wife. Each man has a different relation to the woman, which is what generates the character of the tie between the men; Strathern even notes that in Melanesian terms, this woman is what divides the men (2011, 94). 'What such a relationship does is create a universe of relations that turn on its enactment. In occupying different positions, then, a person switches not individual viewpoints but relationships' (Strathern 2011, 94).

The absence of choice is crucial here. Again, there is no pre-existing individual who chooses a relation, or a point of view; there are relations that are enacted, and in enacting them, the world is created. The person, who contains the relations (both of difference and similarity), enacts parts of them at any given time; but they are parts of one, they all add up to one. The implication is that there are as many worlds as there are relations, and each world can be understood as being an analogy of another one: it can be understood, even if it is not experienced, because the relational logic that generates the one is the same as that which generates another.

In contrast, within the Euro-American perspectival logic, individuals, as well as things and animals, are pre-existing parts of many different wholes, as distinct entities or (epistemological) domains. Those individual entities (ethnicities, types of beans, cats, trees, whatever) which are classified as being similar to one another may be defined as a group that has a particular perspective on the world. Note it is the *similarity* between the separate entities that creates a connection between separate entities here. Strathern calls this the 'ethnicist' version of relation. Or the entities might be different, in which case they could, given a good reason, come into relation with one another. But there has to be a reason, a reason to *choose* the relation.

In contrast, within perspectivist logic, each entity already contains all relations and therefore all similarities and differences. The entity *is* its relations; there is no 'reason' to come into relation, because the relation has to exist prior to the world that it creates. Within perspectivalism, individual entities that are similar to one another (e.g. English people as a group) have to choose to come into relation with entities that are different from them (e.g. nature or culture as separate domains). Within perspectivism, the differences are already integrally implied: a person who is made from his relations already has the differences embedded within the logic of his kinship integrally implied within him.

This issue of the geometry of similarities and differences is where I began and it is also where I will end this brief excursion, with a final quick look at another one of Strathern's most (re)productive concepts, scale. This involves another impossibly long thread, but I will cut it, in the manner described by Strathern herself: all acts of interpretation must be cut in order to make sense.

> Interpretation must hold objects of reflection stable long enough to be of use. That holding stable may be imagined as stopping a flow or cutting into an expanse, and perhaps some of the Euro-Americans' voiced concern over limits re-runs Derrida's question of how to 'stop' an interpretation . . . 'cutting' is used as a metaphor by Derrida himself. . . for the way one phenomenon stops the flow of others. (Strathern 1996, 522)

My cutting draws on the fact that Strathern's use of the concept of scale often involves fractal geometry as well as the Euclidian sort (to which Venn diagrams belong, for example). She carefully renders the term 'scale' so that it simultaneously refers to size (magnitude – bigger or smaller) and to domain (classification of the type of thing being measured, e.g. natural or cultural things). That way, she can draw upon both a merographic understanding of scale (the overlapping of different domains, which generates partial fragments of many separate wholes) and a fractal one (the overlapping of different magnitudes, which generates fractions of an always singular whole). This understanding of scale also allows her to consider an interplay between them, given that scale incorporates both meanings. That has allowed her to analyze differences between, and changes in, how relations work and how persons appear (and sometimes disappear). This is, of course, a reiteration of what I have already discussed, but it takes things in a slightly different direction.

One point about fractal geometry is that it eludes scale understood as magnitude: the same thing happens at the largest and smallest levels. Branches of a tree, veins in the leaf, roots of the tree – all the same structure working at different magnitudes, but none of them fragment into different domains. All the similarities, and all the differences, are fractions of one; all are encompassed within one. Partitioning within fractal geometry does not create the dissolution of entities/persons which break up into bits and parts once there are no clear-cut domains to hold them together: fractal geometry does not generate plurality in the merographic sense and thus also does not generate a postplural condition.

In 'Binary License', Strathern draws on the example of the concept of 'Balkanization' to demonstrate a logic which is precisely *not* fractal in that sense, but is instead an embattlement caused by a plural logic. By reputation, the Balkans famously contain ethnic/nationalist groups whose claim to territory overlap with claims to the same territory by other ethnic/nationalist groups, and there appears to be no way to resolve the overlaps: too much similarity between the groups which ought to be entirely separate makes it difficult to *choose* which group 'naturally' belongs to one territory and which group belongs to another. Yet in this logic, there are pre-existing groups (ethnic/national groups), and in the end, all they can do is choose (Strathern 2011, 100). The problem is that there is no means for separating out one domain from the other (the plural towards postplural problem), no way to establish which choice is the 'right' one.

This analysis loops one of my texts into the discussion, as Strathern draws on my redescription of the issue of Balkans/Balkanization in order to make this point (Green 2005). And once again, Strathern brilliantly extends and refracts one part of the logical problem I discussed there. Both my account and hers describe how Euro-American logic (in Strathern's terms), when confronted with too much similarity and therefore no clear way to distinguish so as to be able to choose how to separate things out, creates a problem that, in practice, has generated major conflicts in the Balkan region. Strathern extends that to show the persistence of that plural Euro-American logic, that sense that in the end the world is made up of pre-existing entities that *must* choose, even if there is no final way to do that to everyone's satisfaction.

Yet there was also another part in my account where I evoked fractals rather than this Euro-American perspectivalist logic, and that was in my discussion of the history of Ottoman statecraft in the region. This was not about too much similarity, too much connection, but on the contrary, about difference, about cuts that make no sense and that subsequently cause trouble. The point was a relatively simple one: the logic used by the late Ottoman regime to generate a relation between people and location was quite different from the logic that replaced it, involving modern, nationalist claims to territory. These two logics were not only different: they directly contradicted one another. The Ottoman state structure, and particularly the *millet* system, was built on the logic that differences exist within the territory and that each part (e.g. Orthodox, Jewish, Catholic and the majority Muslim religious institutions) makes up the whole (the Ottoman Porte).

Nationalist logic, in contrast, asserted that each territory should be coterminous with a single, self-similar group: a nation for the nationals and what Strathern has rightly called the 'ethnicist' understanding of difference and similarity. In the part of my description concerning Ottoman logic, my interest was in what happened when the Ottoman logic came into direct contact with the nationalist logic in the Balkan region and how the considerable and repeated conflicts that resulted were accounted for in ideological terms from the Euro-American perspective (i.e. how the concept of Balkanization came into existence). And my reasons for doing that, for trying to understand what happens when different geometrical logics come together in a place, especially when there is political power behind both of them as was the case here, was the same as the reason I pursued Strathern's work even when it initially baffled me: I wanted to understand something more about it, because there was clearly some kind of important thread in there about the dynamics of social life.

The significance of the thread regarding Ottoman logic for me came from my encounters with people on the Greek-Albanian border: many of their descriptions seemed to contradict Balkan logic (the perspectivalist/ ethnicist logic, in Strathern's terms), even while they evoked the concept of 'Balkans' to explain why it all seemed so complicated. What that led into, and it is something that I am still exploring, was what happens in the encounter between different logics.

So what is that sense of geometry that provoked me into rereading *The Phantom Tollbooth* when I was asked to say something about Strathern's work? The answer of course has to be both partial and personal. Geometry is not any kind of mathematics; it is the part that fundamentally has to do with relations and, in having both Euclidian and fractal versions, it captures the variations in parts, wholes, fragments, fractions, divisions, binaries, fractals, one and many, extensions, connections and disconnections that has proven to be so evocative in thinking about sociality. It is good to think.

NOTES

1. Juster 1962: loc. 1794–1813 of Kindle version of the book.
2. Alfred Gell helpfully drew a series of what he called 'strathernograms' to depict this thinking as it was expressed in *Gender of the Gift* (Strathern 1988; Gell 1999).
3. Although it could be noted that this is also another looping back. In *Shifting Contexts,* Strathern adds an afterword called 'Relocations' (1995, 176)

REFERENCE

Gell, Alfred. 1999. 'Strathernograms, or, the Semiotics of Mixed Metaphors'. In *The Art of Anthropology: Essays and Diagrams,* edited by Eric Hirsch, 29–75. New Brunswick, NJ and London: Athlone Press.

Green, Sarah. 2005. *Notes from the Balkans: Locating Marginality and Ambiguity on the Greek-Albanian border.* Princeton: Princeton University Press.

——. 2015. 'Making Grey Zones at the European Peripheries'. In *Ethnographies of Grey Zones in Eastern Europe: Relations, Borders and Invisibilities,* edited by Ida Harboe Knudsen and Martin Demant Frederiksen, 173–86. Anthem Series on Russian, East European and Eurasian Studies. London and New York: Anthem Press.

Juster, Norton. 1962. *The Phantom Tollbooth.* London: Collins.

Strathern, Marilyn. 1988. *The Gender of the Gift: Problems with Women and Problems with Society in Melanesia.* Berkeley, Los Angeles and London: University of California Press.

——. 1991. *Partial Connections.* Savage: Rowman & Littlefield.

——. 1992. *After Nature: English Kinship in the Late Twentieth Century.* Cambridge: Cambridge University Press.

——. ed. 1995. *Shifting Contexts: Transformations in Anthropological Knowledge.* London and New York: Routledge.

——. 1996. 'Cutting the Network'. *Journal of the Royal Anthropological Institute* 2(3): 517–35.

——. 2004. *Partial Connections.* Updated ed. Walnut Creek and Oxford: AltaMira Press.

——. 2011. 'Binary License'. *Common Knowledge* 17(1): 87–103.

Viveiros de Castro, Eduardo. 2004. 'Exchanging Perspectives: The Transformation of Objects into Subjects in Amerindian Ontologies'. *Common Knowledge* 10(3): 463–84.

Sarah Green is Professor of Social and Cultural Anthropology at the University of Helsinki. Broadly, she is interested in the dynamics of location, particularly questions of establishing where people are as opposed to who they are. In earlier years, this focused on questions of the politics of gender and sexuality and then later on the introduction of digital technologies to people's spatial lives. For many years since then, she has been studying the logic of borders in the Balkan and European regions more widely and the relative locations involved. More recently, she has shifted her attention from the Greek-Albanian border to the Aegean and the Mediterranean region more widely, and is studying how locations overlap and the relations and separations between them.

Afterword
The Disappearing of an Office

Marilyn Strathern

‸

The authority structure has changed very considerably.
– Alan Macfarlane 'Notes on the Wyse Chair'

It is appropriate to end with a few words on the transformation to which Alan Macfarlane has pointed – the detachment of the William Wyse Professorship from the headship of the Department of Social Anthropology at the University of Cambridge. Does this make the chair more akin to that of a traditional Cambridge head of house, not a head at all but merely first among equals, or is this the point at which changes in university administration rehearse a rationality that has also been changing the face of public conduct and national politics over the past twenty years? I would not have the audacity to summon both a thoroughly local Cambridge phenomenon and recent changes in UK bureaucratic structures at large without the help of some arguments on Weber and the expectations of office.

In a provocative chapter on the way concepts connect and disconnect, the educationalist Ian Stronach (2009) talks of the 'semantic collisions' with which they can be made to crash into one another: benevolent hegemony, for instance, or liberal empire. The adjacencies and juxtapositions of an early postmodernism, the laying of ideas, images, information side by side, have given way to a (mature postmodern?) appetite for 'word crashes'. In his own work, he found himself describing Summerhill School[1] in terms of a benevolent panopticon or working dystopia. If there is a deliberate search for novelty in the drive to create fresh meanings, he suggests, a conscious attempt at coipseity or coappearance in the proliferation of 'copossibilities',[2] a creative embrace of contradiction, paradox and oxymoron as the new stasis, then the conjunctions play on a tension or initial resistance between the terms. Irresolution, as he says, keeps contradiction in play. What came to mind, as I read the chapter, were conjunctions that have lost their frisson.

The conjunction I want to talk about has lost its frisson twice over. Anthropological interest in the relationship between 'person' and 'office' belongs to a very particular stretch of twentieth-century theorizing, one that did not even ask itself whether it was modern or not and, indeed, far from waiting for the sparks of collision never hyphenated the two words. Yet there were situations in which the two concepts, each thereby essentializing the other, were opposed, paired, linked or elided to great creative effect. The second loss of frisson comes from the wider intellectual and political climate in Britain within which academic departments, including departments of anthropology, today flourish. On the one hand while many pursue concepts of the person, the idea of office is all but effaced from British anthropological attempts to understand what was once called social organization.[3] On the other hand there has been a sustained attrition, encouraged by UK government policy, of what was once understood as office in the organizational heartland where Weber put it: in the bureaucracies of public administration. In lieu of the distinctive persona of an official comes a personalized proprietorship in all kinds of role. The substitution makes appeals to the ethos of office holding well-nigh impossible – the substitution disappears[4] it and disappears any latent frisson between person and office.

These thoughts about person and office have been stimulated by a sociologist, Paul du Gay (2008, 2006, also 2000),[5] who has long made it his business to comment on changing administrative conventions in the United Kingdom. But what has this to do with the William Wyse Professorship?

NEW RATIONALITIES?

I cannot improve on Alan Macfarlane's (2009) succinct account of changing administrative conventions in the Cambridge Department of Social Anthropology. The only, and hardly original, observation to add is that the separation of the headship of department from the chair[6] appeared at the time as a rational and practical response both to increasing paperwork and to a (possibly populist) sense that 'power' should not be concentrated. Much of the increase of paperwork was driven by the university's ever growing reliance on information technologies. This was the period when everyone and their computer became a work station unto themselves. Secretarial staff, who once got to know something of what anthropologists were up to in the papers they typed and correspondence they dealt with, were being increasingly drawn into an administrative machinery or, after Weber again, life order, with its own aims and objectives. Indeed the persona of departmental administrator was born. It was also the period when the schools into which departments and faculties are now grouped emerged as a middle tier of management to which heads of department became directly responsible. New alignments of responsibility in turn seemed consonant with an increasingly prominent discourse of accountability. A kind of institutional mistrust[7] of the old-style autonomous head of department [hereafter HoD], whose connections to a central administration had been rather remote, was fuelling new procedures. That decision-making over resources was being devolved from the centre to the schools meant that the HoD was at once faced with an expanded order of operations, over budgets for example, and with a more intimate sense of accountability to a now visible management.

Among these procedures were technocommunication devices in the form of templates, spreadsheets and the like. In a way these became the impersonal repositories of responsible leadership, impersonal because their format was a fait accompli of school (and university) management. They in turn helped mould the HoD's attachment to the institution. Traditionally, the HoD occupied an office defined by the university's administrative needs. The office holder's willing submission to the aims of the institution was now in part abducted by the managerial template[8] – with all the potential for a sense of powerlessness that one can encounter filling in online forms. (The boxes only function with one kind of data.) At the same time, the HoD was also being expected to act a bit like an entrepreneur. Responsibility for resources was 'opportunity', strategic plans were 'visions' and fundraising was always on the horizon of challenges. Information about the department now came in the form of self-promotion (websites). Things were becoming complicated in new directions.

This was rather different from the old complications. When the HoD was axiomatically the holder of the foundation chair, there was a performative requirement made of the office holder as the Professor. The expectations of the administration did not encompass the role. Indeed administrative leadership was only a part, even if an important one: the professor served the university in diverse ways, most notably – and by statute – in giving instruction. The institution had to invest trust in the office holder to manage different elements of his or her position.[9]

So what, then, is a William Wyse Professorship [hereafter WWP] detached from the headship? In Cambridge one answer seems to lie in the promotions regime (mentioned by Macfarlane) introduced over this period to enhance the career grades of academic staff. Alongside fundraising for endowments, it gave a new currency to Professorships as well as readerships. Across the university the posts began multiplying, personal chairs becoming a regular part of a reformed, and much welcomed, career structure. The new title of Professor is exactly that: a title that confers prestige on a person. The accompanying expectations amount to the generalized responsibility and public spiritedness to be assumed by a senior member of department. There is little tension between the holder and the position. In this context, the foundation chair starts to look like a kind of first among equals, in which the element of personal prestige – like that of the promotional reward – attaches to the incumbent in a more overt way than before. The person becomes personalized. The WWP becomes less of an office.

Of course similar moves can be found, and not only for anthropology departments, across the country. In Cambridge there is, however, an entrenched local version of the first among equals model in the heads of house (college masters and, in my case, mistresses). Often to the bemusement – if not alarm – of outsiders, a head of house is very much primus inter pares, college government being equally in the hands of the fellows. The range of duties that the head of a university department would be expected to oversee is distributed across other senior office holders: senior tutor, bursar and so forth.[10] But at the same time a head of a college has a significant representational and ceremonial dimension to his or her post. The person is evident, although less through a personalized character as in the case of the promotional chair that signifies individual merit than in being required to personify, or embody, the college. From the point of view of the incumbent, the position remains very much an office to be occupied, coterminous with the institution not the individual, with duties to discharge, a persona to maintain.

Yet what does it mean to say that, under the present regime, the WWP becomes less of an office? What kind of office was it anyway? I answer the questions indirectly, first, through the lens of someone who regrets a diminution in the sense of office when it occurs not in academia but in public life and, second, by recalling the concept in its heyday in social anthropology, a theoretical turn superseded to general relief or recalled with interest rather than regret.

PUBLIC PERSONA

My account is obviously very partial. The particular constellation of foundation chair, personal chair, head of department (and the Cambridge head of college) exists alongside other posts, such as chair of the school, academic secretary in the department and departmental administrator, not brought into the picture here. It is unlikely to compare strictly with constellations outside academia. Nonetheless one can discern elsewhere elements of new arrangements that also affect what appears as a relationship between person and office.

Paul du Gay has delivered a devastating criticism of changing government mores in the United Kingdom under the late Margaret Thatcher and New Labour, spanning roughly the period over which Cambridge University has been self-consciously modernizing (it is still called that). His subject is the role of the state bureaucrat or career civil servant. Basically, he argues, the entrepreneurial management ethos that is obsessed 'with individual creativity and autonomy' (du Gay 2008, 140; compare Osborne 2003) drops from its analytical repertoire, as modes of behaviour are dropped in practice, the ethics of office as a model of bureaucratic effectiveness (Gay 2008, 134). Indeed he argues that 'many of the experiments in public management that have been foisted upon state bureaux over the last two decades have had the effect of undermining the "core business" of public administration: running a state and operating a constitution' (du Gay 2006, 3). It was once thought fundamental to the constitution that the civil servant be differentiated from the politician, as an office is differentiated from a vocation.[11] In referring to the ethics of office, he summons Max Weber.[12]

Weber is important to the argument for his depiction of the bureau's distinctive ethos or life order, one that affords its own kind of moral agency to office holders.[13] It is worth repeating its two broad characteristics. The first is that an office exists within a structure of offices that gives the state an impersonal set of instruments enduring beyond individual incumbents – in effect, an impersonal repository of responsible functioning. The second is that those individuals occupy multiple positions in their lives, manage separate elements of their office(s) and move as different personae between them. The specific persona of the bureaucrat is one who takes pride in preserving impartiality and overcoming his or her own opinions. The moral agency here involves initiative and independent judgement on the part of the incumbent, although it is an agency that has its source not in the individual but in institutionally given obligations. However, while authority comes from outside the individual, this does not mean that individuals doff and don personae at will. On the contrary, personal dedication to instituted (impersonal) purposes becomes an index of the bureaucrat's ethical habitation of his or her office (du Gay 2008, 132, 136).

The point is not to rehearse Weber but to set this model against the changes that du Gay describes. Today's civil servants are supposed to be champions for policies and to show an enthusiasm for and possessiveness towards their duties that are called from within, a personalization of self-action much closer to the ethical framework of the traditional politician. The politician's persona always involved taking personal responsibility for what one does. What du Gay points to is the encroachment of an entrepreneurial and performative ethos of personal striving necessary for politicians onto former ideas about civil servants; self-interest and opportunism become taken for granted everywhere.

The disappearance of the office disappears the state.[14] (and see footnote 16). This is reinforced by a populist regime that imagines a public accessible to direct consultation and in which the demands of office are, in his words, trumped by the normative power of the democratic mandate. He sees many dangers. I quote one:

> The danger ... is that an ethic of responsibility associated with an ethos of bureaucratic office is transmuted by mechanisms of populist participative democratic rule into an acceptance of private interest as the means ... of evaluating performance, of deciding when there has been a failure of administration ... [and so forth] (du Gay 2006, 19). Public office becomes an extension of an individual's own will and commitment.[15] Now the politician's frisson, I surmise, comes from a tension between person and power. Did a frisson once exist for the bureaucrat in the opposition-elision between person and office? Here indeed we might make concepts collide in registering that by contrast with the much more staid 'office', we might even expect something of a frisson to come from playing (internally so to speak) with the relationships among distinct overlapping meanings of 'person'.

For in the way in which these concepts are drawn into political and social commentary, and into anthropological description, the person emerges as thoroughly labile. Thus there is a repeated play on 'person' (often taken to refer to an individual) and 'persona' (an actor). In turn, du Gay (2008, 133) notes that the term persona itself has varied widely in its usage, from the notion of a performed role subject to individual will (it can be put off and on) to a manifestation of and representation of an office, in his words, as an embodiment of a moral economy.[16] 'Person' can in fact occupy either side of the apparent divide between self/individual and office. This is not the place to recall long arguments in the anthropology of personhood, only perhaps to note the fact that a perpetual equivocation, contradiction even, is part of the penumbra that the concept carries. But when it is in tandem with the concept of office, from an officeholder's point of view its multiple theoretical locations echo the delicious-awkward – heroic-antiheroic – tension of being at once part and not part of an institution.

A CAMBRIDGE-STYLE OFFICE HOLDER

Much of the above would have been completely familiar to mid–twentieth-century students of British social anthropology, whether they attributed some of the original thinking to Weber or not. This was the time when Meyer Fortes could open his chapter on ritual and office in tribal society by saying, 'Few concepts in the vocabulary of sociology and social anthropology are so lavishly used as are "role" and "status"' (1962, 53). It has long ceased to be true.

Fortes set out to do something rather creative with these by then hackneyed terms. His interest was in the practices of legitimation by which accountability is made apparent and asked why ritual was so often involved. I leave him to answer his own question and comment briefly on how he extends the concepts of role and status. As he expounds, insofar as roles and statuses are not chosen at will but conferred, they are like offices. 'Office', he proposed, should be considered the generic term (1962, 57).[17] And something like personal commitment may also be at play: an actor 'is made to appropriate his [acting] part to himself because it is in a sense outside himself' (1962, 57).[18] A corollary is that the concept of office is, in Fortes' view, present in all social systems. It is an index of instituted (institutionalized) practice.

Whatever instrumental end is served, an office is also placed in a moral order; it is roles that endure in perpetuity, always occupied, that most qualify, and Fortes dwells on the example of lineage head. Here one can talk of a specific relationship between the office and the officeholder. In Tallensi, each such office holder is accountable to his ancestors. Here, too, is a twist: in arguing for a relationship between individual and office, and thus for the distinction between them, Fortes states that these same practices must also assign individuality to the individual 'so that he may be able to take on diverse roles, statuses and offices in order to play his part in society' (1962, 87). Those parts show at once the individual and the fact that the individual appears socially in his or her[19] persons or personae, office-like in their instituted capacity.

The picture that emerged was a refinement of much that had gone on before, a fresh way in which to appreciate society as a moral order; it, too, was bound in turn to fade. Where it had once seemed so creative to add to understandings of 'social organization', a structure imagined in terms of a constellation of offices, it was to become creative to do anything but that. The disappearance is best put in Fortes' own words.

In 1984 he wrote a foreword to a book by a Melanesianist, acknowledging a theoretical shift that he had to make himself. Now office was one element in a conceptualization of social order that also took on concrete manifestation as group structure, and the foreword largely addresses the ostensible absence of 'groups'. He had been afraid that society in terms of continuity and cohesion had also disappeared, and with it in turn the notion of office.

> I recollect very well my first encounter with the Garia thirty-two years ago. When, fresh from the field, Peter Lawrence enthusiastically described Garia social organization to me, my initial reaction was, shall we say, cautious. What later came to be designated the African segmentary descent group model was still a novelty and to many of us full of promise. Melanesia meant, above all, the Trobriands, Dobu, Manus, the Solomon Islands, and descent groups resembling those of the African Model seemed to occur in all of them. The Garia were conspicuously different . . . no genealogical boundaries marking off one group of people from another . . . no local boundaries fixing village sites . . . no closed ritual associations or exclusive access to economic resources . . . Coupled with the absence of leadership offices corresponding to chieftainship or headmanship, this fluidity of structure posed the problem of how any sort of social continuity or cohesion could be maintained. (Fortes 1984, ix)

Implicit here is the power that notions of group structure were to have on the British anthropological imagination. In explaining his initial distrust of Lawrence's ethnography in the early 1950s, Fortes goes on to explicate the organizational principles of Garia social order as it subsequently appeared to him. His handsome admission of a different perspective meant (indicated) that he was writing from a world that had shifted again.

*   *   *   *   *

Within the microcosm of the Cambridge department, disassociating the HoD from the WWP does not mean that the WWP ceases to play important multiple roles; but within the university it will be principally the HoD who finds new administrative relationships with its developing institutions. It certainly does not mean that the concept of office has disappeared from the system; I suggest that some of it is re-embedded in technology, some (I owe the suggestion to du Gay [personal communication]) is to be found in specialist mechanisms of accountability and ethical practice guidelines and some taken on by the now separate HoD. However, in the case of the HoD, the nature of that office may be changing under the pressures of personalization. This leads to an issue of description: how one might think anthropologically about any of these changes will be coloured by the comparisons one brings to mind.

Two short excursions have sketched this out. I have noted a writer concerned with the consequences of the disappearing office in the day-to-day life of public administrators. For constitutional reasons, there are dangers to be voiced. They do not necessarily apply in the case of academia; nonetheless the account makes salutary reading with respect to enthusiasts of managerial experimentation, and these enthusiasts can be found anywhere. I then turned to a different kind of disappearance altogether, from within social anthropology, and what one might call a willing departure. Anthropology has very largely discarded the whole apparatus of theorization that rested on a premise of social order. What is disappeared, to be replaced by other models, then, is one way of modelling societal process. At the time (I was in my second undergraduate year in 1962) role and status were commonplaces; it was Fortes who quite compellingly brought the notions to life by pursuing a connection with concepts of office.

Yet is the notion of office re-embedded in subsequent theories of societal process too? I am not sure the question is to be easily answered. It would certainly entail thinking with rather larger material than is presented here. Perhaps through the endlessly 'creative' production of apparent tensions between concepts, with which this piece began, one would in fact find abundant counterparts. But they are hardly going to do the work that person and office did when the desirability of the search for order – and for society – needed no justification.

NOTES

1. See Stronach and Piper (2008). On my own interest in this school, see Strathern (2008).
2. Stronach is following the work (and vocabulary) of J-L Nancy (e.g. *Being Singular Plural* [Stanford: Stanford University Press, 2000]).
3. By contrast with the 'upsurge of interest' du Gay (2006, 1) remarks among scholars of public law and public management.
4. 'Disappearing' after the colloquialism, in which 'to disappear' becomes a verb for the removal of 'unwanted' persons in guerrilla and other undercover conflict.
5. With a hinterland of references to allied works not noted here.
6. Over my previous eight years at Manchester University (1985–1993), being head of department and foundation chair went together.
7. The systemic mistrust that relies on rules and procedures to compel good practice.
8. All that is being ceded is apparent willingness to use the technology: it externalizes the will to conform. The devices I have in mind are familiar from financial accounting; there they are intended to make available and transparent the dimensions of resource allocation predictions, business plans and the like.

9. This applied to all professors, foundation chairs or not. The statutes of Cambridge University used to specify 'The duties of Professors' but do so no longer. Chapter XV of Statute D, as it was enforced when I was appointed, put in this order, first, the duty of a professor to devote himself to the advancement of knowledge in his subject, second to promote the interests of the university.

10. Reminiscent of Godelier's (1986) contrast between Baruya big men (head of department) and great men (head of house).

11. With reference to what follows, in the case of the bureaucrat, the office becomes the incumbent's vocation.

12. Not the Weber of the instrumental rationalization of modern life but 'Weber as a sort of historical anthropologist whose polymath interests are linked by a set of ethical-cultural concerns' (du Gay 2008, 130).

13. 'The bureau is a "life order" or "office" comprising the technical and "spiritual" (ethical-cultural) conditions of a distinctive and independent organization of a persona' (du Gay 2008, 135). The bureaucrat is an archetype office holder, just as chiefship is an archetype office in certain African polities (Fortes 1962, 71).

14. 'The conduct of government . . . is [now] represented first and foremost as a particular sort of managerial enterprise. Here, the statist and constitutional dimensions of the work of public officials disappear from view entirely' (du Gay 2006, 27). Also, see footnote 16.

15. And reaching out to, bouncing off, a public understood as a mass of individual wills and commitments, the 'greenhouse effect' that became apparent in Thatcher's Britain (Strathern 1992, 169).

16. Close to Radcliffe-Brown's abstract concept of person, a bundle of rights and duties that is a fulcrum of social relations. We may compare the conceptualization of society that follows with the conception of the state as a structure of offices. 'As a person the human being is the object of study for the social anthropologist. We cannot study persons except in terms of social structure, nor can we study social structure except in terms of the persons who are the units of which it is composed' (Radcliffe-Brown [1940] 1952, 194). Taking up a characterization offered by Udo Wolter, du Gay (2006) describes the sovereign state as an abstract structure of offices endowed with powers, warrants and resources (to be distinguished from the contingent human occupants of these offices).

17. Du Gay (2008, 134) uses 'status' as an alternative to 'persona'.

18. In extreme situations, an office may absorb the whole person during his tenure, citing the case of Ashanti chiefship.

19. There is a distinct gender equivocation here in the Tallensi and similar cases as they were analyzed at the time, a male being the archetype 'full person'. Fortes (1955, 337–38) had argued similarly, and incidentally reinforcing the point about gender, in an article on Tale names: 'The individuals themselves are, so to speak, hidden behind the mask of chief or priest . . . for purposes of the situation and the relationship. Yet the individual himself, the common basis of the several offices and ranks and kinship statuses he may exercize, is not thus

extinguished. His very existence as an individual . . . affects everything in which he plays a part and must therefore receive social recognition [as in naming]'.

Marilyn Strathern had the good fortune to receive initial – and indelible – training in Papua New Guinea, which led to work, among other things, on kinship and gender relations. In the United Kingdom she subsequently became involved with anthropological approaches to the new reproductive technologies, intellectual property, audit cultures and interdisciplinarity. Now retired from the Cambridge Department of Social Anthropology, she is (honorary) life president of the Association of Social Anthropologists (ASA). Strathern is currently working on issues in the conceptualization of relations, some of which were sketched out in her 2005 book, *Kinship, Law and the Unexpected: Relatives Are Often a Surprise.*

REFERENCES

du Gay, Paul. 2000. *In Praise of Bureaucracy.* London: Sage Publications.
——. 2006. 'Re-instating an Ethic of Office? Office, Ethos and Persona in Public Management'. Working Paper no. 13, ESRC Centre for Research on Socio-Cultural Change. University of Manchester.
——. 2008. 'Max Weber and the Moral Economy of Office'. *Journal of Cultural Economy* 1: 129–44.
Fortes, Meyer. 1955. *Names among the Tallensi of the Gold Coast.* Afrikanistische Studien no. 26. Berlin: Akademie-Verlag.
——. 1962. 'Ritual and Office'. In *Essays on the Ritual of Social Relations*, edited by M. Gluckman. Manchester: Manchester University Press.
——. 1984. 'Foreword'. In *The Garia: An Ethnography of a Traditional Cosmic System in Papua New Guinea,* edited by Peter Lawrence. Melbourne: Melbourne University Press.
Godelier, M. 1986. *The Making of Great Men: Male Domination and Power among the New Guinea Baruya.* Translated by R. Swyer. Cambridge: Cambridge University Press.
Macfarlane, Alan. 2009. 'Notes on the Wyse Chair and the Department of Social Anthropology at Cambridge.' Special issue of *Cambridge Anthropology: The William Wyse Professorship, the Organisation of Knowledge and the work of Marilyn Strathern,* edited by Sabine Deiringer and Ashley Lebner, 28(3): 6–19.
Osborne, T. 2003. 'Against Creativity – a Philistine Rant'. *Economy and Society* 32: 507–25.
Radcliffe-Brown, A.R. [1940] 1952. *Structure and Function in Primitive Society.* London: Cohen and West.

Strathern, M. 1992. *After Nature: English Kinship in the Late Twentieth Century.* Cambridge: Cambridge University Press.

——. 2008. 'Sharing, Stealing and Borrowing Simultaneously'. Paper presented at the ASA Annual Conference Ownership and Appropriation, Convenors Veronica Strang and Mark Busse, Auckland, December 2008.

Stronach, I. 2009. *Globalizing Education, Educating the Global: How Method Made us Mad.* London: Routledge.

Stronach, I., and H. Piper. 2008. 'Can Liberal Education Make a Comeback? The Case of "Relational Touch" at Summerhill School'. *American Educational Research Journal* 45: 6–37.

Appendix

Marilyn Strathern: A Complete Bibliography

(Professor Dame Marilyn Strathern FBA)
January 2015

PUBLICATIONS

BOOKS

1972   *Women in Between: Female Roles in a Male World. Mt Hagen, New Guinea.* London: Academic (Seminar) Press. Re-issued by Rowman and Littlefield, Lanham, MD. 1995.

1981   *Kinship at the Core: An Anthropology of Elmdon, Essex.* Cambridge: Cambridge University Press.

1987 (ed)   *Dealing with Inequality. Analysing Gender Relations in Melanesia and Beyond.* Cambridge: Cambridge University Press.

1988   *The Gender of the Gift: Problems with Women and Problems with Society in Melanesia.* Berkeley and Los Angeles: University of California Press.

Translated by André Villalobos, edited by Mariza Corrêa, as *O gênero da dávida: Problemas com as mulheres e problemas com a sociedade na Melanésia.* Campinas, São Paulo: Editoria da Unicamp, 2006.

1991   *Partial Connections.* Savage, MD: Rowman and Littlefield. Reissued by AltaMira Press, Walnut Creek, CA, 2004.

Translated by Marija Zidar, edited by Maja Petrovic-Steger, as *Pisanje antropologijo.* Ljubljana: Koda, Studentska zalozba, 2008.

1992   *After Nature: English Kinship in the Late Twentieth Century.* Cambridge: Cambridge University Press.

1992   *Reproducing the Future: Essays on Anthropology, Kinship and the New Reproductive Technologies.* Manchester University Press / Routledge, Chapman and Hall. [Essays, 1988–91] Translation, under direction of Dimitra Gefou-Madianou, Ellenika Grammata, Athens, 2008.

1995 (ed) *Shifting Contexts: Transformations in Anthropological Knowledge.* London: Routledge.

1999   *Property, Substance and Effect: Anthropological Essays on Persons and Things.* London: Athlone Press. [Essays, 1992–98]

2000 (ed) *Audit Cultures. Anthropological Studies in Accountability, Ethics and the Academy.* London: Routledge.

2005   *Kinship, Law and the Unexpected: Relatives are Always a Surprise.* Cambridge: Cambridge University Press.

2013   *Learning to See in Melanesia. Four Lectures Given in the Department of Social Anthropology, Cambridge University, 1993–2008.* With Introduction by Giovanni da Col, HAU Masterclass Series, vol. 2. [online].

With Andrew Strathern (joint author)
1971   *Self-Decoration in Mount Hagen.* London: Duckworth.

With Carol MacCormack (joint editor)
1980   *Nature, Culture and Gender.* Cambridge: Cambridge University Press. Ch. No nature / no culture: The Hagen case. Reprinted in *Cultural Anthropology.* K. and M. Fortun (eds). London: Sage, 2009.

With Maurice Godelier (joint editor)
1991   *Big Men and Great Men. Personifications of Power in Melanesia.* Cambridge: Cambridge University Press; Paris: MSH.

With Jeanette Edwards, Sarah Franklin, Eric Hirsch and Frances Price (joint authors)
1993   *Technologies of Procreation: Kinship in the Age of Assisted Conception.* Manchester: Manchester University Press. Second edition. London: Routledge, 1999

With Eric Hirsch (joint editor)
2004   *Transactions and Creations: Property Debates and the Stimulus of Melanesia.* Oxford: Berghahn Books.

Further translations

2014   *O efeito etnográfico e outros ensaios* [The ethnographic effect and other essays]. Coordinating editor Florencia Ferrari, translated by Iracema Dulley, Jamille Pinheiro and Luísa Valentini. São Paulo: Cosac Naify.

RESEARCH MONOGRAPHS, REPORTS AND WORKING PAPERS

1972   *Official and Unofficial Courts: Legal Assumptions and Expectations in a Highlands Community.* Canberra: New Guinea Research Bulletin No 47.

1975   *No Money on our Skins: Hagen Migrants in Port Moresby.* Canberra: New Guinea Research Bulletin No 61.

1975   Report on *Questionnaire relating to sexual offenses in the criminal code.* Prepared for the Papua New Guinea Administration, Department of Law.

1975   Report on *Villagers' attitudes towards Corrective Institutions.* Prepared for the Papua New Guinea Corrective Institutions Service.

1991   *The Representation of Kinship in the Context of the New Reproductive Technologies.* Research Report to ESRC (Award R000 23 2537).

2000   Supplementary notes, to accompany L. Kalinoe, *Background Paper in Intellectual Rights and Related Social and Cultural Issues in Papua New Guinea.* Prepared for the PNG National Intellectual Property Rights Committee.

2002   *Property, Transactions and Creations: New Economic Forms in the Pacific.* Research Report to ESRC (Award R000 23 7838).

2004   *Commons and Borderlands: Working Papers on Interdisciplinarity, Accountability and the Flow of Knowledge.* Wantage: Sean Kingston Publishing.

2011   [Report] *Human Bodies: Donation for Medicine and Research.* London: Nuffield Council on Bioethics. Outcome of panel deliberations [nonresearch, indirect authorship].

ARTICLES AND CHAPTERS

With Andrew Strathern (joint author)

1964   'Minj Open Electorate (PNG) First National Election'. *Journ. Polynesian Soc.*, 73: 209–11.

1966   'Dominant Kin Relationships and Dominant Ideas.' *American Anthropologist,* 68: 997–99.

1968   'Marsupials and Magic A Study of Spell Symbolism Among the Mbowamb'. In E R Leach (ed), *Dialectic in practical religion.* Papers in Social Anthropology, No 5. Cambridge: Cambridge University Press.

1969   'Marriage in Melpa'. In R Glasse and M Meggitt (eds), *Pigs, Pearlshells and Women.* Englewood Cliffs: Prentice-Hall.

With Jeanette Edwards (joint author)

2000   'Including our own'. In J Carsten (ed), *Cultures of Relatedness: New Approaches to the Study of Kinship.* Cambridge: Cambridge University Press.

With Elena Khlinovskaya Rockhill (joint author)

2013   'Unexpected Consequences and an Unanticipated Outcome'. In G Born and A Barry (eds), *Interdisciplinarity: Reconfigurations of the social and natural sciences.* London: Routledge.

JOURNAL / REFEREED ARTICLES

1965   'Axe Types and Quarries: A Note on the Classification of Stone Axe Blades from the Hagen Area, New Guinea'. *Journal Polynesian Society,* 74: 182–91.

1966   'Note on Linguistic Boundaries and the Axe Quarries'. *Proc Prehistoric Society,* 32: 117–21.

1968   'Popokl: the Question of Morality'. *Mankind,* 6: 553–62.

1969   'Why is the Pueraria a Sweet Potato?' *Ethnology,* 8: 189–98.

1969   'Stone Axes and Flake Tools: Evaluations from Two New Guinea Highlands Societies'. *Proc Prehistoric Society,* 35: 311–29.

1972   'Legality or Legitimacy: Hageners' Perception of the Judicial System'. *Melanesian Law Journal,* 1: 5–27.

1972   'Absentee Businessmen: The Reaction at Home to Hageners Migrating to Port Moresby'. *Oceania,* 43: 19–39. Reprinted in R May (ed), *Change and Movement.* Canberra: ANU Press, 1977.

1976   'Crime and Correction: the Place of Prisons in Papua New Guinea'. *Melanesian Law J.,* 4: 67–93.

1979   'The Self in Self-Decoration'. *Oceania,* 49: 241–57.

1979   'Sexual Offences and Criminal Codes'. *Cambridge Anthropology,* 5: 4–31.

1981   'Culture in a Netbag: The Manufacture of a Subdiscipline in Anthropology'. *Man* (NS), 16: 665–88 [Malinowski Memorial Lecture].

1984   'Marriage Exchanges: a Melanesian Comment'. *Ann. Rev. of Anthrop,* 13: 39–71.

1984   'Localism Displaced: a 'Vanishing Village' in Rural England'. *Ethnos,* 49: 43–61. [Revised version of 'The social meaning of localism', 1984].

1985   'Kinship and Economy: Constitutive Orders of a Provisional Kind'. *American Ethnol.,* 12: 191–209.

1985   'Discovering "Social Control"'. *Journal of Law and Society,* 12: 111–34. Reprinted in T D Campbell (ed), *The International Library in Essays of Law and Legal Theory.* Aldershot: Dartmouth, 1991. Also reprinted in P Sack and J Aleck (eds), *Law and Anthropology.* Aldershot: Dartmouth, 1993.

1985   'Dislodging a World View: Challenge and Counter-Challenge in the Relationship between Feminism and Anthropology'. *Australian Feminist Studies,* 1: 1–25.

1985   'John Locke's Servant and the Hausboi from Hagen: Some Thoughts on Domestic Labour'. *Critical Philosophy,* 2: 21–48.

1987   'An Awkward Relationship: the Case of Feminism and Anthropology'. *Signs. Journal of Women in Culture and Society,* 12: 276–92. [Revised version of 'Dislodging a world view', 1985].. Translated as Una relación dificultosa: el caso del feminismo y la antropología, *Feminaria,* 6: 1–9. Buenos Aires, 1990. Also translated as Ein schiefes Verhaltnis: Der Fall Feminismus und Anthropologie. *Unberschreiblich weiblich: Texte zur feministischen Anthropologie,* ed. H von G Rippl. Frankfurt: Fischer Taschenbuch Verlag, 1993; Uma relação incômoda: O caso do feminismo e da antropologia, *Revista Mediações,* 14(2): 83–104, 2009.

1987   'Out of Context: the Persuasive Fictions of Anthropology'. *Current Anthropology,* 28: 251–81 [Frazer Lecture]. Reprinted in M Manganaro (ed), *Modernist Anthropology: from fieldwork to text.* Princeton: Princeton University Press, 1990. Excerpt translated as Poza kontekstem: sugestywnosc fikcji literackiej w antropologii, *Konteksty,* 3/4: 166–68 (Institut Sztuki Polskiej Akademi Nank), 1995. Translated as Fuera de contexto. Las ficciones persuasivas de la antropología, C Geertz, J Clifford (eds), *El surgimiento de la antropología posmoderna,* compilación de C Reynoso. Barcelona: Editorial Gedisa, 2003.

1987   'The Study of Gender Relations: A Personal Context'.
        Anthropologie et sociétés, 11: 9–18.
1988   'Concrete Topographies'. *Cultural Anthropology* (special theme
        issue), 'Place and voice in anthropological theory', 3: 88–96.
1989   'Between a Melanesianist and a Deconstructive Feminist'.
        Australian Feminist Stud., 10: 49–69.
        Translated as Entre uma Melanesianista e uma feminista,
        Cadernos Pagu: Gênero, narrativas, memórias [Campinas, São Paulo],
        8/9: 7–49, 1997.
1990   'Enterprising Kinship: Consumer Choice and the New
        Reproductive Technologies'. *Cambridge Anthropology*, 14: 1–12.
        Translated as Parentesco por iniciativa: a possibilidade de escolha
        dos consumidores e as novas technologias da reproduçao, *Análise
        Socias*, 114: 1000–1022. Lisbon, 1991. Reprinted in P Heelas and
        P Morris (eds), *The values of the enterprise culture: The moral debate*.
        London: Unwin Hyman Press, 1992. Excerpted in M Fraser and
        M Greco (eds), *The body: A Reader*. London: Routledge, 2005.
1991   'Partners and Consumers: Making Relations Visible'. *New
        Literary History*, 22: 581–601. Reprinted in A Schrift (ed), *The
        Logic of the Gift*. New York: Routledge, 1997.
1991   'Disparities of Embodiment: Gender Models in the Context of
        the New Reproductive Technologies'. *Cambridge Anthropology*, 15:
        25–43.
1992   'Writing Societies, Writing Persons'. *Writing as a Human Science*
        (theme issue), 'History of the Human Sciences', 5: 5–16.
1992   'The Decomposition of an Event'. *Cultural Anthropology*, 7: 244–54.
1993   'One-Legged Gender'. *Visual Anthropology Review*, 9: 42–51.
        Reprinted in L Taylor (ed), *Visualizing theory*. New York:
        Routledge, 1994.
1994   'New Knowledge for Old? Reflections following Fox's *Reproduction
        and Succession'*. *Social Anthropology / Anthropologie Sociale*, 2: 263–79.
1994   'Cultural Diversity'. *Bull. of Institute of Ethnology, Academia Sinica*,
        78: 1–26.
1996   'Potential Property: Intellectual Rights and Property in Persons'.
        Social Anthropology / Anthropologie Sociale, 4: 17–32. Reprinted in
        M Mundy (ed), *Law and Anthropology*, Int. Library of Essays in
        Law and Legal Theory, 2nd series, Aldershot: Ashgate, 2002.
1996   'Cutting the Network'. *Journal of Royal Anthropological Inst.* (NS)2:
        517–35. Reprinted in H Moore and T Sanders (eds), *Anthropology
        in theory: Issues in epistemology*. Oxford: Blackwell, 2005.

1996   'No Culture, No History'. *Anthropological notebooks* (special issue), 'Multiple identities', ed. B Telban, Ljubljana, Slovenia Anthrop. Society, 11:118–36.

1997   'A Return to the Native'. *Social Analysis* (special issue), 'Technology as skilled practice', ed. P Harvey, 41: 15–27.

1997   'From Improvement to Enhancement: An Anthropological Comment on the Audit Culture'. *Cambridge Review*, 118: 117–26. [Founders' Memorial Lecture, Girton College]. Revised as 'Improving ratings': Audit in the British university system, *European Review*, 5: 305–21, 1997. Translated as 'Melhorar a clasificação': a avaliação no sitema universitário britânico, *Novos Estudos*, 53: 15–31, 1999.

1998   'New Economic Forms: A Report from the Highlands of Papua New Guinea'. Translated as 'Novas formas econômicas: um relato das Terras Altas de Papua Nova-Guiné'. *Mana: Estudos de Antropologia Social*, 4: 109–39.

1998   [with M Carneiro da Cunha, P Descola, C Alberto and P Harvey] 'Exploitable Knowledge Belongs to the Creators of It: A Debate'. *Social Anthropology / Anthropologie Sociale*, 6: 109–26. Introduction, Circulating knowledge, translated for *Sexta Feira antropologia, artes e humanidades*, São Paulo, Brazil, 2000.

2000   'The Tyranny of Transparency'. *British Education Research Journal*, 26: 309–21. Also published in H Nowotny and M Weiss (eds), *Shifting Boundaries of the Real: Making the Invisible Visible*, Zürich: vdf Hochschulverlag AG an der ETH, 2000. Reprinted in A Corsín Jiménez (ed), *The anthropology of organisations*, International Library of Essays in Anthropology, Aldershot: Ashgate, 2007.

2000/01 'Abstraction and Decontextualisation: An Anthropological Comment [ESRC conference 'Virtual Society? Get Real!']'. *Cambridge Anthropology*, 22: 52–66. Revised in S Woolgar (ed), *Virtual Society? Technology, cyberbole, reality*. Oxford: Oxford University Press, 2002.

2001   'The Patent and the Malanggan'. *Theory, Culture, & Society*, 18: 1–26. Also published in C Pinney and N Thomas (eds), *Beyond aesthetics: Art and the technologies of enchantment*. Oxford: Berg, 2001. [Essays for Alfred Gell].

2002   'Externalities in Comparative Guise'. *Economy & Society* (special issue), 'The technological economy', ed A Barry and D Slater, 31: 250–67. Reprinted in A Barry and D Slater (eds), *The technological economy*. London: Routledge, 2005.

2002   'Still Giving Nature a Helping Hand? Surrogacy: A Debate about Technology and Society'. *J. Molecular Biology*, 319: 985–93 [New version of 'Surrogates and substitutes' (1998)]. Abridged as Surrogacy: A case study in ethics, in R Levinson and M Reiss (eds), *Key issues in bioethics: A guide for teachers.* London: Routledgefalmer, 2003. Also published in S Day Sclater and R Cook (eds), *Surrogate motherhood: International perspectives.* Oxford: Hart Publishing, 2003.

2004   'Laudable Aims and Problematic Consequences, or: The 'Flow' of Knowledge is Not Neutral'. *Economy and Society* (special issue), ed J Squires, 33: 550–61. Also published in original version as Universities – and Society!, *Anthropology in Action*, 12: 11–19, 2005.

2004   'Social Property: An Interdisciplinary Experiment'. *PoLAR (Political and Legal Anth. Review),* 27: 23–50. Abridged as Experiments in interdisciplinarity, *Social Anthropology,* 13: 75–90, 2004.

2005   'Resistance, Refusal and Global Moralities'. *Australian Feminist Studies,* 20: 181–93.

2006   'A Community of Critics? Thoughts on New Knowledge'. *J. Royal Anthropological Institute* (NS) 12, 191–209. [Huxley Memorial Lecture].

2007   'Interdisciplinarity: Some Models from the Human Sciences'. *Interdisciplinary Science Reviews,* 32(2): 123–34.

2009   'Comparing Concerns: Some Issues in Organ and Other Donations'. *Suomen Antropologi: Journal of the Finnish Anthropological Society,* 34(4): 5–21. [Westermarck Lecture].

2010   'Binary License'. *Common knowledge,* 17: 87–103; *What Politics? A Response,* 123–7, 2010. [Symposium on Comparative Relativism].

2010   'Writing in Kind'. *Interdisciplinary Science Reviews* (special issue), Geoffrey Lloyd's 'History and human nature', 35(3–4): 291–301.

2010   'An End and a Beginning for the Gift?' *Journal de la Société des Oceanistes* (special issue), 'Hommage à Bernard Juillerat', ed D Monmerie and P Lemmonier, 130–1: 119–27.

2012   'Gifts Money Cannot Buy'. *Social Anthropology* (special issue), 'The debt issue', ed H High, 20(4): 397–410.

2012   'Eating (and Feeding)'. *Cambridge Anthropology,* 30(2): 1–14.

2014   'Innovation or Replication? Crossing and Criss-Crossing in Social Science'. *Arts and Humanities in Higher Education,* 13(1–2): 62–76. [OnlineFirst, doi: 10.1177/1474022212467603].

2014   'Reading Relations Backwards'. *JRAI* (NS) 20(1): 3–19. [Marett Memorial Lecture, 2013].

2014   'Kinship as a Relation'. *L'Homme,* 210: 43–61.

2014   'Anthropological Reasoning: Some Threads of Thoughts'. *HAU, Journal of Ethnographic Theory,* 4(2) 245–59.

2015   'Being One, Being Multiple: A Future for Anthropological Relations'. *NatureCulture* (special issue), 'Acting with nonhuman entities', ed G Mohácsi and A Morita, 3: 122–57. [online].

BOOK CHAPTERS

1974   'Managing Information: The Problems of a Dispute-Settler (Mount Hagen)'. In A L Epstein (ed), *Contention and dispute.* Canberra, ANU Press.

1975   'Sanctions and the Problems of Corruption in Village Courts'. In J Zorn and P Bayne (eds), *Lo bilong ol manmeri.* Port Moresby: University of Papua New Guinea.

1976   'An Anthropological Perspective'. In B Lloyd and J Archer (eds), *Exploring sex differences.* London: Academic Press.

1978   'The Disconcerting Tie: Attitudes of Hagen Migrants Towards "Home"'. In R May (ed), *Change and movement. Readings on internal migration in Papua New Guinea.* Canberra: ANU Press. Revised in M Chapman and R M Prothero (eds), *Circulation in population movement: Substance and concepts from the Melanesian case.* London: Routledge and Kegan Paul, 1985. Reissued by Routledge, 2012.

1978   'The Achievement of Sex: Paradoxes in Hagen Gender-Thinking'. In E Schwimmer (ed), *Yearbook of Symbolic Anthropology* 1. London: Hurst.

1980   'No Nature, No Culture: The Hagen Case'. In C MacCormack and M Strathern (eds), *Nature, culture and gender.* Cambridge: Cambridge University Press. Reprinted in M Evans (ed), *Gender.* Feminist International Relations. London: Routledge, Forthcoming.

1981   'Self-Interest and the Social Good: Some Implications of Hagen Gender Imagery'. In S Ortner and H Whitehead (eds), *Sexual meanings. The cultural construction of gender and sexuality.* Cambridge: Cambridge University Press. Reprinted in P Erickson and L Murphy (eds), *Readings for a history of anthropological theory.*

Ontario: Broadview Press, 2001. Reissued 2006, University of Toronto Press, 2009.

1982   'The Village as an Idea: Constructs of Village-ness in Elmdon, Essex'. In A P Cohen (ed), *Belonging: Identity and social organisation in British rural cultures.* Manchester: Manchester University Press.

1982   The Place of Kinship: Kin, Class and Village Status in Elmdon, Essex'. In A P Cohen (ed), *Belonging: Identity and social organisation in British rural cultures.* Manchester: Manchester University Press.

1984   'Subject or Object? Women and the Circulation of Valuables in Highlands New Guinea'. In R Hirschon (ed), *Women and property, women as property.* London: Croom Helm.

1984   'Domesticity and the Denigration of Women'. In D O'Brien and S W Tiffany (eds), *Rethinking women's roles: Perspectives from the Pacific.* Berkeley and Los Angeles: California University Press.

1984   'The Social Meaning of Localism'. In A. Bradley and P. Lowe (eds), *Locality and Rurality: Economy and Society in Rural Regions.* Norwich: Geo Books

1985   'Knowing Power and Being Equivocal: Three Melanesian Contexts'. In R Fardon (ed), *Power and knowledge: Anthropological and sociological perspectives.* Edinburgh: Scottish Academic Press.

1985   'Women's Studies in Social Anthropology'. In A Kuper and J Kuper (eds), *The Social Science Encyclopaedia.* London: Routledge and Kegan Paul.

1986   'The Limits of Auto-Anthropology'. In A Jackson (ed), *Anthropology at home.* ASA Monograph 25. London: Tavistock.

1987   'Relations Without Substance'. In L Lindstrom (ed), *Drugs in Western Pacific Societies.* ASAO monograph no 11. Lanham: University Press of America.

1987   'Producing Difference: Connections and Disconnections in Two New Guinea Highland Kinship Systems'. In J Collier and S Yanagisako (eds), *Gender and Kinship: Essays Towards a Unified Analysis.* Stanford: Stanford University Press.

1990   'Negative Strategies in Melanesia'. In R Fardon (ed), *Localizing Strategies: Regional Traditions of Ethnographic Writing.* Edinburgh and Washington: Scottish Academic Press, Smithsonian Institution.

1990   'Artefacts of History: Events and the Interpretation of Images'. In J Siikala (ed), *Culture and History in the Pacific.* Helsinki: Finnish Anthropological Society. Translated as Acontecementos históricos e a interpretacão di imagens. Um commentário do ponto de vista da Melanésia. *Artefactos Melanesios: reflexoes post-modernistas.* Exhibition catalogue, Museu de Etnologia, Lisbon, 1988.

1991 'One Man and Many Men'. In M Godelier and M Strathern (eds), *Big Men and Great Men: Personifications of Power in Melanesia.* Cambridge: Cambridge University Press.

1991/1992 'Naming People'. In A Pawley (ed), *Man and A Half: Essays on Pacific Anthropology and Ethnobiology in Honour of Ralph Bulmer.* Auckland: Polynesian Society.

1992 'Artificial Life' [Introduction] and 'A Partitioned Process' [ch. 7],.contributions to *Reproducing the Future.* Not previously published. Manchester: Manchester University Press.

1992 'Parts and Wholes: Refiguring Relationships in a Postplural World'. In A Kuper (ed), *Conceptualising Society.* London: Routledge. Abridged in R Borofsky (ed), *Assessing Cultural Anthropology.* New York: McGraw-Hill, 1994. Translated by G Kubica-Heller as Czesci i calosci. Przeobrazenia zwiazkow w swiecie postpluralistycznym. In M Kempny and E Nowicka (eds), *Bedanie kultury: elementy teorii antropologicznej.* Warsaw: Wydawnictwo Naukowe PWN.

1992 'Qualified Value: The Perspective of Gift Exchange'. In C Humphrey and S Hugh Jones (eds), *Barter, Exchange and Value.* Cambridge: Cambridge University Press. Translated as Valor calificativo: la perspectiva del intercambio de regales. In C Humphrey and S Hugh Jones (eds), *Trueque, intercambio y valor: aproximaciones Antropológicas,* Quito: Ediciones Abya-yala, 1998.

1992 'The Meaning of Assisted Kinship'. In M Stacey (ed), *Changing Human Reproduction: Social Science Perspectives.* London: Sage.

1992 'Reproducing Anthropology'. In S Wallman (ed), *Contemporary futures.* ASA Monograph. London: Routledge.

1992 'The Mother's Brother's Child'. In B Juillerat (ed), *Shooting the Sun: Ritual and Meaning in West Sepik.* Washington: Smithsonian Institution Press.

1993 'Future Kinship and the Study of Culture'. In A Cohen and K Fukui (eds), *Humanising the City? Social Contexts of Urban Life at the Turn of the Millennium.* Edinburgh: Edinburgh University Press. Reprinted in *Futures: Journal of forecasting, planning and policy* (special issue), 'Anthropological perspectives on the future', 4: 423–35, 1995.

1993 'A Question of Context' [Introduction]; 'Regulation, Substitution and Possibility' [ch. 5]; 'A Relational View' [Postscript]. In

J Edwards et al, *Technologies of Procreation: Kinship in the Age of Assisted Conception.* Manchester: Manchester University Press.

1993   'Making Incomplete'. In V Broch-Due, I Rudie and T Bleie (eds), *Carved Flesh/Cast Selves: Gendered Symbols and Social Practices.* Oxford: Berg. Translated as Fare incompleto. In Consigliere S (ed), *Mondi multipli. Vol. 2. Lo splendore dei mondi,* 151–66. Naples: Kaiak, 2014.

1994   'Displacing Knowledge: Technology and its Consequences for Kinship'. In I Robinson (ed), *Life and Death under High Technology Medicine.* Manchester: Manchester University Press. Abridged In F Ginsburg and R Rapp (eds), *Conceiving the new world order: The global politics of reproduction.* Berkeley and Los Angeles: California University Press, 1995.

1995   'The Nice Thing about Culture is that Everyone has It' [ch. 8]; also 'Shifting Contexts' [Foreword] and 'Relocations' [Afterword]. In M Strathern (ed), *Shifting Contexts Transformations in Anthropological Knowledge.* London: Routledge.

1995   'Bisogno di padri, bisogno di madri. Le 'madri vergini' in Inghilterra'. In G Fiume (ed), *Madri: storia di un ruolo sociale.* Venice: Marsilio Editori. And as Gender: ein Frage der Vergleiches. In U Davis-Sulikowski, H. Diemberger, A Gingrich, J Helbling (eds), *Korper, Religion und Macht: Sozialanthropologie der Geschlechterbeziehungen.* Frankfurt: Campus Verlag, 2001. Translated as Necessidade de pais, necessidade de maes, *Revista Estudos Feministas,* Rio de Janeiro, 3: 303–29, 1995.

1995   'Gender: Division or Comparison?' In N Charles and F Hughes-Freeland (eds), *Practising Feminism: Identity, Difference, Power.* London: Routledge. Reprinted in K. Hetherington and R Munro (eds), *Ideas of Difference: Social Spaces and the Labour of Division.* Sociological Review Monograph. Oxford: Blackwell, 1997.

1995   'Disembodied Choice'. In L Rosen (ed), *Other Intentions: Cultural Contexts and the Attribution of Inner States.* Santa Fe: School of American Research Press.

1995   'Nostalgia and the New Genetics'. In D Battaglia (ed), *Rhetorics of self-making.* Berkeley and Los Angeles: California University Press.

1995   New families for old? In C Ulanowski (ed), *The Family in the Age of Biotechnology.* Aldershot: Avebury.

1996   'Double Standards'. In H. Levine and A Ploeg (eds), *Work in Progress: Essays in New Guinea Highlands Ethnography in Honour of Paula Brown Glick.* Frankfurt am Main: Peter Lang. Also in S

Howell (ed), *The ethnography of moralities*. London: Routledge, 1997.

1997 'Pre-figured Features: A View from the Papua New Guinea Highlands'. In J Woodall (ed), *Portraiture: Facing the Subject*. Manchester: Manchester University Press. Revised as 'Pre-figured features: A View from the Papua New Guinea Highlands', *Australian J. of Anthropology*, 8: 89–103, 1997.

1998 'Divisions of Interest and Languages of Ownership'. In C Hann (ed), *Property Relations: Renewing the Anthropological Tradition*. Cambridge: Cambridge University Press.

1998 'Surrogates and Substitutes: New Practices for Old?' In J M M Good and I Velody (eds), *The Politics of Postmodernity*. Cambridge: Cambridge University Press.

1998 'The New Moderntities'. In V Keck (ed), *Common Worlds and Single Lives: Constituting Knowledge in Pacific Societies*. Oxford: Berg.

1998 'Social Relations and the Idea of Externality'. In C Renfrew and C Scarre (eds), *Cognition and Material Culture: The Archaeology of Symbolic Storage*. Cambridge: McDonald Institute Monographs.

1999 'The Ethnographic Effect' [ch. 1]; 'The Aesthetics of Substance' [ch. 3]; 'Refusing Information; [ch. 4]. In M Strathern, *Property, Substance and Effect: Anthropological Essays on Persons and Things*. London: Athlone Press. Ch. 3 Abridged in N Cummings and M Lewandowska (eds), *Capital: A Project by Neil Cumings and Mariysia Lewandowska*. London: Tate Publishing, 2001. Ch. 3 Reprinted in V Buchli (ed), *Material Culture: Critical Concepts. A Reader*. New York: Routledge, 2004.

1999 'What is Intellectual Property After?' In J Law and J Hassard (eds), *Actor Network Theory and After*. Sociological Review Monograph. Oxford: Blackwell.

2000 'Environments Within: An Ethnographic Commentary on Scale'. In K Flint and H Morphy (eds), *Culture, Landscape, and the Environment: The Linacre Lectures 1997*. Oxford: Oxford University Press.

2000 'New Accountabilities' [Introduction]; 'Accountability and Ethnography' [Afterword]. In M. Strathern (ed), *Audit Cultures*. London: Routledge.

2001 'Rationales of Ownership' [Introduction]; 'Global and Local Contexts'. In L Kalinoe and J Leach (eds), *Rationales of Ownership: Ethnographic Studies of Transactions and Claims to Ownership in Contemporary Papua New Guinea*. New Delhi: UBS Publishers'

Distributors. As above, in vol. reissued as *Rationales of Ownership: Ethnographic Studies of Transactions and Claims to Ownership in Contemporary Papua New Guinea.* Wantage: Sean Kingston Publishing, 2004.

2001   'Same-Sex and Cross-Sex Relations: Some Internal Comparisons'. In T Gregor and D Tuzin (eds), *Gender in Amazonia and Melanesia: An Exploration of the Comparative Method.* Berkeley and Los Angeles: University of California Press.

2002   'On Space and Depth'. In J Law and A-M Mol (eds), *Complexities: Social Studies of Knowledge Practices.* Durham: Duke University Press. Translated as Sobre o espaço e a profundidade, *Cadernos de campo* (University of São Paulo), 20: 241–58.

2004   'Losing (out on) Intellectual Resources'. In A Pottage and M Mundy (eds), *Law, anthropology, and the constitution of the social: Making persons and things.* Cambridge: Cambridge University Press.

2004   'The Whole Person and its Artefacts'. *Annual Review of Anthropology*, 33: 1–19.

2004   'Knowledge on its Travels: Dispersal and Convergence in the Make-up of Communities'; 'Accountability across Disciplines'. In M Strathern, *Commons and Borderlands.* Wantage: Sean Kingston Publishing. Reprinted in *Interdisciplinary Science Reviews*, 31: 149–62.

2004   'Transactions: an Analytical Foray'. In E Hirsch and M Strathern (eds), *Transactions and Creations: Property Debates and the Stimulus of Melanesia.* Oxford: Berghahn Books.

2005   'Robust Knowledge and Fragile Futures'. In A Ong and S Collier (eds), *Global Assemblages: Technology, Politics, and Ethics as Anthropological Problems.* New York: Blackwell.

2006   'Intellectual Property and Rights: An Anthropological Perspective'. In C Tilley, W Keane, S Küchler, M Rowlands and P Spyer (eds), *Handbook of Material Culture.* London: Sage. Abridged as Social invention. In M Biagioli, P Jaszi and M Woodmansee (eds), *Making and Unmaking Intellectual Property: Creative Production in Legal and Cultural Perspective.* Chicago: Chicago University Press, 2011.

2006   'Divided Origins and the Arithmetic of Ownership'. In Bill Maurer and Gabriele Schwab (eds), *Accelerating Possession: Global Futures of Property and Personhood.* New York: Columbia University Press. [Earlier version of ch. 6, *Kinship, Law and the Unexpected*].

2006   'Protecting Channels of Communication: Some Challenges from the Pacific'. In F Macmillan (ed), *New directions in copyright law,* 2, Cheltenham: Edward Elgar.

2006   'Bulletproofing: A Tale from the United Kingdom'. In A Riles (ed), *Documents: Artifacts of Modern Knowledge.* Ann Arbor: University of Michigan Press.

2007   'Knowledge Identities'. In R Barnett and R di Napoli (eds), *Changing Identities in Higher Education: Voicing perspectives.* London: Routledge.

2008   'Old and New Reflections.' In L Chua, C High and T Lau (eds), *How Do We Know? Evidence, Ethnography, and the Making of Anthropological Knowledge.* Newcastle: Cambridge Scholars.

2009   'Using Bodies to Communicate'. In H Lambert and M McDonald (eds), *Social Bodies.* Oxford: Berghahn Books. Revised version of 'Can one rely on knowledge?' In P W Geissler and C Molyneux (eds), *Evidence, Ethics and Experiment: The Anthropology and History of Medical Research in Africa.* Oxford: Berghahn Books, 2011.

2009   'Land: Intangible or Tangible Property?' In T Chester (ed), *Land Rights: The Oxford Amnesty Lectures 2005.* Oxford: Oxford University Press.

2010   'The Tangible and Intangible: A Holistic Snalysis?' In A Iteanu (ed), *La Cohérence des sociétés. Mélanges en hommage à Daniel de Coppet.* Paris: Maison des sciences de l'homme. [Another version of 2009 immediately above].

2011   'Sharing, Stealing and Borrowing Simultaneously'. In V Strang and M Busse (eds), *Ownership and appropriation.* ASA Monograph. Oxford: Berg.

2011   'Social Invention'. In M Biagioli, P Jaszi and M Woodmansee (eds), *Making and Unmaking Intellectual Property: Creative Production in Legal and Cultural Perspective.* Chicago: University of Chicago Press. [Abridged version of 2006, see above].

2011   'An Experiment in Interdisciplinarity: Proposals and Promises'. In C Camic, N Gross and M Lamont (eds), *Social Knowledge in the Making.* Chicago: Chicago University Press.

2012   'Currencies of Collaboration'. In M Konrad (ed), *Collaborators Collaborating: Counterparts in Anthropological Knowledge and International Research Relations.* New York: Berghahn Books.

2013   'Cambridge'. In R J McGee and R L Warms (eds), *Theory in Social and Cultural Anthropology: An Encyclopedia.* London: Sage, 101–4.

2014 'The Academic as Examiner'. In L Gornall, C Cook, L Daunton, J Salisbury and B Thomas (eds), *Academic Working Lives: Experience, Practice and Change.* London: Bloomsbury Academic, 143–52.

2014 'Introduction to Marie Reay'. In F Merlan (ed), *Wives and Wanderers in a New Guinea Highlands Society: Women's Lives in the Wahgi Valey.* Canberra: ANU Press, xlix–lxi.

2015 'Detaching and Situating Knowledge: Comment'. In M Candea, J Cook, C Trundle and T Yarrow (eds), *Detachment: Essays on the Limits of Relational Thinking,* 256–63. Manchester: Manchester University Press.

2015 'Afterword: Taking Relationality to Extremes'. In L Broz and D Münster (eds), *Suicide and Agency: Anthropological Perspectives on Self-Destruction, Personhood and Power,* 205–11. Studies in death, materiality and the origin of time series. Farnham: Ashgate.

2016 'Inroads into Altruism'. In A Amin and P Howell (eds), *Releasing the Commons: Rethinking the Futures of the Commons,* 161–76. London: Routledge.

In press

'The Authority of Value, and Abjection from Value'. In S Ladkin et al. (eds), *Against value.* Lanham: Rowman and Littlefield.

In press

'Opening-up Relations'. In M de la Cadena and M Blaser (eds), *Indigenous Cosmopolitics: Dialogues about the Reconstitution of Worlds.* Durham: Duke University Press.

In preparation

'Questions for Answers'. In S Bamford, J Robbins, J Shaffner and J Weiner (eds), *Roy Wagner: Symbolic Anthropology and the Fate of the New Melanesian Ethnography.*

Under consideration

'Questions for Answers'. In S Bamford, J Robbins, J Shaffner and J Weiner (eds), *Roy Wagner: Symbolic Anthropology and the Fate of the New Melanesian Ethnography.*

OCCASIONAL PAPERS

1994 *New Certainties for Old. The Case of Enabling Technology.* Centre for the Study of Cultural Values, University of Lancaster Occasional Paper. Revised as *Enabling Identity? Biology, Choice and the New Reproductive Technologies.* In S Hall and P du Gay (eds), *Questions of cultural identity.* London: Sage, 1996.

1995   *The Relation: Issues in Complexity and Scale.* Prickly Pear Pamphlet 6. Cambridge: Prickly Pear Press. [Inaugural lecture 1994].

2001   *Emergent Properties.* Rothschild Distinguished Lecture 2000. Department of the History of Science, Harvard University. Revised as Emergent relations. In M Biagioli and P Galison (eds), *Scientific Authorship: Credit and Intellectual Property in Science.* New York: Routledge, 2003.

2011   'What is a parent? Unedited Text (1991)', *Hau: Journal of Ethnographic Theory* 1(1): 245–78. [online].

2011   'What's in an Argument? Reflections on Knowledge Exchanges'. University of Delhi, Working Paper series xi, 28pp [with comments by Rita Brava].

2013   *Fora de contexto: As ficções persuasivas da Antropologia.* Translated by T Lotierzo and L F K Hirano as 'Out of Context', *Current Anthropology*, 1987, with new Preface. São Paulo: Terceiro Nome. With CA commentaries, and new postscript by R. Sztutman, 154 pp.

PROCEEDINGS, CONTRIBUTIONS TO DEBATE (INCLUDING TEXTS OF TALKS/ABSTRACTS)

1990   'The Concept of Society is Theoretically Obsolete [proposer of motion]'. Group for Debates in Anthropological Theory 2. Manchester: GDAT. Reprinted in T Ingold (ed), *Key Debates in Anthropology*, 60–66. London: Routledge, 1996.

1993   Contribution to *Virgin Birth.* Proceedings of symposium. London Hospital Medical College, ed. Robert Silman. London: WFT Press, 1991.

1995   'Sex Selection: Social Issues'. In D Morgan and R Lee (eds), *Designer Babies? Legal and Social Dimensions.* Aldershot: Dartmouth. Sex selection conference, BMA, 1993.

1997   'The Work of Culture: An Anthropological Perspective'. In A Clarke and E Parsons (eds), *Culture, Kinship and Genes: Towards a Cross-Cultural Genetics.* London: Macmillan.

1997   'Kinship Knowledge [abstract]'. In L Weir (ed), *Governing Medically Assisted Human Conception: Report of an International Symposium.* Toronto: Centre for Criminology, University of Toronto, 1996.

1998   'Scale, Culture and the Imagination: An Anthropological Puzzle from Papua New Guinea'. *The British Psycho-Analytical Society*

Bulletin. Revised as Puzzles of scale. In M Strathern, *Property, Substance and Effect.* London: Athlone, 1999.

2000   'Multiple Perspectives on Intellectual Property'. In K Whimp and M Busse (eds), *Protection of Intellectual, Biological and Cultural Property in Papua New Guinea.* Canberra and Port Moresby: Asia Pacific Press at the Australian National University and Conservation Melanesia Inc.

2001   'The Social Dimensions of "Culture"'. In R Higham (ed), *Building on Plurality: Cultures in an Evolving Global Context.* Ottawa: Centre on Governance, University of Ottawa.

2001   'The Reinvention of Kinship'. In Rong Ma (ed), *21st Century: Cultural Consciousness and Cross-Cultural Comunication.* Centennial Lecture series, Institute of Sociology and Anthropology. Peking: Peking University, 1998. [in Mandarin].

2003   British Academy Conversazione [with Alain Pottage], 'Who Owns Academic Knowledge?' *Cambridge Anthropology,* 23(3): 1–17. [Working paper 3 in *Commons and borderlands,* 2004].

2003   'In Crisis Mode: A Comment on Interculturality'. In L Kosinski and K Pawlik (eds), *Social Science at the Crossroads.* Proceeding of the International Conference on Social Science and Social Policy in the 21st century. Paris: ISSC (International Social Science Council). [Working paper Introduction to *Commons and Borderlands,* 2004].

2005   'Imagined Collectivities and Multiple Authorship'. In R Ghosh (ed), *Code: Collaborative Ownership and the Digital Economy.* Cambridge, MA: MIT Press.

2005   'Emblems, Ornaments and Inversions of Value'. Epilogue to S Küchler and G Were (eds), *The Art of Clothing: A Pacific Experience.* London: UCL Press.

2005   'Money Appearing and Disappearing: Notes on Inflation in Papua New Guinea'. In C Gross, H Lyons and D Counts (eds), *A Polymath Anthropologist: Essays in Honour of Ann Chowning.* Research in Anthropology and Linguistics Monographs, no. 6. Auckland: University of Auckland, Department of Anthropology.

2006   'Useful knowledge'. *Proceedings of the British Academy,* 139: 73–109. [Isaiah Berlin Lecture]. Abridged as Measures of usefulness: A diatribe. In B Somekh and T Schwandt (eds), *Knowledge Production: Research Work in Interesting Times.* London: Routledge, 2007.

2013 'Reproducing the Future, in Conversation with Marysia Lewandowska'. In M Lewandowska and L Ptak (eds), *Undoing Property?* Berlin: Sternberg Press and Tensta konsthall, 207–20.

2013 'Die Aufteilung: Explorations and Exchanges across the Seas'. In N Hirsch, S von Olfers, C Carrara and M de la Garza (eds), *Michael Stevenson: An Introduction / una introducción.* Frankfurt: Portikus, 145–66 [includes Spanish translation].

2013 'The Jester' [epilogue to debate], in S Venkatesan (ed), 2011 Annual GDAT debate, 'Non-dualism is philosophy not ethnography', *Critique of Anthropology,* 33(3): 300–360 [pp 356–59].

2014 'Engaging Interests' [Afterword]. In J Leach and L Wilson (eds), *Subversion, Conversion, Development: Cross-Cultural Knowledge Exchange and the Politics of Design,* 223–29. London: MIT Press.

2015 'Dialogue' [contribution to], in L Josephides (ed), *Knowledge and Ethics in Anthropology: Obligations and Requirements.* London: Bloomsbury, 191–229 *passim.*

2015 Personne est divisible, in H Fulgence (dir), *Persona: étrangement humain* [catalogue], Musée du Quai Branly et Actes Sud, 149–50.

REVIEW ARTICLES, COMMENTARIES

1978 On Leacock's 'Women's status in egalitarian society', *Current Anthropology,* 19: 267.

1978 'Gender as it Might Be'. Review of Ardener/Cassell/Lipshitz, *RAIN,* October: 4–7, 1978.

1983 'The Punishing of Margaret Mead'. On Freeman's 'Margaret Mead and Samoa'. *London Review of Books,* 5(8): 5–6. Reprinted in *Canberra Anthropology,* 6: 70–79, 1983.

1984 'The Anthropologist as Poet'. On Modell's biography of Ruth Benedict, *The Times Literary Supplement.* 29 June: 721.

1984 'The Fertilised Cosmos: On Yeatman's "Procreative Model"'. *Social Analysis,* 16: 16–20.

1984 Obituary: Audrey Richards. *RAIN,* October: 11–12, 1984.

1985 'Not a Field Diary'. Report on 'Anthropology at home', ASA Conference, *Anthropology Today,* 1: 25–26.

1985 'Them and Us ...' [For series 'Human interest']. *Times Higher Education Supplement,* 13 December, 15.

1985 Introduction to *Domestic Violence in Papua New Guinea.* Monograph no. 3. Port Moresby: Law Reform Commission of Papua New Guinea.

1987   'Intervening'. On Crapanzano's 'Waiting: the whites of South Africa'. *Cultural Anthropology,* 2: 264–76.

1987   'On Keesing's "Anthropology as Interpretive Quest"', *Current Anthropology,* 28: 173–74.

1989   'On Roth's "Ethnography without tears"', *Current Anthropology,* 30: 565–66.

1989   'On Kirby's "Capitalising Difference"', *Australian Feminist Studies,* 9: 25–29.

1989   'Stopping the World: Elmdon and the Reith Lectures'. *Cambridge Anthropology* (special issue), 'Sir Edmund Leach', 13: 70–74.

1990   'Anthropology and the Time Factor'. *Cultural Anthropology: A Perspective on the Human Condition,* E A Schultz and R H Lavender (eds). St Paul: West Pub. Co. [guest editorial].

1990   'Or, Rather, On Not Collecting Clifford'. *Social Analysis* (special issue), 29: 88–95.

1991   'Primate Visionary: On Haraway's "Primate Visions"', *Science as Culture,* 2: 282–95.

1992   'The Mirror of Technology' [Foreword]. In R Silverstone and E Hirsch (eds), *Consuming Technologies: Media and Information in Domestic Spaces.* London: Routledge.

1992   'Ubiquities: On "The New Cultural History"'. *Annals of Scholarship* (special issue), 9: 199–208.

1992   Response to Book Review Forum, 'The Gender of the Gift', *Pacific Studies,* 15: 123–59.

1992   'Annuals and Decennials'. *Anthropology Today,* 8: 21–22.

1992   'Unanticipated Contexts: The Representation of Kinship in the Context of the New Reproductive Technologies'. *Anthropology in Action,* 11: 5–7.

1992   Die Entsorgung der englischen Gesellschaft, *Freibeuter,* 54: 49–64 [excerpts from *After Nature,* trans. R Cackett]. Also appears as Efter naturen: Samhallets retratt in i individen, *Ord & Bild,* 1: 23–30, 1993.

1993   Audrey Isabel Richards, 1899–1984 [memoir], *Proc. of the British Academy,* 82: 439–53.

1993   'Society in Drag'. *The Times Higher Education Supplement,* 2 April: 19.

1993   'Entangled Objects: Detached Metaphors'. *Social Analysis* (special issue), 34: 88–101.

1994   'On Escobar's "Welcome to Cyberia: Notes on the anthropology of cyberculture"'. *Current Anthropology,* 35: 225–26.

1995   'On Stolcke's "Talking Culture: New Boundaries, New Metaphors of Exclusion in Europe"'. *Current Anthropology*, 36: 16.

1995   Multiple review of Bell, Caplan and Wazir / Gillison / Spector / Wolf, *Signs*, 21: 163–67.

1996   'Family work. Multiple Review of Delphy and Leonard / Clark / Bertraux and Thompson / Katz and Monk', *Gender and History*, 8: 143–47.

1996   'People Too Much Like Us: Comment on Ingold's "People like us"'. *Cultural Dynamics*, 8: 373–76.

1997   'Dear David: Correspondence in "An Exchange with David Schneider": On Gay and Lesbian Kinship'. *Cultural Anthropology*, 12: 281–82.

1997   'Less Nature, More Technology: Excerpts from *After Nature* (1992)'. In S. Kemp and J. Squires (eds), *Feminisms: An Oxford Reader*. Oxford: Oxford University Press, 494–97.

1998   'Mirror of the World's Working [on critical theory]', *The Times Higher Education Supplement*, 20 February: 21.

1998   'On Brown's "Can culture be copyrighted"'. *Current Anthropology*, 39: 216–17.

1988   'Self-Regulation: An Interpretation of Peter Lawrence's Writings on Social Control in Papua New Guinea'. *Oceania*, 59: 3–6.

1998   'The Father's Tears'. Review article on Kelly's 'Constructing Inequality', *Pacific Stud.*, 20: 164–72.

1999   'Criticizing Best Practice', special section on 'Knowledge for What? The Intellectual Consequences of the Research Assessment Exercise', I Velody (ed), *History of Human Sciences*, 12: 139–40.

1999   'No limite de uma certa linguagem'. Interview with M Strathern, Rio de Janeiro, translated by D Rodgers and E Viveiros de Castro, *Mana: Estudos de Antropologia Social*, 5: 157–75.

2000   Introduction to C Banks (ed), *Developing Cultural Criminology: Theory and Practice in Papua New Guinea*. Institute of Criminology Monographs. Sydney: Federation Press.

2001   'Living Complexity', with L Braddock and Eileen Rubery, 'Educating Everyone', *Oxford Magazine*, 190: 4–5.

2001   Foreword to *The Commodification of Bioinformation: The Icelandic Health Sector Base*, by Hilary Rose. London: Wellcome Trust. [Occasional paper].

2002   Professor Sir Raymond Firth, Obituary, *The Independent*, 5 March 2002.

2002   'Not Giving the Game Away'. Foreword to A Gingrich and R
            Fox (eds), *Anthropology, by Comparison*. New York: Routledge.

2002   Afterword to 'Reinventing "The Invention of Culture"'. *Social
            Analysis* (special issue), D Murray and J Robbins (eds), 46:
            90–91.

2003   'Re-describing Society'. Essay review, *Minerva, A Review of
            Science, Learning and Policy* (special issue), H Nowotny and
            P Gibbons (eds), 'Reflections on the New production of
            Knowledge', 41: 263–76. [Working paper Endnote, in *Commons
            and borderlands*, 2004].

2003   Kinship in Flux, *Encyclopaedia of the Human Genome*. London:
            Nature Publishing Group, Macmillan.

2003   Contribution to 'Three Perspectives'. Girton College conference
            on 'Changing Roles: the Work-Life Conundrum', *New Academy
            Review*, 2: 83–87 (67–91).

2004   'Audrey Richards'. Entry for the *Oxford Dictionary of National
            Biography*. Oxford: Oxford University Press.

2005   'Missing Men'. Comment on E Blackwood's 'Wedding bell
            blues', *American Ethnol.*, 32: 28–29.

2005   'Anthropology and Interdisciplinarity'. *Arts and Humanities in
            Higher Education*, 4: 125–35. [Interviewed by L Jordanova].

2005   'Rethinking Audit and Inspection: a Response to M Rustin'.
            Soundings: a Journal of Politics and Culture, 29: 141–43.

2005   'In Other People's Shoes'. In A Ahmed and B Forst (eds), *After
            Terror: Promoting Dialogue among Civilizations*. Cambridge: Polity
            Press.

2005   'Comment on Carrithers' "Anthropology as a Moral Science of
            Possibilities"'. *Current Anthropology*, 46: 452–53.

2006   Prologue to M Mosko and F Damon (eds), *On the Order of Chaos:
            Social Anthropology and the Science of Chaos*, xii–xv. New York:
            Berghahn Books.

2006   [with Penny Harvey] Afterword to E Hirsch and S Macdonald
            (eds), 'Creativity and Temporality'. *Cambridge Anthropology* (spe-
            cial issue), 25: 108–10.

2006   'Don't Eat Unwashed Lettuce: Commentary on AE Forum,
            "IRB's, bureaucratic regulation, and academic freedom"'.
            American Ethnologist, 33: 532–34.

2009   Afterword to J Copeman (ed), 'Blood Donation, Bioecomony,
            Culture'. *Body and Society* (special issue),15: 217–22.

2009   Afterword to D Oliver (ed), *Justice, Legality, and the Rule of Law: Lessons from the Pitcairn Prosecutions.* Oxford: Oxford University Press, 221–29.

2009   'The Disappearance of an Office'. Afterword to A Lebner and S Deringer (eds), *Cambridge Anthropology* (special issue), 28(3),127–38, 2008–2009.

2010   'Learning' ('Prickly Pear Polemics', ed S Brandstädter and K Sykes). *Critique of Anthropology,* 30(1): 102–9. Reprinted in D Scott (ed), *Theories of Learning.* London: Sage, 2012.

2010   'Response to Gordon Matthews' "On the Referee System as a Barrier to Global Anthropology"'. *Asia Pacific Journal of Anthropology,* 11(1): 64–65.

2010   'Ars Synthetica: A Rehearsal, Book Review Forum'. *Biosocieties,* 5(3): 393–95.

2010   'Boundary Objects and Asymmetries'. Commentary on D Garrow and T Yarrow (eds), *Archaeology and Anthropology: Understanding Similarity, Exploring Difference.* Oxford: Oxbow Books, 171–78.

2010   Afterword to M Candea (ed), *The Social after Gabriel Tarde: Debates and Assessments.* London: Routledge, 271–77.

2010   Foreword to L King and C Moutsou (eds), *Rethinking Audit Cultures: A Critical Look at Evidence-Based Practice in Psychotherapy and Beyond.* Ross-on-Wye: PCCS Books, i–ii.

2010   'A Tale of Two Letters: Reflections on Knowledge Conversions'. *Insights,* 3 (16): 1–15. [online].

2011   'Reflections on Gamete Donation'. *Bionews,* 24 October [written by NCOB under my name].

2011   [with Katherine Wright] 'Donating Bodily Material: The Nuffield Council Report'. *Clinical Ethics,* 6: 191–94.

2012   'Epilogue: Expectations, Auto-Narrative and Beyond'. In J Skinner (ed), *The Interview: An Ethnographic Approach.* London: Berg, 261–66.

2012   'Afterword: A Last Word on Futures' for R Fardon et al. (eds), *The Sage Handbook of Social Anthropology.* London: ASA and Sage, 431–36.

2012   Contribution to discussion of Sergei Sokolovsky's article, 'On Copyright and Culture'. *Antropologichesky Forum,* 16: 234–244 [in Russian]. *For Anthropology and culture, Forum,* 9, 2013: 51–60 [in English].

2013   'Gender Ideology, Property Relations and Melanesia: The Field of "M"'. In C Shore and S Trnka (eds), *Up Close and Personal: On*

        Peripheral Perspectives and the Production of Anthropological Knowledge, 233–46. Oxford: Berghahn Books. [interview].

2013   'Epilogue'. In J Robb and O Harris (eds), *The Body in History: Europe from the Palaeolithic to the Future.* Cambridge: Cambridge University Press, 235–36.

2013   [by Janaki Abraham and Yasmeen Arif] 'A Conversation with Marilyn Strathern'. *Contributions to Indian Sociology,* 47(3): 423–38.

2014   Reflections. In R Kaur and P Dave-Mukherji (eds), *Art and Aesthetics in a Globalizing World,* 259–64. ASA Monograph Series. London: Bloomsbury Academic.

2014   'Maurice Godelier's Metamorphoses of Kinship'. *Anthropological Forum,* 24(1): 71–85.

2014   Preface to *ISRF Bulletin* on 'Freedom', 5: 2–3.

2015   'Outside Desk-Work: A Reflection from Marilyn Strathern'. *JRAI* (NS) 21(1): 244–45.

Index